The Maritime Heritage of the Cayman Islands

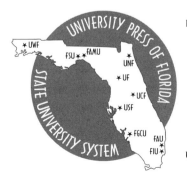

Florida A&M University, Tallahassee
Florida Atlantic University, Boca Raton
Florida Gulf Coast University, Fort Myers
Florida International University, Miami
Florida State University, Tallahassee
University of Central Florida, Orlando
University of Florida, Gainesville
University of North Florida, Jacksonville
University of South Florida, Tampa
University of West Florida, Pensacola

ROGER C. SMITH

The Maritime Heritage

NEW PERSPECTIVES ON MARITIME HISTORY AND NAUTICAL ARCHAEOLOGY
James C. Bradford and Gene A. Smith, Series Editors

This series is devoted to providing the reading public with lively and important books that cover the spectrum of maritime history and nautical archaeology broadly defined. It includes works that focus on the role of oceans, rivers, lakes, and canals in history; on the economic, military, and political use
of those waters; and upon the people, communities, and industries that support maritime endeavors. Limited neither by geography nor by time, volumes
in the series contribute to the overall understanding of maritime history and
can be read with profit by both general readers and specialists.

of the Cayman Islands

UNIVERSITY PRESS OF FLORIDA

Gainesville ~ Tallahassee ~ Tampa ~ Boca Raton ~ Pensacola ~ Orlando ~ Miami ~ Jacksonville ~ Ft. Myers

06 05 04 03 02 01   c 6 5 4 3 2
07 06 05 04 03 02 01 p 6 5 4 3 2 1

Library of Congress Cataloging-in-Publication Data
Smith, Roger C., 1949–
The maritime heritage of the Cayman Islands / Roger C. Smith.
p.   cm. — (New perspectives on maritime
history and nautical archaeology)
Includes bibliographical references and index.
ISBN 0-8130-1773-4   (cl.: alk. paper)
ISBN 0-8130-2447-1 (pbk.: alk. paper)
1. Cayman Islands—History. 2. Cayman Islands—History, Naval.
3. Cayman Islands—Antiquities. 4. Underwater archaeology
—Cayman Islands. I. Title. II. Series
F2048.5 .S656 2000
972.92'1—dc21   00-025144

The University Press of Florida is the scholarly publishing agency
for the State University System of Florida, comprising Florida
A&M University, Florida Atlantic University, Florida Gulf Coast
University, Florida International University, Florida State
University, University of Central Florida, University of Florida,
University of North Florida, University of South Florida,
and University of West Florida.

University Press of Florida
15 Northwest 15th Street
Gainesville, FL 32611
http://www.upf.com

For KC

Contents

List of Figures ix

Foreword by James C. Bradford and Gene A. Smith, Series Editors xiii

Preface xv

Acknowledgments xix

1. The Cayman Islands Project 1

2. Founded Upon the Seas 18

3. Shoal of Sea Turtles 51

4. Crocodiles and Pirates 84

5. Catboats and Schooners 112

6. A Graveyard of Ships 147

Conclusion 177

Appendix 1. The Deposition of Samuel Hutchinson 183

Appendix 2. Lieutenant Alfred Carpenter's Observations 185

Appendix 3. The First Census of Cayman 189

Notes 197

Bibliography 207

Index 219

Figures

Tables

2.1. Hurricanes Affecting the Cayman Islands   43
A3.1. First Census of the Cayman Islands, 1802   192

Illustrations

1. Wreck of *Ridgefield* at East End, Grand Cayman   6
2. Cayman Islands Project Team 1979   7
3. "Uncle Joe" Grizzel situating a shipwreck   8
4. Sheli Smith and Kathryn Boeckman recording anchor of *Maggie Gray*   9
5. Cayman Islands Project Team 1980   11
6. Louisa Kirkconnell of Cayman Brac   12
7. Surveying the Cayman reef line using water scooters to pull snorkelers   14
8. Denise Hoyt drawing a site plan in midwater   15
9. Archaeological materials drawn, photographed, and studied   16
10. Spanish olive jars found throughout the Caymans   17
11. The Cayman Islands' location south of Cuba   19

12. Admiralty chart of Cayman Brac, 1882   21
13. Admiralty chart of Little Cayman, 1882   23
14. Admiralty chart of Grand Cayman, 1882   24
15. Detail of 1502 world map of Alberto Cantino, with unnamed islands in approximate position of Caymans   25
16. Detail of 1580 map from *Theatrum Orbis Terrarum*, showing Grand Cayman and the Sister Islands   27
17. Author sampling sediments from a karst solution feature   30
18. First chart of Grand Cayman, by English surveyor George Gauld, 1773   32
19. George Town harbor, circa 1910   34
20. George Town harbor today   35
21. Detail of Gauld's 1773 chart, showing Grand Cayman's Careening Place and Duck Pond   39
22. Test excavation at the Careening Place   40
23. Marine fasteners recovered from the Careening Place   40
24. Stingray spine, used as a needle to repair turtling nets   41
25. Sketch of the careening process   42
26. Detail of Gauld's 1773 chart, noting effects of a 1751 hurricane   45
27. Coat of arms of the Cayman Islands, featuring sea turtle and three stars on a field of waves   52
28. Sea turtle image, detail of a 1589 map   55
29. Eighteenth-century sailor turning a sea turtle on its back   56
30. Indians of Miskito Coast fishing for turtles from a small boat   65
31. Miskito Coast turtlers removing portions of shell for supposed regeneration   66
32. Turtlers from schooner *Adams* setting nets, 1961   69
33. Caymanians hauling ensnared turtle into a catboat, circa 1950   70
34. Filled catboat returning to *Adams*, 1961   71
35. Turtles being hoisted aboard *Adams*   72
36. Turtles, flippers tied together, marked "AD" to show they are *Adams*'s catch   73
37. Green turtle from turtle crawl at Miskito Cay   74
38. Schooner *Rainbow* discharging a catch at Kingston, Jamaica, circa 1910   75
39. Schooner *Adams* under sail, circa 1938   76
40. Turtles awaiting slaughter or shipment, circa 1955   80
41. Crocodile image, detail of a 1589 map   85
42. Fossil skull of *Crocodylus rhombifer*   88

43. Deposition of Samuel Hutchinson describing Spanish privateer attack, 1669 92

44. Portuguese privateer Manuel Rivero Pardal's challenge to Henry Morgan 94

45. Fragments of clay pipes from Turtle Wreck site, Little Cayman 96

46. Length of slow match, from Turtle Wreck site 97

47. Brass sewing thimble, from Turtle Wreck site 97

48. Matchlock musket and broken Spanish olive jar, clues to seventeenth-century attack on Little Cayman 98

49. Author cleaning matchlock musket 99

50. Reconstruction drawing of buried olive jar 101

51. Pirate captain Edward Teach, aka Blackbeard 105

52. Career criminal and pirate Edward Low 107

53. Mutineer and pirate George Lowther 108

54. Sloop, from *Falconer's Marine Dictionary* (1780) 116

55. Remains of colonial vessel in South Hole Sound 117

56. Site plan of Turtle Wreck 119

57. Caymanian catboat under sail, 1938 125

58. Catboat *Defiance,* with weatherboard for balance 125

59. *Ajax,* one of few surviving catboats 126

60. Reconstructed lines of catboat *Ajax* 127

61. George Town shipbuilding, circa 1910 129

62. Vessel under construction, circa 1942 130

63. Schooner *Goldfield* under sail, 1938 132

64. Annual Yacht and Sailing Club regatta 133

65. Schooner *Rembro* competing in 1935 133

66. A "rope walk" used to produce rope 134

67. Coils of "twenty-five fathoms ropes" 135

68. Launching of motor boat *Cimboco,* 1927 139

69. Site plan of Deep Wreck, Grand Cayman 141

70. Site plan of Duck Pond Wreck 143

71. *Goldfield* as a private yacht, before returning to the Caymans in 1986 145

72. Bob Adams inspecting cannons from HMS *Convert,* wrecked with nine merchantmen in 1794 159

73. Bicentennial monument to Wreck of the Ten Sail 162

74. Prominent East End shipwrecks *Rimandi Mibaju* and *Ridgefield,* 1980 163

75. Windlass of sailing freighter *Cali* today 165

76. *Cali* in 1949, five years after grounding   165

77. Ghost ship *Soto Trader,* sunk in 1975   167

78. Seven hundred feet down, freighter *Kirk Pride* lodged precariously on vertical coral wall   168

79. Iron mast of 1895 wreck *Prince Frederick*   176

80. Wreck of *Evening Star*   179

81. Cayman Islands National Museum, in the Old Court House, George Town   180

82. Exhibit of Cayman Brac catboat *Independent*   181

Foreword

Water is unquestionably the most important natural feature on earth. By volume the world's oceans compose ninety-nine percent of the planet's living space; in fact, the surface of the Pacific Ocean alone is larger than that of the total of all land bodies. Water is as vital to life as air is. Indeed, to test whether the other planets or the moon can sustain life, NASA looks for signs of water. The story of human development is inextricably linked to the oceans, seas, lakes, and rivers that dominate the earth's surface. The University Press of Florida New Perspectives on Maritime History and Nautical Archaeology is devoted to exploring the impact of the earth's water while providing lively and important books that cover the spectrum of maritime history and nautical archaeology broadly defined. The series includes works that focus on the role of oceans, rivers, lakes, and canals in history; on the economic, military, and political use of those waters; and upon the people, communities, and industries that support maritime endeavors. Limited neither by geography nor by time, volumes in the series contribute to the overall understanding of maritime history and can be read with profit by both general readers and specialists.

Few societies have been as directly dependent on the sea for as long as that of the Cayman Islands. Thus Roger C. Smith's *Maritime Heritage of the Cayman Islands* is an excellent volume to inaugurate the series. His study offers a fascinating historical and archaeological view of how the sea influenced the three small western Caribbean land forms—Grand

Cayman, Cayman Brac, and Little Cayman—that together comprise a tiny island group. Roger Smith possesses the perfect combination of experience and knowledge to write this history. A nautical archaeologist, he has conducted a comprehensive survey of Caymanian waters; an expert on early modern sailing vessels, he has written the standard study of the ships used in the earliest explorations of American waters by Europeans. In this book he judiciously blends archaeological, ethnological, and archival historical sources to provide a well-rounded and readable story describing five centuries of maritime change—change that molded the islanders into a unique sea-hardened people whose nautical skills became renowned throughout the Caribbean world.

Initially uninhabited, the islands abounded in sea turtles that came seasonally to sandy, isolated beaches to lay their eggs. From the moment Christopher Columbus discovered the Caymans in 1503, those reptiles and their eggs helped sustain early explorers of the Caribbean. The settlers who followed harvested the turtles, which provided an important food resource, along with other bounties of the sea. Meanwhile, the low-lying islands proved to be a dangerous trap for Spanish treasure galleons, Dutch and English merchantmen, and warships that wrecked on the coral-lined coasts. To this day islanders still reap what the sea providentially brings to their shores.

During the late seventeenth and early eighteenth centuries the Cayman Islands' remote location also made them a favorite rendezvous for pirates, including Edward Teach, the famed Blackbeard. Other freebooters retreated to the Caymans to escape authorities or to lie in wait for unsuspecting passing merchant ships. While the pirates contributed little to the development of the islands, the romanticism surrounding their feats has proved a boon to modern tourism.

The sea and the marine life beneath it have been the driving forces behind the development of the Cayman Islands. The island people—whether harvesting sea turtles and the cargoes of wrecked ships, constructing specialized boats for turtling and salvaging, or evolving an economy based on tourists (drawn to the islands by the opportunity to soak up the sun's rays on pristine beaches, dive in coastal waters teeming with beautiful sea creatures, and go angling offshore for game fish)—have adapted their culture to and played a vital role in the growth and development of the West Indies. Theirs is truly a maritime society and economy worthy of examination.

James C. Bradford and Gene A. Smith, Series Editors

Preface

Because of their remote geographical location and comparatively small population, the Cayman Islands sometimes were called "the islands that time forgot." Emerging from an unpretentious, insular existence into the fervor of twentieth-century banking, real estate, and tourism, a historically maritime people have adapted to new lifestyles as the legacy of the sea is submerged beneath the roar of jet aircraft and the rumble of cement trucks.

Scientific and scholarly research dealing with the Caymans first arose with the need to plot the islands' location on maps. English surveyor George Gauld completed a map of Grand Cayman in 1773, showing some of the water depths at anchorages and in sounds.[1] However, systematic hydrographic surveys for the purpose of making accurate navigational charts of the island group were still being undertaken by the Royal Navy as late as the 1880s.[2] Shortly thereafter, British naturalists arrived to make observations and collections of plants, birds, reptiles, and mollusks.[3]

Although Jesse Walter Fewkes, an anthropologist with the Peabody Museum at Harvard University, visited the Caymans briefly from 1912 to 1913, his investigations were confined to the search for prehistoric cultures.[4] Finding no evidence of aboriginal populations, he continued his quest elsewhere in more profitable regions, and archaeology took a backseat to other fields of inquiry directed at the small island group.

In the early decades of the twentieth century, naturalists continued to discover the distinctive wildlife of the Caymans, commenting in journals about birds, insects, reptiles, sea turtles, and mollusks.[5] Several of these studies were results of the Oxford University Cayman Islands Biological Expedition of 1938, which included entomologists, botanists, and other biologists, who made large collections of most plant and animal groups. The unusual limestone formation of the island group soon was noted by geologists,[6] and eventually geographers turned their attention to the region and helped to end its remoteness with their physical and cultural observations.[7]

These diverse researchers all encountered one thing in common: the Caymans' enormous population of mosquitoes, a serious pest that had been endured by residents for more than a hundred years. The principal species was the black salt marsh mosquito (*Aedes taeniorhynchus*), which breeds in the mangrove swamps that comprise portions of the islands.[8] The government established in 1965 the Mosquito Research and Control Unit (MRCU) and a laboratory, under the direction of Dr. Marco Giglioli, which began spraying insecticide and building dikes to manipulate water in the swamps. In the course of this work, Giglioli became increasingly concerned with environmental issues related to modern development, and between 1974 and 1975 a massive study to determine the nature and extent of the natural marine resources of the islands was sponsored by the British Ministry of Overseas Development. Researchers in marine biology, oceanography, and fisheries sought to identify threats to the resources and make recommendations on ways in which to utilize and preserve them. The resulting six-volume study contained reports on additional and timely topics such as dredging, oil pollution, tourism, beach litter, and marine parks and conservation.[9] The natural resources study paved the way for an expedition to Little Cayman in 1974, jointly sponsored by the Royal Society and the Cayman Islands government, with assistance from the MRCU. Participants included a botanist, marine biologist, zoologist, entomologist, ornithologist, and mangrove specialist, who published their findings in a detailed bulletin.[10]

With the establishment of the MRCU, Giglioli encouraged a number of researchers and graduate students to pursue various studies in the Cayman Islands; his laboratory contained simple accommodations made available to visiting overseas scientists including, on several occasions, this author. The growing number of investigators working in the islands in the 1970s and 1980s included geologists, malacologists, biologists, hydrogeologists, entomologists, sedimentologists, ichthyologists, zoologists, and paleontologists. In addition to an astonishing number of university theses and dissertations written on the resources of the Cayman Islands,[11] and scores of articles published in academic journals,[12] much of this research has been compiled into a large volume on the natural history and biogeography of the islands, which was published in 1994 and dedicated to the memory of Dr. Giglioli, who passed away in 1984.[13]

In comparison with natural resources, the study of cultural resources has lagged far behind. While the history of the Cayman Islands has not been neglected by interested researchers, it has been presented either piecemeal or in summary fashion.[14] Although the nature of Caymanian culture and its changing situation have been addressed by political scientists and social anthropologists, only small strata of society in specific areas were studied, leaving broader implications unformulated for the islands as a whole.[15]

Realization of the significance of the Cayman Islands' role in the course of West Indian affairs has awaited an explanation of how and why they came to be the way they are today. This realization undoubtedly rests on the accumulation of additional data that only recently have been provided by archaeological discoveries, anthropological inquiry, and archival testimony. The formulation of this book resulted from several years of research conducted by the author under the auspices of the Institute of Nautical Archaeology (INA) of Texas A&M University, at the invitation of the government of the Cayman Islands. During 1979 and 1980, the INA team recorded seventeen archaeological sites on Little Cayman, five sites on Cayman Brac, and fifty-five sites on Grand Cayman. The archaeological record compiled during two seasons of field work on land and under water encompasses more than three centuries of cultural information and reflects seafaring activities, external and internal trade practices, and fishing and wrecking pursuits. By combining this record with archival and cartographic information collected from several repositories on both sides of the Atlantic, as well as ethnographic data gathered from island inhabitants, the unique maritime heritage of the Cayman Islands is assembled and unfolded for the reader.

The essence of this heritage centers on the sea turtle and the human pursuit of it. Once the New World's largest turtle fishery, the islands for several centuries possessed a resource that not only made a distinct impact on the development of the West Indies but also shaped the cultural framework of Cayman Islanders for posterity. Until the middle of the twentieth century, turtle fishing was the basic thread of Caymanian existence. It was the principal impetus in the evolution of a race of seafarers unique to the Caribbean world.

The extent to which this maritime activity contributed to the early history and colonization of the region is rarely recognized by those familiar with West Indian culture. And as the resource has dwindled, the special folkways that evolved from the utilization of the resource also have begun to fade. Hopefully they will not be forgotten. While this book cannot pretend to provide a complete picture of the Caymans' past, significant elements of maritime culture are explored, explained, and celebrated so that they may provide a starting point for future inquiry.

Acknowledgments

The formulation of this book resulted from the combined assistance of a great many individuals who helped to conduct the actual investigations and of organizations that made possible the successful completion of field and archival work.

At the very beginning, there was an invitation from Mr. and Mrs. C. Charles Adams, founders of the Caymanian Heritage Trust, whose generous encouragement and friendship constantly fueled the entire undertaking. It was due largely to their foresight, and to the diplomatic courtesies of former U.S. ambassador to Jamaica Sumner Gerard and of His Excellency Thomas Russell, CBE, former governor of the Cayman Islands, that a pleasant working relationship in the islands was established so smoothly. Without the assistance and support of Mr. J. M. Bodden and other members of the Executive Council of the Cayman Islands government, this research would not have been possible. I owe equal thanks to the late Brian Lauer, principal secretary for agriculture, lands, and natural resources, and to the late Dr. Marco E. C. Giglioli and the staff of the Mosquito Research and Control Unit in the Cayman Islands, who graciously offered their advice and resources in a quest for history and archaeology.

Special appreciation is directed to Drs. George F. Bass, Frederick van Doorninck, J. Richard Steffy, Henry C. Schmidt, and Vaughn M. Bryant for their invaluable assistance and encouragement during various phases of the investigation. This book is a reflection of their academic guidance and practical advice.

A successful field expedition to remote islands requires a dedicated and imaginative team of people with a myriad of talents ranging from the mastery of special skills—engineering, surveying, cartography, archaeology, photography, diving, conservation—to the more ordinary chores of cooking, equipment maintenance, record keeping, and washing dishes. Combined with unselfish enthusiasm and a large dose of humor, the ingredients of productive research were shared by these colleagues: Robert Adams, Kathryn Boeckman, William Crow, Alison Darroch, Dennis Denton, Hugh Dutton, Patricia Gibson, Emily Graves, Denise Hoyt, Steven Hoyt, Paul Hundley, Margaret Leshikar, Pilar Luna Erreguerena, Charles Mazel, Ricardo Menes, Michelle Scudder, KC Smith, and Sheli Smith. Their untiring energy and determination helped to make the first survey of its kind in the Cayman Islands a reality.

Encouragement and support for the publication of this book came from Martin Golob of Miami, Florida; Benson O. Ebanks, former Cayman Islands Executive Council member; Anita Ebanks, director of the Cayman Islands National Museum; Margaret Leshikar-Denton, archaeologist of the Cayman Islands National Museum; Dennis Denton of Atlantis Submarines Ltd.; and KC Smith of the Museum of Florida History. Thanks too for the enthusiasm and patience of Meredith Morris-Babb, editor in chief of the University Press of Florida.

I should like also to acknowledge the kind assistance of the following additional individuals, whose contributions of financial support, expertise, advice, time, or other help made the first archaeological survey of the Cayman Islands and the writing of this book possible:

On Grand Cayman: Charles and Lori Adams, Michael Adams, Richard Beswick, Darby Bodden, Dinah Bodden, Edroy Bodden, Ernest Bodden, Floyd Bodden, Haig Bodden, Halkeith Bodden, Norman Bodden, "Sonny Boy" Bodden, Brent Bush, Brian E. Butler, Stanley Cook, Mary Cooper, Roger L. Craig, James Dailey, Mr. and Mrs. John Doll, Clinton Ebanks, Kent Eldermire, Richard Emory, James Graves, Hugh Hart, James Hawthorne, Richard Heath, Wilton Hercules, Samuel Jackson, Barton Kirkconnell, Captain Charles Kirkconnell, Eldon Kirkconnell, Jerry Kirkconnell, Mr. and Mrs. James Lawrence, Jan Liebaers, His Excellency G. P. Lloyd, Michael McGowen, Woodrow McLaughlin, Lester MacLean, Goldborne Mascal, Mr. and Mrs. Eric Nelson, Dr. Philip Pedley, Mark

Pimbert, Douglas Rollings, Geoffrey Rutty, Tamara Selzer, Maggie and Doug Seward, Mr. and Mrs. Earl Smith, Deborah Tabora-Barnes, Ralph Terry, Stacy Tibbetts, Ira Thompson, Christopher Thorne, Mr. and Mrs. Michael Villani, Mr. and Mrs. Cordel Watler, Mr. and Mrs. Marshall Watler, W. Burnatt Webster, Mr. and Mrs. Randy White, C. J. Whitelock, Clinton Whittaker, and Mr. and Mrs. Percy Whorms.

On Cayman Brac: Floyd Banks, Harold Banks, William Cass, Marvin Ebanks, Ernest Eggler, Captain Ashland Foster, Hebe Foster, Minnie Foster, Nolan Foster, Daryl Grant, Mr. and Mrs. Elvern Hurlstone, Garlon Jackson, Mr. and Mrs. Lee Jervis, Dean Kelso, James Ketrow, Louisa Kirkconnell, Captain Mabry Kirkconnell, Willie Kirkconnell, Delano Lazzari, Russell Loggins, Crelon MacFarlon, Gilbert MacLean, Captain Kenneth Ritch, Frederick Ryan, J. Alger Ryan, Richard Sanders, Bramwell Scott, Mr. and Mrs. Carroll Scott, Clyde Scott, Durwin Scott, Mr. and Mrs. Eston Scott, Raymond Scott, Shelby Scott, Vetie Smith, Captain Keith Tibbetts, Linton Tibbetts, Marky Walter, Mathan Walters, and Henry Watson.

On Little Cayman: Eleanor Bodden, Mr. and Mrs. Franklin Bodden, Mr. and Mrs. Jody Bodden, Nada Bodden, Mr. and Mrs. Douglas Chisholm, Burt Ebanks, Mr. and Mrs. Jack Ebanks, Cissie Grizzel, Joseph Grizzel, Gladys Howard, Mr. and Mrs. Basil Kassa, Mike Lewis, and Astley McLaughlin.

In the United States: Mr. and Mrs. Jeffrey Apple, Charles Beeker, Diane Bond, Louise Brown, Denise Clarke-Hundley, Marcia Cook Hart, Edwin Doran, William Fife, Diane Foley, James Frazier, Donald Geddes, Robert Goswick, Dr. and Mrs. Donny Hamilton, William Hart, Donald Keith, Denise Lakey, David Langworthy, Keith Langworthy, Wilson Langworthy, Jay Lewallen, Mr. and Mrs. Rob Lewallen, Stanley Lopata, Robert F. Marx, Alan Nelson, Brent O'Brian, Carol Olsen, Desmond Rolfe, Dory Slane, T. K. Treadwell, and Joanne Treat.

Other colleagues, scholars, and supporters who provided unique and valued assistance include:

In Jamaica: Anthony G. Aarons, Port Royal Archaeological Research Centre; Dr. David Buisseret, Department of History, University of the West Indies; Mrs. Charles Cotter, Lime Hall, St. Ann; Donald Dacosta, Kingston; the Honorable John Drinkall, British high commissioner; Mr. and Mrs. Maurice Facey, Kingston; Richard Issa, Kingston; and Father Francis J. Osbourne, Jamaica National Trust Commission.

In the United States: F. Hebert, Hispanic Division, Library of Congress; Donald G. Shomette, Graphics Division, Library of Congress; John A. Wolter and Patrick Dempsey, Geography and Maps Division, Library of Congress; and Susan Danforth, the John Carter Brown Library.

In Great Britain: Phillip Annis, National Maritime Museum, Greenwich; Lieutenant Commander Andrew David, Hydrography Department, Ministry of Defence, Taunton; Hugh and Peter Dutton, London; David Lyon, National Maritime Musem, Greenwich; Colonel Max Robinson, West India Committee, London; Dr. Rogers and Miss Harding, Public Record Office, Kew; and Jane Weeks, Conway Maritime Press, Greenwich.

In the Netherlands: P. C. Emmer, Institute for the History of European Expansion, Leiden; Bas Kist, Rijksmuseum, Amsterdam; M. van Opstall, Algemeen Rijksarchief, The Hague; and Jan Pirt Puype, Nederlands Scheepvaartmuseum, Amsterdam.

In Spain: Rosario Parra Cala, Archivo General de Indias, Seville; Santiago Jiménez, Museo Naval, Madrid; Victoria Stapells-Johnson, Seville; Rick Thornburgh, Madrid; and Dalmiro de la Valgoma, Real Academia de la Historia, Madrid.

In Mexico: Pilar Luna Erreguerena, Ricardo Menes, and Hortensia de Vega Nova, Instituto Nacional de Antropología y Historia, Mexico City.

Organizations that assisted field research in the Cayman Islands included the following firms, to which I remain most grateful:

In the Cayman Islands: Bank of Nova Scotia; Canadian Imperial Bank of Commerce; Cayman Airways; Cayman Energy; Cayman National Bank; Cayman Property Corporation Ltd.; Elizabethan Developments Ltd.; Guinness Mahon Trust Ltd.; Jacques Scott & Company Ltd.; National Employees Mutual; Onions, Bouchard & McColluch; R. B. Kirkconnell Bros. Ltd.; and Red Carpet Flying Services.

In the United States: Agfa-Gevaert; Allied Safety Equipment; American R Corporation; Cobart Marine, Inc.; Cutter Laboratories, Inc.; Dickens Corporation; Ehrenreich Photo-Optical, Inc.; Outboard Marine Corporation; Fuji Photo Film Corporation; Gerard Foundation; Igloo Corporation; Institute of Nautical Archaeology; Johnson and Johnson, Inc.; Kenlee's West; Koh-i-noor Rapidograph, Inc.; Pentax Corporation; P. R. Mallory & Co., Inc.; S. C. Johnson and Sons, Inc.; Sonic Research; Texas A&M Research Foundation; Texas A&M University Anthropology Program; Texas A&M University Department of Engineering; Texas Trunks; Tom Padgitt, Inc.; U.S. Divers Corporation; U.S. Naval Oceanographic Office; and Zodiac of North America, Inc.

The Cayman Islands Project

As the summer of 1980 drew to a close, most of the offshore waters and coastal lagoons of Grand Cayman had been surveyed. Work had progressed smoothly, and the weather had been excellent. But, as is usual in the West Indies, the month of August brought increased awareness that the hurricane season was under way. Throughout the expedition, the British Broadcasting Corporation had been a daily source of radio news about the outside world. One morning the broadcast included mention of a depression forming in the mid-Atlantic. In the days that followed we learned that the first hurricane of the season, named Allen, slowly was gaining force and heading into the Caribbean Sea. We began tracking Allen's progress on a dog-eared National Geographic map of the West Indies. The previous season had given us plenty of practice packing up project equipment in a hurry, with not one but two hurricanes on the way. Both, however, had moved to the north of Cuba rather than remaining on a course toward the Cayman Islands. Now we waited and prepared to batten down should the new hurricane head in our direction.

The Caymans probably have suffered storm damage more often than any other island group in the Caribbean, because they are located on the path of least resistance along prevailing hurricane tracks. The year 1980 proved to be no exception, and as reports from Jamaica described the storm's destruction on that island's north coast, it became clear that Allen was pointed northwest toward the Cayman Islands. Radio warnings became more frequent, and offshore, as the oncoming storm gathered strength over water again, the air became ominously still and the seas flat calm.

Before long the wind and sea signaled a change in the atmosphere, and the sky grew dark. We began to collect our boats from the water, dragging them into the bush and tying them down to the stoutest trees. Loose equipment was carried into the house, and sheets of plywood and scraps of timber were assembled to secure every window, door, and opening. Although the project headquarters was the windwardmost building on the island, it had been built with cement blocks on a rock bluff above the sea. We trusted the house to withstand a major storm, especially when we compared it with other dwellings of wood and mortar along the beach.

Around-the-clock preparations began in earnest before dawn on August 6. Every container in the house was filled with fresh water. Kerosene lamps and stoves were made ready, and extra blankets, cots, and provisions were brought to the second floor, where we planned to weather the approaching storm. By midmorning several of the crew members were down in the village in howling winds and driving rain to offer assistance and shelter to whoever felt unsafe at the water's edge. The town hall and village school had been designated as hurricane shelters and soon were filled with reluctant townspeople. No one seemed frightened, only resigned to the workings of nature.

Seventy miles to windward, the islands of Little Cayman and Cayman Brac had lost communication with the outside world as the hurricane passed nearby. Incredible seas began to pound the eastern edge of Grand Cayman. We watched thirty- and forty-foot waves smash over the outside reef. The steel hulls of two large freighters, grounded on the reef in the early 1960s, gradually came apart. The larger one buckled in two before our eyes, while the other freighter spun around and almost disappeared beneath the raging waves. Contemplating what it must have been like to be at sea in a small ship during a hurricane in the days of sail, we began to feel more reverence for the unfortunate crews of the wrecks that we had been investigating for the past two years.

Eight-foot seas pushed across the normally placid lagoon, broke over the bluff, and sprayed the side of the house. East End Sound became a churning mass of muddy turbulence, and we began to count fragments of docks, boats, and fishing huts as they floated by the bluff, wrenched from the shore. Retreating into the house, we listened to the radio, which barely was audible over the sound of the storm. Word came in the late afternoon that Allen had passed to the north of the island, pushing winds of up to 215 miles per hour in the open sea. Although rough weather and heavy rains continued for several days, no lives had been lost in the Cayman Islands, and damage was minimal compared with that sustained on Haiti, Jamaica, and Cuba. We later learned that this storm, which narrowly missed Grand Cayman, was considered one of the most powerful Caribbean hurricanes of the decade.

New beaches had appeared on either side of our headquarters where mangroves had been torn away and replaced by sand from the bottom of the lagoon. After the project dried out and began survey operations once more, the reef line was explored again to see what had happened to familiar wrecks and their environments. We were flabbergasted to discover the seabed transformed into a wasteland, barren even of the fish that usually congregated in profusion. They had retreated into deeper water for protection. Incredibly, portions of wrecksites that we were recording had vanished, other sections of the seabed had eroded to expose wreckage we hadn't seen before, and several of the larger modern sites had been totally rearranged.

As the field season came to a close, our inventory of wrecksites around Grand Cayman had grown to more than fifty, each carefully examined and documented. Now, entire days were spent indoors, despite good weather, because the paperwork was piling up. In addition to older sites, we had investigated the remains of a wrecked PBY flying boat, a trading ship laden with cases of Cuban beer, and a copper-sheathed turtling schooner. A wrecked yacht loaded with drugs smuggled from Colombia naturally was off limits to the survey crew, but we did have an opportunity to help the government to locate the remains of its mosquito-spraying aircraft that had crashed into the water one evening during a low-altitude turning maneuver.[1]

The project had come full circle since its inception. I had first visited the Cayman Islands in 1978 as a young graduate student at Texas A&M University's Institute of Nautical Archaeology. Late one afternoon in the spring semester, Professor George F. Bass called another student, Donald Keith, and me into his office. As was typical for a widely published scholar in a unique field, he had been contacted by representatives of another country, who sought his assistance in matters relating to ancient shipwrecks. However, this request came from the Caribbean, a region with which he was unfamiliar, having worked primarily in the Mediterranean.

He asked Don and me whether we knew where the Cayman Islands were. We looked at one another with blank stares, and had to admit to our professor that we aspiring young archaeologists hadn't a clue.

Instead of going home that evening, I went to the library. The next morning as Professor Bass walked toward his office, I was waiting for him with a briefing based on bits and pieces of information I had gathered. Several weeks later I found myself on an airplane to Grand Cayman via Miami. As the cabin door opened on arrival in George Town, I descended the stairs into a tropical world of brilliant colors, salty breezes, and exotic fragrances—a transitional experience that was to be repeated many times in the coming years. Charles Adams, a distinguished attorney with a love of West Indian history and culture, met me at the gate with a firm, warm handshake. He had formed a foundation called the Caymanian Heritage Trust, with the idea of promoting and preserving local history, architecture, and folkways. With a twinkle in his eye, he asked whether I had brought my mask and fins.

Thus began a whirlwind of meetings with government officials, civil servants, local divers, and fishermen, all of whom displayed the openness and sincerity for which the Caymanian people are known. Adams explained that, despite the islands' legendary reputation as a trap for ships and a haven for pirates and wreckers, there had not yet been a proper examination of the many ancient shipwrecks that dotted the reefs around each island. No one knew how many there were or what they contained. He showed me several rusting cannons from offshore sites, now adorning private residences. He took me to meet his friend Ira Thompson, a local taxi driver who had spent years collecting artifacts and relics of the past—from an old kerosene lamp that had lit the lighthouse on the windward side of the island to Spanish pots that fishermen had recovered from the sea. Thompson had carefully catalogued hundreds of objects and arranged them for display in a private building that he called the Keimanos Museum. Adams explained that "Mr. Ira" hoped one day to make his collection available to the government as the basis for a national museum.

On the last day of my visit, Adams drove me to the east end of the island, which is surrounded by a vast, treacherous reef. On the horizon were two large steel freighters, rusting in the sun, which provided stark testimony to the nautical hazards that lay beneath the waters of this tranquil, tropical Eden. Adams had arranged with Woody McLaughlin, a tall, soft-spoken East Ender, to take me into the lagoon on his boat to show me an old shipwreck. As we made our way across the shallow, clear waters over patches of crystalline sand and emerald eel grass, McLaughlin told me the names of the two freighters and what he knew about each of them. He explained that there were many, many shipwrecks outside, on top of, and inside the reef. He and his friends, their fathers, and their grandfathers before them all had seen the wreckage of old ships under the sea, but no one knew much about where they had come from or how old they were. He told me the story of how ten ships had wrecked together on the reef one night in the 1700s, and how local East Enders helped to rescue the survivors. But he wasn't sure exactly where on the reef the ships had gone aground.

We were well offshore when Woody cut the boat engine and picked up a long pole. He looked back at the land, then out to the reef, and began to maneuver us with the sun at his back toward a dark patch in the surrounding grass flat. Then he picked up a wooden box, enclosed at one end with a pane of clear glass, and leaned over the gunwale to look through the water. I noticed that his broad-brimmed straw hat shaded the entire open end of the box as he hunched over it. He sat up with a smile and handed me the box. As I peered into it, I was startled by a magnified vision that seemed to be close enough to touch. Poking up through the thick sea grass below were the encrusted remains of an old sailing ship, surrounded by small, brightly colored fish. It was like an optical illusion.

After Woody anchored, I slid into the water. As far as I could see, a long line of frames and tackle stretched across the seabed, creating a ghostly outline of the side of a sunken ship. At intervals, remnants of the vessel's standing rigging became recognizable, strewn in more or less predictable fashion on the bottom. Gradually the fish showed me where other nearby features were located. I swam transfixed by the magic and mystery of the scene below, until Woody banged his pole on the bilge of his boat, indicating that it was time to go. As we headed to shore toward the setting sun, I sat speechless in the bow of the boat, occasionally looking back over my shoulder at the monster freighter wrecks glowing distinctly in the sharp evening light. I looked at Woody, and he smiled and nodded his head. As we pulled his boat up on the beach, he presented me with a queen conch shell and said that he hoped that I would come back soon. Thus the genesis of a shipwreck survey of the Cayman Islands was formed.

The Institute of Nautical Archaeology began its first Caribbean project in the summer of 1979 on the island of Little Cayman. There were ten in our survey crew, eager to explore the secrets of the remote island. The fifteen people living on the island were curious to learn our names when

Fig. 1. Silhouetted in the setting sun, the wreck of *Ridgefield* stands guard at the entrance to the sound of East End, Grand Cayman. Photo by KC Smith.

they discovered that we were not tourists. We had two boats, one of which was fitted with a magnetometer for detecting iron objects such as cannons and anchors, and a digital trisponder unit for accurate positioning of submerged sites. Cayman Energy had donated a Jeep that was towed to Little Cayman from nearby Cayman Brac on a small barge behind the crewboat *Cayman Mariner.* We set up our headquarters in a small waterfront compound on South Hole Sound and began to assemble our equipment. But before we even had a chance to test it, local residents began to tell us about several shipwrecks in close proximity. Frankie and Jody Bodden, energetic owners of a small fishing lodge, showed us several sites, and a pattern was set. It turned out that we had much to learn—not about finding shipwrecks, but about recording and interpreting those that local people showed to us.[2]

We soon became acquainted with all of the residents of Little Cayman, each of whom participated in one way or another in our research. Elderly islanders, in particular, generously shared their stories and customs, helping us to begin to understand the unique maritime culture of the islands. "Uncle Joe" Grizzel, veteran mariner and master boatbuilder, had a soft spot for the female members of our survey team and spent hours relating seagoing anecdotes and offering information about the island's shipwrecks. One day I helped him to gather whelks along the tidal ironshore. As we waded in rubber boots at low tide across sharp limestone pinnacles, looking in the crevasses for the largest mollusks, Joe told me about how the sea had provided for him and his sister, Cissie, and about the various watercraft that he had built with his own hands. After each of us had filled our buckets with whelks, we made our way back to his modest seaside house. He showed me how to extract the snails from their shells and grind them for Cissie, who made us a tasty local dish called sea pie.

Gradually the crew became familiar with the waters of Little Cayman, recording and studying seventeen archaeological sites that included the remains of small colonial sailing vessels, several merchant ships that had struck the reef, nineteenth-century composite-built trading vessels, and a modern freighter with cargo still in the hold.[3] After a site was located, its precise position was surveyed from existing benchmarks and plotted on a master chart of the areas covered by the investigation. Features such as

Fig. 2. Cayman Islands Project Team 1979. *Front row:* Emily Graves, Bill Crow, Alison Darroch, KC Smith; *back row:* Sheli Smith, Charles Mazel, Kathyrn Boeckman, Roger Smith, Paul Hundley; *not shown:* Hugh Dutton, Michelle Scudder. Photo by KC Smith.

Fig. 3. Drawing in the sand, "Uncle Joe" Grizzel (*right*) describes for the author the location of one of Little Cayman's many shipwrecks. Photo by KC Smith.

anchors, cannons, ship's structure, and fittings were carefully measured and recorded (fig. 4). Limited testing by selective excavation or surface sampling was undertaken to obtain diagnostic artifacts useful in determining a general date or cultural affiliation for each site. These artifacts often included pottery sherds, clay smoking-pipe fragments, bits and pieces of ship's equipment, or crew's possessions.[4]

The most significant site dated to the seventeenth century, the heyday of buccaneering in the Caribbean. Evidence of a battle, including discarded arms and spent ammunition, burned ship's timbers, and charred turtle bones, was uncovered beneath the sandy floor of a shallow lagoon, and an obscure reference in a local book provided a clue to what had happened. In 1669 an English captain had complained to officials in Jamaica about the capture of his vessel and the destruction of huts and boats belonging to a turtle fishing station on Little Cayman. The chief villain appeared to have been a Portuguese corsair, who carried a royal Spanish commission of reprisal against the English for Henry Morgan's raids on Portobelo and Maracaibo the previous year. The privateer claimed responsibility for attacking the Caymans, nailing to a tree a piece of sailcloth on which was written a challenge to the chief of the English buccaneers to come out and witness "the Valour of the Spaniards."

Our curiosity was aroused by this and other discoveries on Little Cayman, but the first season came to a close as hurricanes David and Frederick forced the expedition to move to neighboring Cayman Brac, which has higher ground and sheltering caves. It was evident that additional historical research might shed light on finds that we had made, and that further investigation of the general history of the islands would be necessary before the second season's survey of Cayman Brac and Grand Cayman.[5]

Since virtually no early written records survived in collections in the Cayman Islands, archival materials would have to be searched for in other countries. The islands' government generously provided a grant through the Caymanian Heritage Trust for archival research abroad, and I planned a winter itinerary to search for more information about the Caymans' maritime past. The most obvious place to begin was Jamaica, the English administrative center for the Cayman Islands in colonial times. The Island Record Office in old Spanish Town, and the West India Reference Collection (now the National Library) of the prestigious Institute of Jamaica yielded early correspondence between the governor and Grand Cayman's chief islanders. The earliest official census of the Caymans was located in a cedar box and copied for the first time in its entirety.

Fig. 4. Sheli Smith and Kathryn Boeckman record the anchor of *Maggie Gray,* a phosphate ship that sank off the west end of Little Cayman circa 1892. Photo by KC Smith.

The vast Library of Congress in Washington, D.C., was my next stop. Surrounded by one of the world's largest collections of books, I managed to wangle a stack pass. I searched old descriptions of the West Indies, poked through journals of voyages and records of ship losses, and scanned rare manuscripts for references to the remote Cayman Islands. In the Geography and Maps Division, in a building almost as large as the main library, the director kindly allowed early charts to be photographed in an effort to assemble a unique cartographic record of the Caymans as they appeared to mariners of yesterday.

In Europe, I began research at Great Britain's Public Record Office, located in an imposing building near Kew Gardens, outside London. Armed with lists of references to specific records, I was assigned a computer number, a reserved reader's seat, and an electronic beeper. In the days that followed, documents were requested by computer, delivered when the beeper sounded, and carefully examined, one by one. Soon I had compiled several folders of photocopied documents full of clues to the islands' past. An historical jigsaw puzzle was being pieced together from diplomatic correspondence, official depositions, captured Spanish papers, ships' logs, proceedings of courts martial, and captains' letters.

A visit to the Admiralty Hydrography Office in Somerset was equally worthwhile. I located documents from the first Royal Navy survey of the Cayman Islands that included official field notes, reports, and handwritten sailing directions compiled in the 1880s aboard the survey schooner HMS *Sparrowhawk*. The original watercolored navigational chart of the islands was taken from the map vault for me to examine. This is the map on which all modern charts of the area are based, containing details that have, of course, changed since it was drawn. Remark books from various Royal Navy ships also were consulted, several of which provided descriptions of the topography, inhabitants, and other remarkable features of the Cayman Islands.

Vague mention of an early Dutch West India Company ship wrecked on Grand Cayman in 1628 led to a quick trip across the English Channel to the Netherlands. Disappointment accompanied a visit to the Algemeen Rijksarchief in The Hague, where I discovered that a nineteenth-century fire had consumed the majority of the West India Company records. However, the Nederlands Scheepvaartmuseum in Amsterdam yielded several chronicles of Dutch voyages to the Cayman Islands.

Of major importance to students of Spanish New World history is the Archivo General de Indias in Seville, which I hoped would shed light on the mysterious activities of the Spanish corsair who attacked Little Cayman. Situated in the sixteenth-century House of Trade, next to the Gothic cathedral containing the tomb of Columbus, the collection contains millions of documents pertaining to Spain's once-vast overseas empire. After passing through a stately marble entryway and elegant red curtains, I was assigned an oak desk and leather-covered chair in the *salón de investigación,* and began the task of examining bundles of handwritten papers in an unfamiliar script and lexicon that, at first, seemed indecipherable. Although determined to learn the Spanish side of early Caymanian history, I found the going slow and frustrating.

After several days of studying dusty folios—some with blotting sand still between the papers—words and sentences began to emerge from the paleography on the pages. Bits and pieces of information about the Caymans were hidden in royal correspondence, declarations of prisoners, lists of prize ships, testimonies of unfortunate mariners, and the like. Finally, on the last day of my scheduled stay in Seville, a report to the king dealing with the corsair attack on the islands was found in a section of the archive known as Indiferente General (General Miscellaneous).[6]

Fig. 5. Cayman Islands Project Team 1980. *Left to right:* Pilar Luna Erreguerena, Dennis Denton, Pat Gibson, Bob Adams, Margaret Leshikar, Roger Smith, Steve Hoyt, Denise Hoyt, Ricardo Menes, KC Smith. Photo by KC Smith.

Fig. 6. Native Cayman Bracker Louisa Kirkconnell tells Margaret Leshikar about her family's involvement in the local shipping industry. Photo by KC Smith.

Bolstered by the newly acquired historical data, the survey expedition continued with a new team, which arrived on Cayman Brac in the summer of 1980. Headquarters were established in the old mansion of the Kirkconnell family, a successful merchant clan. Situated on the shore with a small cove for our boats, the abandoned house was reputed to be haunted by "duppies," or island ghosts. However, considering that we were given free use of the building by the family, we didn't mind a few unexplained noises and incidents during our stay. Aside from searching for shipwrecks, the project crew became adept at collecting oral histories from elderly Brackers eager to recount the past. Living memories, legends, and anecdotes passed down through generations were recorded on tape and later transcribed to provide ethnographic data important to the survey. Other pursuits involved examining old boats hidden in sheds or left forlorn on the beach. Several caves were explored in hopes of finding evidence of prehistoric occupation.[7]

Absorbed in our work, we found the summer days slipping quickly away, and soon it was time to transfer operations to the largest island, Grand Cayman, which was noted for its shipwrecks. The monthly inter-island trading vessel left the Brac with our survey boats lashed on deck and our equipment safely in her hold. Our departure on the small island-hopping airplane was a sad affair; many of our newly made friends showed up to see us off, offering going-away presents of homemade breadfruit cakes, sea pies, and coconut jellies.

On Grand Cayman, we were fortunate to find accommodations in a large, round cement house overlooking the East End lagoon from a rocky promontory called Gun Bluff. Built around a circular cistern, the building had plenty of living and working space for crew and visitors. It looked more like a fortress than a dwelling, with a tall flagpole on its roof. Cement steps led down to a small cove where we moored our project boats. We immediately met Marshall Watler, an elderly sailor and fisherman who lived down the road with his wife, Victorine, and their children. Watler had decided at age fifty that it was time to settle down, marry, and have a family, so he retired from the sea. Now, twenty-five years later, he supported his brood by working on the island road crew; in his spare time, he set fish traps in the lagoon. Eventually, he showed us where he had seen wrecks.

Our survey team now had three boats that could be deployed simultaneously around the island, always finding an area of calm water in which to search for shipwrecks. Fiberglass towboards with handles were used to pull snorkelers in tandem behind the boats. Skimming through the sea, some ten to twelve fathoms behind a boat, with dive mask strap tightened down, snorkel firmly clenched between teeth, and swimming suit cinched up, was great fun. It was like an aerial reconnaissance in the island's clear waters; as targets along the seabed came into view, the towboards could be angled down toward the bottom for closer inspection. We learned early on to look periodically over our shoulders as we towed the reef line to keep tabs on curious fish that followed us through their territory.

The towboards allowed us to visually survey large inner and outer tracts of the reef around the island. However, our boats could not operate up on the crest of the reef, since it usually was too shallow and turbulent. For this job, we acquired two Italian-made "water scooters," each consisting of a tiny two-stroke engine mounted to a fuel tank float that drove a small, caged propeller. Promoted as watertight, each scooter had a long upright snorkel to supply air to its carburetor. We weren't sure about their other attributes until we began to test the units at sea. One female team member discovered that the scooters were only designed to operate on the surface; when she tried to submerge the machine under power, the propeller stole her swimming suit top, which promptly stalled the unit. Another crew member found that when he let go of the machine, it continued to run through the water making a wide arc, eventually returning to him. Fully fueled, each unit was rated to run for two hours.

Fig. 7. Surveying large tracts of the Cayman reef line is facilitated by the use of small water scooters to pull snorkelers through shallow water. Photo by KC Smith.

The scooters allowed us to navigate among coral heads and in the surf on top of the reef. Deployed from the boats, they sometimes carried crew members so far away that we couldn't see them anymore, even with binoculars. So we lengthened the snorkels and tied fluorescent streamers to them. Other times, a unit quit and couldn't be restarted without cleaning its carburetor. So we devised a small waterproof tool pouch for scooter operators to carry with them.

We were not disappointed by the reefs and sounds of Grand Cayman, discovering them to be virtual graveyards of ships. On the weather-beaten windward reef in front of our headquarters alone, careful survey and mapping revealed twenty-four wrecksites, some lying on top of each other. Scattered remains of wooden sailing ships extended over coral heads into the sand, leaving tracks through the reef and trails of ballast and hull fasteners along the seafloor. Outside, in deeper water, anchors and windlasses and hardware marked the impact points of unfortunate vessels. Heaps of broken iron hulls and masts were located by the unmistakable dark shadows they cast through the clear water. Other sites were camouflaged by coral, and some were half buried in sand or grass. Recovery of

Fig. 8. Denise Hoyt draws a site plan of a colonial shipwreck on the reef off the east end of Grand Cayman. Photo by KC Smith.

Spanish olive jars, French floor tiles, English trade ceramics, wine and beer bottles, encrusted ammunition, and rigging and hardware helped us to untangle individual sites and identify them by date and origin. It wasn't long before the crew coined a jocular motto at the breakfast table: "A wreck a day!" Some days we found two.

After four months, the second season of the Cayman Islands Project came to a close. During the last weeks of the expedition, we were honored with an official reception organized by the government and held at our Gun Bluff house. The occasion provided an opportunity to show the governor and Executive Council of the Cayman Islands, as well as local residents and supporters, the results of our work. On all three islands, seventy-seven sites of archaeological significance had been recorded during the project.

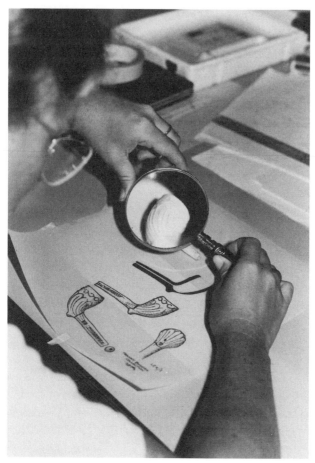

Fig. 9. Archaeological materials are drawn, photographed, and studied for information about their place and date of manufacture. Photo by KC Smith.

Fig. 10. Typical earthenware containers for colonial commerce, these Spanish olive jars were found on various archaeological sites throughout the Cayman Islands. Photo by KC Smith.

A series of portfolios had been assembled, detailing site locations, features, and tentative interpretations. Presented to the Caymanian Heritage Trust, the survey records would form the nucleus of a national archaeological inventory. In addition to data and artifacts, the project offered several formal recommendations for consideration by the government of the Cayman Islands. These included revision of the existing Abandoned Wreck Law to accommodate shipwrecks as archaeological and historical monuments; formal governmental regulation of terrestrial and marine cultural resources, with guidelines for issuing of research permits, and additional surveys prior to development projects that might impact these resources; and suggestions for the establishment of a national museum with curatorial and conservation staff, in addition to exhibit and educational capabilities.

Founded Upon the Seas

Thrust up from the abyss and coated with life between wind and water, three isolated islands were discovered half a millennium ago by seafarers from distant shores. Named after remarkable reptiles that crawled along white beaches or swam in profusion offshore, the islands gradually were charted by navigators and given their place in modern geography. As mariners became familiar with the remote land forms and their attributes, names for the islands became standardized, yet their accurate locations on charts of the region had to wait for refinements in navigational instruments. The first settlers brought with them a maritime outlook that characterized patterns of human existence for posterity. Living on the sea was not without hazards, since the low islands lie in the path of seasonal storms. In time, their seaward exposure provided Cayman Islanders with a distinctively nautical culture that is reflected in their language and customs today.

Landforms from the Ocean

Three small satellites of the Greater Antilles, the Cayman Islands are located in a remote corner of the western Caribbean Sea. Grand Cayman, the largest island, is situated 150 miles south of Havana, 180 miles west-northwest of Jamaica, and 480 miles south of Miami. The Sister Islands,

Cayman Brac and Little Cayman, lie approximately 75 miles east-north-east of Grand Cayman, separated from it by open sea (fig. 11). Surrounded by deep water, the Cayman Islands are emerging peaks of the Cayman Ridge, a underwater continuation of Cuba's Sierra Maestra mountain range. This ridge runs parallel to the Cayman Trench, an abysmal ocean trough that includes the Oriente, Bartlett, and Misteriosa Deeps, each more than 3,000 fathoms deep.

The islands consist of two distinct limestone formations. The central core and elevated areas of each island are composed of bluff limestone, an ancient fault-block of white Oligocene and Miocene strata. A much younger formation, termed ironshore limestone, consists of deposits of coral reef, sand, and marl laid down in a low, porous plateau surrounding the perimeter of each uplifted block.[1] This coastal plane of hardened crust has been eroded constantly by rain and surf, producing what has been described as a karstland in an advanced stage of development.[2] Sharp pinnacles of rock that produce a metallic ring when struck contrast with crevices and cavities of hollowed solution features, giving the ironshore a barren and treacherous appearance. It has been suggested that subse-

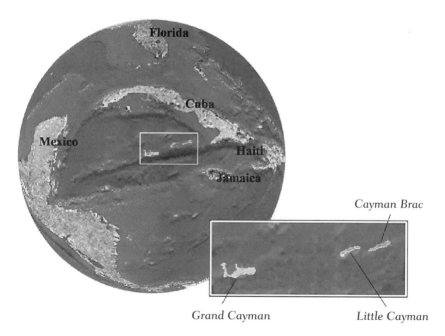

Fig. 11. The Cayman Islands are located south of Cuba along the Cayman Trench, one of the deepest parts of the Caribbean Sea. Illustration by Redell Akins.

quent to the first uplifting, the surface of the bluff limestone was planed flat by the sea, after which a second uplifting occurred that tilted the original fault-block slightly to the west.

This tilt is demonstrated by the shape of Cayman Brac, which when viewed in profile resembles a wedge. The twelve-mile-long block comprising the backbone of the island slopes gradually from a sheer cliff 144 feet high on the eastern end into the sea at the western end (fig. 12). The flat top of this steep-sided bluff is nearly a mile wide and is distinguished by numerous caves and hardwood forests around the perimeter. Alleged to have been used by pirates to conceal their plunder, the Brac's caves mainly have served as hurricane shelters over the years. The forests gradually have been thinned out, with the larger trees cut for shipbuilding purposes. The surface of the bluff traditionally has been used by islanders as a provision ground, yielding plantains, cassava, sweet potatoes, and yams on broken plots of cleared land. As the most windward of the Caymans, this prominent outcropping of rock in the ocean has supported generations of closely knit seafaring people, who became known for their resilient and independent nature. The population of Cayman Brac, second largest of the islands, has remained relatively stable for decades at around two thousand.

Little Cayman, situated five miles to the lee of Cayman Brac, is the smaller of the two Sister Islands (fig. 13). Stretching ten miles in length, and in some places less than a mile wide, Little Cayman is the lowest island of the group, its highest point being only forty-three feet above sea level.[3] Three small elevations—Weary Hill, Sparrowhawk Hill, and Salt Rocks—rise almost imperceptibly above the flat contour of the land form. Unlike its sister island, Little Cayman is almost entirely surrounded by coral reefs. A large shallow lagoon, South Hole Sound, dominates the southwestern coast of the island. Sandy beaches and mangrove swamps border the shoreline of the lagoon; nearby, a large pond supports an important and undisturbed seabird rookery. Inside the sound there is a small cay called Owen Island that, at one time, may have been connected to the main island by a mangrove spit. According to local inhabitants, the force of the 1876 hurricane opened a narrow channel separating the two. Another lagoon, also enclosed by coral reefs, is located on the eastern tip of Little Cayman. Slightly deeper than South Hole Sound, this sound is divided by a large expanse of treacherous coral and a ridge of bluff limestone. A sandy spit, called Point of Sand, constantly shifts its configuration, owing to its windward exposure to storms and ocean currents. Along

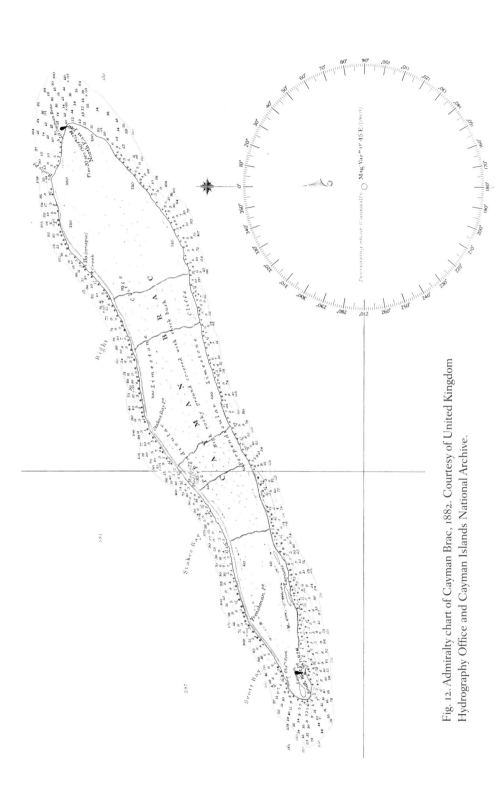

Fig. 12. Admiralty chart of Cayman Brac, 1882. Courtesy of United Kingdom Hydrography Office and Cayman Islands National Archive.

the south coast of the island, a ridge of coral rock and rubble separates the shore from the fringing reef line.

Although Little Cayman presently is the least populated of the three islands, with not more than a hundred residents, seasonal fishing and cultivation traditionally were carried out there by Cayman Brackers, who crossed the deep channel separating the two islands in small boats. Today, cultivation on the island has been abandoned, and old farming trails through the bush are overgrown with vegetation. Visited now by sport fishermen and offshore divers, Little Cayman is being developed as a secluded resort destination with modern conveniences.

Grand Cayman is nearly twenty-two miles long, and four miles wide at the broadest point (fig. 14). More than half of the land consists of low, swampy terrain that drains into a large body of water called North Sound. Grand Cayman often is said to resemble a crab's claw in shape, with North Sound comprising the area between the claw's pincers. Encompassing more than forty square miles of shallow water, the sound is fringed by small creeks and coves that harbor the largest stands of inland mangrove in the Caribbean. Access to the sea from North Sound is limited to natural breaks in the nearly continuous reef line that encloses the sound along its northern border.[4]

Another distinctive feature of the island's topography is a long, natural beach of white coral sand extending along the western shore. Once hosting seasonal fleets of sea turtles that emerged from the water to lay their eggs at night, this beach also provided a convenient anchorage in the lee of the land, which otherwise is encircled by dangerous reefs. Today this part of the island is the focus of a large tourist and diving industry adjacent to the main center of population and commerce for the entire island group.

In the past, large areas of Grand Cayman have supported a certain amount of subsistence agriculture, although farming was a secondary pursuit to the traditional occupations of turtling and wrecking. Coconut trees, planted in measured tracts called coconut walks, provided an important export item in the nineteenth century until a disease known as lethal yellowing caused many of them to perish. Mining of guano for fertilizer also was undertaken briefly in the latter part of the nineteenth century. Today, since the decline of cultivation, Grand Cayman supports its population of native Caymanians, expatriate colonials, and immigrants, as well as numerous visitors, with massive importation of staple foods from abroad.

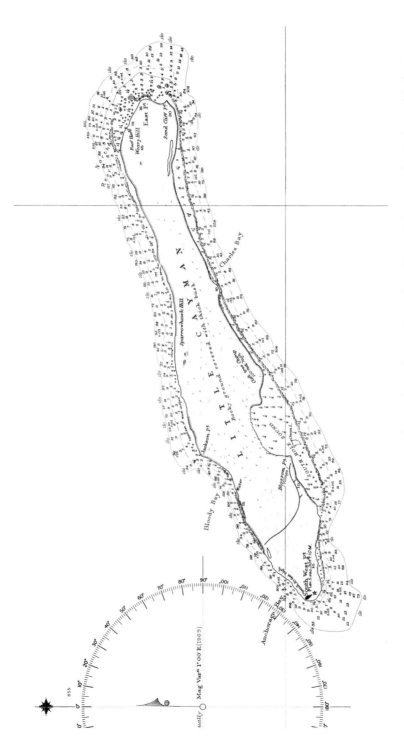

Fig. 13: Admiralty chart of Little Cayman, 1882. Courtesy of United Kingdom Hydrography Office and Cayman Islands National Archive.

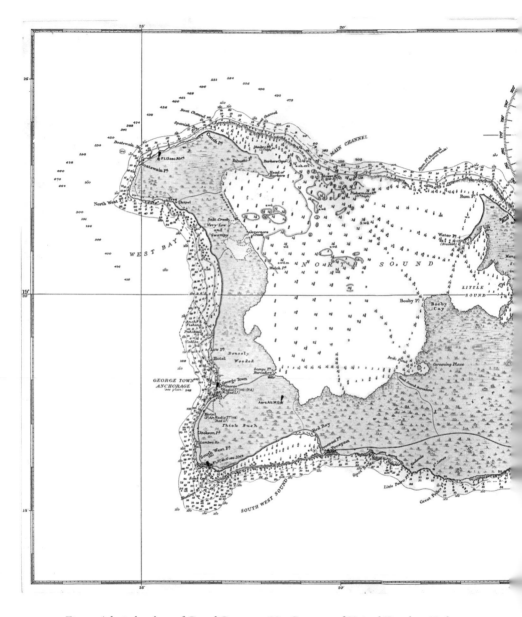

Fig. 14. Admiralty chart of Grand Cayman, 1882. Courtesy of United Kingdom Hydrography Office and Cayman Islands National Archive.

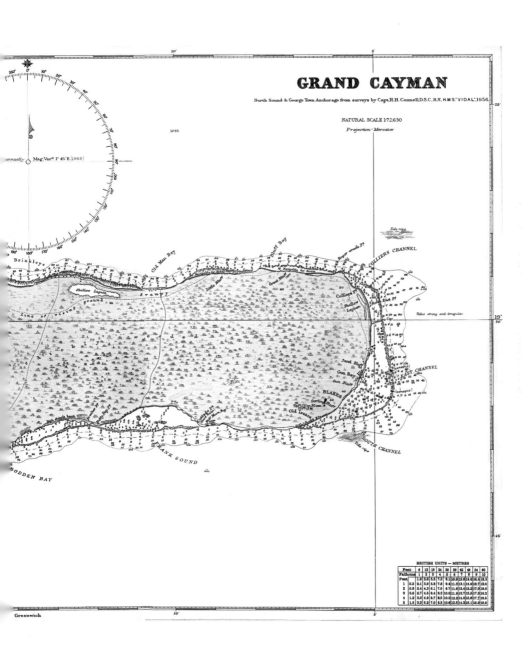

GRAND CAYMAN

North Sound & George Town Anchorage from surveys by Capt. R.H. Connell, D.S.C., R.N., H.M.S. "VIDAL", 1956.

NATURAL SCALE 1:72,630

Projection~Mercator

Naming the Islands

From their first discovery by European mariners, the Cayman Islands have undergone an interesting evolution in nomenclature. Forced off course by winds and currents west of Jamaica on his fourth and final voyage to the Americas, Christopher Columbus and his men, aboard the leaking caravels *Capitana* and *Santiago,* came across two rocky islands on May 10, 1503. Astonished by the vast numbers of sea turtles swimming in the warm, clear waters of Little Cayman and Cayman Brac, they called the islands Las Tortugas. The discovery of Grand Cayman is not recorded, although as early as 1502 five small unnamed islands are shown northwest of Jamaica on the world map of Alberto Cantino (fig. 15).

As the most distinctive and prevalent creatures figuring in the Caymans' early history, sea turtles continued to be associated with the islands during the sixteenth century on various maps, such as that of Münster (1532), on which they were labeled "Insl. Tor[t]ucarum," and a later copy of 1582, on which they were identified as "Tortues In." Curiously, within two decades after they first were encountered by European sailors, an-

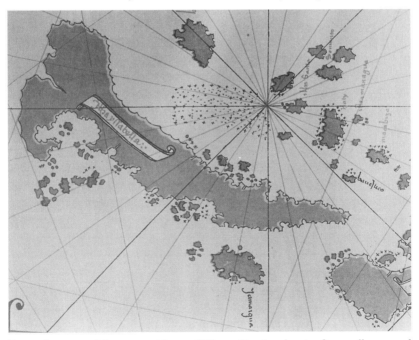

Fig. 15. A portion of the 1502 world map of Alberto Cantino showing five small unnamed islands in the approximate position of the Cayman Islands. Library of Congress Map Collections.

other title had been given to the islands. The name "Lagartos" (lizards) appeared first on the Turin map of 1523, and then in 1527 and 1529 in the cartographic works of Diogo Ribeiro, a Portuguese mapmaker employed by the Spanish crown, as well as in those of Tomaso Porcacchi in 1576.

This new appellation, Lagartos, has been thought by some writers to have been derived from the large land iguanas (*Cyclura nubila*) that still are found today in the Lesser Islands.[5] But ultimately it was the Carib word *caimán*, denoting a general species of Central and South American reptile larger than the iguana but resembling an alligator or crocodile, that led to the present designation of the Cayman Islands. Other hypotheses as to the origin of the name Cayman have been suggested in the past: that Grand Cayman looks like an alligator or *caimán* on the horizon when approached from the east, or that the word was a combination of *cayo* and *mano* because Grand Cayman resembles an outstretched hand in shape, or that *cay* (reef) and *main* (sea) somehow were combined to produce the name Cayman.[6] However, these alternate explanations seem far-fetched.

Early European mariners reported encountering a "multitude of Alligators . . . resembling ye Crocodiles of Egypt."[7] The reptiles were, in fact, crocodilian lizards (*Crocodylus acutus* or *Crocodylus rhombifer*) that once roamed the beaches of the Caymans. Recent fossil finds suggest that the latter, a freshwater variety, were prevalent in the islands until the twentieth century, when they began to disappear. They probably migrated from the southern shores of nearby Cuba, where the word *caimán* still is applied to crocodilians in general.[8] Thus the Cayman Islands were labeled, early on, after the two largest animals found in substantial numbers along their shores: sea turtles and crocodiles.

The first known cartographic representation of the Cayman Islands with a semblance of their modern name was the Wolfenbüttel chart of 1527 or 1530. The label "Caymanes," however, appears upside down on the chart. From then on, curious versions of the name Cayman appear. The island group was referred to as Canuanas by Sebastian Cabot, who may have misread the Wolfenbüttel map in the drafting of his own version for Spain in 1544.[9] The English captain William Jackson, who described the islands in 1643, called them Chimanos, and governor of Jamaica Thomas Lynch in 1672 referred to the Caymans as Caimanos in his official correspondence.[10] The physician Hans Sloane, who wrote in 1707 of his experiences in Jamaica, called the islands Caymanes, and historian Edward Long referred to them as The Caymanas in 1774.[11] The largest island, Grand Cayman, was referred to as Cuny Grand by one of Sir Francis

Drake's officers on a voyage to the West Indies in 1585–86.[12] In the popular nineteenth-century novel *The Pirate,* Sir Walter Scott mentions the Grand Caymains: "'Is he dead?' asked Bunce. 'It is a more serious question here, than it would be on the Grand Caymains or the Bahama Isles, where a brace or two of fellows may be shot in the morning, and no more heard of, or asked about them, than if they were so many wood-pidgeons'."[13]

French, Spanish, and Dutch sources reflect equally diverse spellings of the name. Occasionally, distortions of the root word *caimán* turn up in documents from the early colonial period. A notable example is the corruption "the Kie of Manus," which appears in a diary of the English conquest of Jamaica in 1655.[14] This term may have enjoyed usage among new residents of that island for several years, since the Caymans are similarly referred to as Kiemanas by the governor of Jamaica in 1661.[15] Colonial

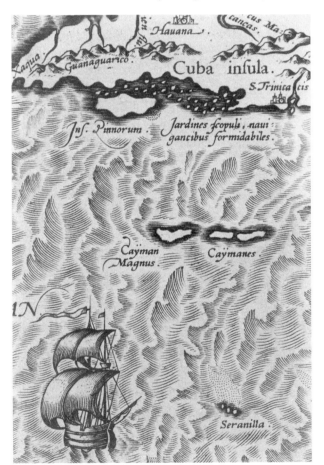

Fig. 16. Part of a map from *Theatrum Orbis Terrarum,* published in Antwerp in 1580 by Abraham Ortelius, showing Grand Cayman and the Sister Islands in their approximate locations. Library of Congress Map Collections.

maps, though, usually denote the larger island Grand Cayman, as distinct from its smaller sisters, Caymanes, suggesting that the islands ultimately retained their Spanish-derived nomenclature until a distinction between Cayman Brac and Little Cayman was made by English-speaking peoples. It appears that the name Brac comes from the Gaelic word *brack,* meaning a cliff, bluff, or rock. Considering the island's high outcropping of bluff limestone and the sheer cliffs on its windward edge, the name seems quite appropriate.

Maritime Geography

More than anything else, the relationship between the marine environment and the geographical configuration of the Cayman Islands determined an early pattern of human activity in the islands and ultimately decided the destiny of the Caymanian people. As small, remote land forms on the open sea, the Caymans initially served as landmarks for passing navigators. They also came to provide way stations for mariners in need of sheltered waters in which to refit and repair their vessels. Although relatively barren and dry compared with other Caribbean islands, the Caymans became known among European seafarers in the West Indies as a marine oasis, offering victuals in the form of sea turtles and limited amounts of fresh water. However, because of their small size and low profile on the horizon, the islands also were veritable traps for unwary sailors, whose ships came to grief along the coral-lined coasts. Eventually, the Cayman Islands were settled by groups of individuals who existed on the marine frontier of the Caribbean colonies.

The extreme insular situation of the Cayman Islands restricted early visitors to seafarers; the same circumstance constrained those who later settled the islands also to make their living primarily from the sea. Maritime geography not only defined the kinds of human endeavor that characterized the Caymans but also determined their specific locations on each island. Selection of suitable areas for habitation, trade, shipbuilding, pilotage, and provisioning depended on such critical factors as protection from and access to the sea—that is, secure anchorages and navigable passages through reefs—and the proximity of fresh water to the shoreline. Human existence, on remote islands such as these, hinges on the essential recognition and appreciation of the marine environment, and the ability to adapt and coordinate lifeways with the sea.

As is the case with mariners sailing on the high seas, an acute awareness of the prevailing weather direction is a vital factor in the life systems of island inhabitants. In contrast with other islands such as the Bahamas, Turks and Caicos, Florida Keys, and those of southern Cuba, all of which are situated on shallow, gradually shelving banks, the Cayman Islands are surrounded by deep water on all sides. Each is directly exposed to the prevailing winds and currents of the open ocean. Windward and leeward exposures dominate the establishment of basic enterprises, whether marine or terrestrial.

Throughout most of the year, the prevailing winds in the Cayman Islands are from the east-northeast or east-southeast. Ocean currents of the Caribbean Sea set along a westerly course in this region. Consequently, safe anchorage areas normally are found on the leeward side of each island—that is, the western or northwestern coasts. The Lesser Caymans, lying on a southwest-to-northeast diagonal, offer extensive lee protection along most of their northern shores. Locations such as the Bight, Stake Bay, and Scott Bay on Cayman Brac have seen the majority of maritime activity. At these places, the combination of sheltered water unfettered by coral reefs and open access between land and sea facilitated the establishment of small communities based on trade, fishing, and shipbuilding. A large, anomalous cleft at the base of the limestone bluff near the Bight produces one of the most abundant sources of fresh water on the Brac. Rainfall percolating down through the top of the bluff emerges at this fracture and traditionally has been collected by islanders and passing mariners. Locally known as the Watering Place, a community dominated by a family of merchant traders and shipbuilders grew up around this water source.

The north coast of Little Cayman is characterized by similar locations sheltered from prevailing weather. Indentations along the shore, such as Bloody Bay and Anchorage Bay, offer calm, open roadsteads. Likewise, two of the oldest-known sources of fresh water are located in these areas. A limestone solution cavity situated inland from Bloody Bay was used seasonally as a well and was indicated as such by the designation "Water" on early English Admiralty navigational charts.

Another well, unmarked on charts, is situated several hundred yards from the beach near Jackson's Point on an overgrown trail leading into the interior of the island. Archaeological sampling of the natural well and surrounding area produced cultural debris such as ceramic fragments,

Fig. 17. The author samples sediments from a karst solution feature that was found by consulting an old nautical chart of Little Cayman. Artifacts found in association with this natural well revealed that it had been used for more than two hundred years. Photo by KC Smith.

tobacco pipes, and bottles, as well as buttons. Analysis of these materials suggests that the water source was used for at least two hundred years. This site has become known locally as "the pirates' well," a reflection of a persistent island legend. In the so-called Battle of Bloody Bay, allegedly fought between local "pirates" and the Royal Navy, "the bay ran red with pirate blood" when the pirates made a last stand on the northern coast of the island. Whatever the origin of the name Bloody Bay, the proximity of these two wells to known anchorages indicates that they frequently were visited by passing mariners to replenish shipboard water casks. An assortment of anchors of various sizes and ages lodged into the coral gardens of Bloody Bay also attests to these activities.

Although less populated today than the other two islands, Little Cayman has not always been so. Evidence of abandoned provision grounds and remnants of coconut harvesting and phosphate collection lie buried in the thick bush of the northern coast. Old trails camouflaged by time lead to areas in the interior that contain clusters of rocks cleared from cultivation tracts. One such location, near the well at Bloody Bay, has been alleged to be the remains of an old stone fort. Small piles of randomly oriented limestone rocks can be seen in this area approximately one acre in size, which probably in fact represents an abandoned provision ground, the stones having been cleared to expose soil for cultivation. However, the almost impenetrable foliage effectively guards the mysteries of the past against all but the most determined and patient investigator.

Grand Cayman has an extensive lee shore along its western edge, which is well protected from the prevailing winds by the bulk of the island (see fig. 18). A broad inlet, originally known as Long Bay, today is called West Bay. Characterized by placid water, white beaches, and a gently sloping submarine terrain, the area historically was a natural and ideal anchorage for ships calling at the island to collect turtles that came ashore at night to lay eggs in the sand. This victualing venture's success depended on the time of year. Occasional mariners such as buccaneer William Dampier, who rode at anchor in Long Bay to search for provisions in 1675, arrived too late in the season to find the reptiles: "We anchored at the West-end, about a half a Mile from the Shore. We found no Water nor any provision. . . . indeed had it been in the Months of June or July we might probably have gotten Turtle, for they frequent this Island some Years as much as they do little Caymanes."[16]

Long Bay also offered the safest approach to Grand Cayman because its white sandy shore, which is unobstructed by reefs, was always easy to distinguish. It was from this roadstead that the survivors of the troop transport *Cumberland,* which wrecked on the east end of the island in 1767, were rescued by HMS *Adventure.*[17] A letter written by Major General Thomas Gage to the British War Office in 1768 described what happened:

> Captain Hodgson of His Majesty's 31st Regiment, on his Passage from this Place to Pensacola with 180 Draughts for the Regiment in West Florida, was unfortunately wrecked on the 28th of last November on an Island called the Great Commander [this is an obvious slip of the good general's military mind], about Fourscore Leagues from Jamaica. Three men only were drowned, but the Provisions, Baggage, & everything else in the Ship was lost. Captain Hodgson dispatched a small Vessel without Delay to inform Admiral Parry who commands His Majesty's Squadron at Jamaica of his Misfortune, and to beg his Assistance; and I have learned from an Officer of the Navy, lately arrived here from that Island, that the Admiral had sent the Troops an immediate Supply of Provisions, & was repairing one of the King's Frigates to transport them to Pensacola.[18]

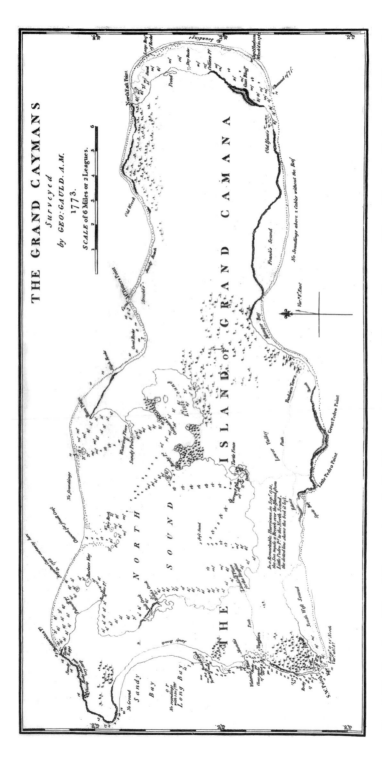

Fig. 18. The first chart of Grand Cayman, drawn by English surveyor George Gauld in 1773. Courtesy of United Kingdom Hydrography Office and Cayman Islands National Archive.

Arriving at Grand Cayman the following January, Captain Thomas Fitzherbert, commander of the rescue frigate *Adventure,* was unwilling to anchor on the eastern side of the island. Instead, he signaled to the castaway troops on shore and ran down to the leeward side of the island for a safer place to embark them. The captain wrote in his log the following notations:

> Friday 22st . . . The SW part of the Caymann West 5 Miles. The first and Middle part [of the day] fresh breezes & fair, the latter d⁰ [ditto] gales & Cloudy Weather at 11 brought to, at 6 AM made Sail, at 9 saw the SE part of the great Caymanns bearing West 13 or 14 Miles, at 11 fired a Gun as a Signal—

> Saturday 23rd . . . NW point of yᵉ Caymains NNE 6 or 7 Miles Modᵉ [moderate] and fair Weaʳ [weather], Employ'd turning in the bay on the NW side of the Caymans, at 2 AM fired a Gun as a Signal for the Troops, at 2 fired another for them to get ready to Embark at 1/2 past 3 Anchor'd with the Best Bʳ [bower anchor] in 7 fms Water & veer'd to 1/2 a Cable, the NW point NW B W the Town ESE. The Boat Embarking the Troops and Getting the Officers things on board . . .[19]

The predicament of Captain Hodgson and his men would be followed by a much greater calamity—the wrecking of ten ships at once—and a similar sequence of events that again brought rescue ships into the tranquil waters of Long Bay. Of this, more in chapter 6.

The sandy stretch of coastline where the shipwrecked soldiers gathered to embark for home, and where Dampier's men landed to look for fresh water, now hosts thousands of vacationing tourists who flock to hotels that advertise the Seven Mile Beach as one of the finest in the world. Where passing mariners once anchored their ships to revictual, scores of modern recreational vessels are moored, ready to take sport divers offshore for a glimpse of the underwater world. Sands that once covered seasonal clutches of sea turtle eggs, collected in daylight by sailors and in moonlight by crocodiles, today are enjoyed by throngs of sunbathers and snorkelers.

South of Long Bay the shore is rocky but continues to be protected from the weather most of the time. A small and once almost insignificant cove today has become the single most important geographical location in the Cayman Islands. On early charts of the island, a village called Hogsties is shown where there is today the busy hub of George Town, seat of gov-

Fig. 19. George Town harbor, circa 1910, was a primary landing place for local fishing and trading vessels. From Vaquero, *Life and Adventure in the West Indies.*

ernment for the Crown Colony. Not surprisingly, the site is situated near another Watering Place, which, like that on Cayman Brac, was a source of potable water for islanders and passing ships. The combination of leeward shelter, good holding bottom, and fresh water encouraged the area's development from a community of swineherds and fishermen to a harbor town, fortified by a small gun battery named Fort George. Few remnants of the stone fortification remain today, the guns having been removed long ago. However, an archaeological excavation sponsored by the Cayman National Trust has ensured the site's preservation. Replica cannons and signage mark its location today, and the fort figures prominently in the annual island celebration of Pirate's Week.

The offshore anchorage at George Town gradually developed into Cayman's principal maritime conduit to the outside world, thanks to its convenient geographical characteristics. Not surprisingly, the town's population grew to become the largest in the islands, employed in shipbuilding, turtle fishing, and maritime commerce. Today the harbor's eminence is even more pronounced, as tons of cargo enter the islands across a modern wharf and thousands of visitors from regular passenger liners converge along the waterfront.

During the winter months, the prevailing weather in the islands is variable. The wind shifts intermittently to the north and west, signaling the onset of a nor'wester. Caused by outbreaks of cold air from the North American continent that descend into the Gulf of Mexico and the Caribbean, nor'westers may last for several days, during which normal anchorages become unsafe for small craft. Alternative protection from the elements is sought in the lee of each island, usually along the southern coasts.

On Cayman Brac, a small lagoon enclosed by reefs is situated at the southwestern extremity of the land. Channel Bay, as the minute harbor is called, provides virtually the only protected haven for small vessels on the Brac; all other locations are exposed to the vagaries of the weather. It has been suggested that the first settlement on the island was located at Channel Bay. When the first group of permanent colonists arrived on Cayman Brac in 1833, they found cooking utensils and other artifacts, as well as cleared sections of land that suggested the region had previously been occupied and cultivated.[20] Lieutenant Archer of HMS *Phoenix,* sailing in August 1780 from Port Royal, Jamaica, to Pensacola, Florida, reported, "In a few days we made two sandy islands that look as if they had just risen out of the sea, or fallen from the sky; inhabited nevertheless by upwards of three hundred English, who get their bread by catching turtles and parrots, and raising vegetables, which they exchange with ships that pass, for

Fig. 20. Today George Town is still is the primary landing place for modern commercial and tourist shipping. Photo by KC Smith.

clothing and a few of the luxuries of life, as rum, etc."[21] Today a small government wharf in Channel Bay is the only stable landing place for seaborne cargo; most of the Brac's traffic in visitors flows through the nearby airport.

Little Cayman, on the other hand, affords a fair degree of security for small craft in both South Hole Sound and East Sound. Each has wide, navigable channels through the reef and enough room to accommodate numerous vessels at anchor. Again, the developing nucleus of population favored areas providing a haven from and an avenue to the sea. Little Cayman's only extant community, Blossom Village, also called South Town, is situated inside South Hole Sound directly opposite the channel. Protected from the sea but with a wide view of the horizon, the village commanded an optimum location for seafaring endeavors.

The eastern tip of the island is equally suitable for these purposes. The region known as Muddy Foots near Point of Sand may have been the earliest site of seasonal occupation by fishermen. According to oral histories, the name is a corruption of Modyford's, after Thomas Modyford, a governor of Jamaica who figured prominently during that island's privateering era. Historical documents suggest that Muddy Foots may have been the site of an English turtling station destroyed by Spaniards in 1669. The deposition of the captain of a ship from Jamaica stationed at the turtling outpost on Little Cayman claimed that the attackers landed some two hundred men on the easternmost point of the island in the middle of the night and proceeded to burn the fishermen's dwellings. As we shall see, the turtlers' huts were not the only English possessions destroyed in the raid. Archaeological verification of Muddy Foots, however, is hampered by extensive alteration of the land by repeated hurricanes and coconut planting in the past.

Patterns of settlement adjacent to sheltered lagoons with access to the sea are demonstrated most clearly on Grand Cayman. Two of the oldest permanent communities, Prospect and Bodden Town, are situated along the southern coast and are well protected by fringing reefs. Of the two, Prospect appears to have been chosen more carefully, as it is in the leeward bight of South Sound, affording a highly secure haven. This settlement also had a small fortification with gun emplacements overlooking the sea. Recent discoveries of occupational sites have produced artifacts that date to the mid-eighteenth century.

Bodden Town, situated midway along the southern shore, appears to have been the oldest village of any size on Grand Cayman. It has been proposed that both George Town and Bodden Town were settled after the village of Prospect had been established.[22] The earliest known map of the island, drawn by George Gauld in 1773 (see fig. 18), depicts Bodden Town as a small community of at least ten dwellings, while Hogsties (the future George Town) appears to have been composed of eight dwellings. The settlement at Prospect does not appear on the map at all; instead, a place named Eden's is shown with two dwellings at the nearby location of modern-day Spotts. Although Bodden Town's location was not as ideal as that of other communities, its small harbor formed by reefs could be approached through a narrow channel, allowing the town to function as an early seaport. The reef entrance was guarded by several cannons placed in an open area known as Gun Square, at which the local militia could assemble if an unfriendly sail was sighted. Legend has it that natural limestone caves near the town were used for concealment by villagers during attacks on the island by pirates.

Another early community, known originally as Old Isaacs but today simply called East End, may have been occupied primarily for its windward situation. Located at the foot of the large, shallow sound that protects the eastern extremity of Grand Cayman, the village commands a broad view of approaching weather and sea traffic. At least two navigable channels through the treacherous offshore reef were available at the time the settlement first was occupied; a third has been widened artificially in recent years. Associated with pirate and wrecking activities in the past, this region includes a particularly distinctive ironshore promontory that bore the name Gun Bluff as early as 1773 on Gauld's map of Grand Cayman. The name suggests that there once were fortifications erected near East End, or that from the bluff a gun was fired to warn ships in danger of striking the reef. While several cannons today remain partially buried under the seabed at the base of Gun Bluff, it is not clear whether they originally were positioned on the promontory or came from a shipwreck offshore.

By far the most secure anchorage in the Cayman Islands is the wide expanse of North Sound on Grand Cayman. Protected on all sides, this large body of shallow water was recognized early by mariners as an ideal natural harbor for vessels in need of shelter or repair.

It was in North Sound that Captain Francis Knighton sought refuge for his sloop-of-war *Jamaica* during a storm in 1715. Scudding before a squall while on patrol for pirates, HMS *Jamaica* lost her steerage when the tiller suddenly broke, and she broached in heavy seas.[23] After lying with her hatches in the water for some time, the vessel finally was righted by cutting her mast and rigging away. However, most of the loose equipment had washed overboard, and the cabin windows were stove in. Still in danger of foundering, Captain Knighton ordered the sloop's eight cannons and three of her swivel guns to be cast overboard, and the ship continued before the wind. That afternoon another Royal Navy sloop, HMS *Drake*, came into sight and the next morning took *Jamaica* in tow toward the nearest land—the Cayman Islands.

Jamaica's pilot was consulted as to the best place to seek refuge to install a new mast, and the "Broad Sound of the grand Caimanas" was chosen. Tragedy followed an attempt to enter North Sound as the pilot mistook the channel entrance—a common error, even today—and ran *Jamaica* over the outer reef in heavy seas, dislodging her rudder. After throwing everything overboard to lighten the ship, the crew managed to get her off the reef, but found themselves in the midst of shoal waters without steerage. They anchored to rehang her rudder, but before they could reach the safety of deeper water, the ship struck another reef, which displaced the rudder and bilged the hull. Given the heavy seas and winds, Captain Knighton ordered his crew to abandon the sloop in order to save their lives. Fortunately, *Drake* managed to get into the sound safely and took the unlucky sailors aboard.

The following morning, it was discovered that water had entered *Jamaica* up to her decks, and despite repeated attempts to pump and to bail her out, she remained fast on the reef. A diver was sent overboard to inspect the hull, which he reported had been stove in by a large rock. In addition, both stem and sternpost had been split, making any further efforts to save the ship futile. Knighton ordered his sloop stripped of remaining stores, and he and his men sailed back to Port Royal, Jamaica, aboard *Drake* to face court martial.[24]

Had he not encountered disaster at the entrance, Captain Knighton would have steered for the lower reaches of North Sound, where a small, protected cove provided the conditions that he needed to repair his sloop. This shallow and tranquil location, situated between two mangrove islets, became known as the Careening Place because of its suitability for hauling over small vessels in order to clean and refit their hulls. In addition, an adjacent cove called Duck Pond became a convenient natural pen for live turtles. Enclosed by a submarine fence, captured turtles brought to the island were left to feed on beds of underwater grass until it was time for them to be marketed.

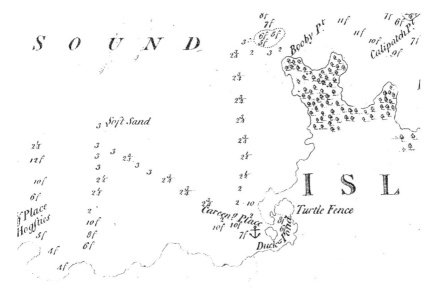

Fig. 21. Close-up of the Careening Place and Duck Pond on George Gauld's 1773 survey chart of Grand Gayman. Courtesy of United Kingdom Hydrography Office and Cayman Islands National Archive.

Test excavations at the Careening Place in 1980 revealed a myriad of nautical implements and artifacts interspersed among numerous layers of discarded ballast stones left by countless ships that underwent this essential operation (fig. 22). Marine hardware such as copper sheathing and patches, deck and hull fittings, pulley blocks and cable, and innumerable planking nails, sheathing tacks, and other fasteners were recorded (fig. 23). Broken fragments of deck lanterns, oil lamps, rusted tools, and numerous spirit bottles and jugs testified to the industrious nature of the undertakings that occurred at this single location. Analysis of materials recovered from three two-meter-square test grids tentatively dated usage of the Careening Place from the first half of the eighteenth century until the first half of the twentieth century. Association of the site with past turtling activities was demonstrated by more than two hundred bone samples from the three gridded squares, which also included pork, beef, and fish remains (fig. 24).

The geographical setting of the Careening Place, coupled with its archaeological interpretation, allows a reconstruction of what must have been a common Caymanian scene in the past. Returning from a turtling voyage with a large catch, fishermen rounded the northern tip of Grand

Fig. 22. A two-by-two-meter test excavation at the Careening Place reveals layers of maritime debris, discarded over several centuries of ship repair and refitting. Photo by KC Smith.

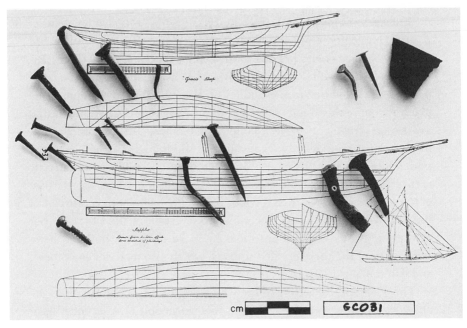

Fig. 23. A variety of marine fasteners recovered from test excavations at the Careening Place. Photo by KC Smith.

Fig. 24. Stingray spines, such as this example from the Careening Place, were used by local fishermen as needles to repair their turtling nets. Photo by KC Smith.

Cayman and entered the broad sound under sail. As the locally built schooner coasted toward the mangrove-lined recesses of the vast lagoon, her crew lowered sail, glad to be home. Small turtling boats were hove overboard, and one by one the live reptiles were hoisted into the smaller craft, taken to the pen at Duck Pond, and released into its shallow waters.

Before another voyage could begin, the schooner was towed between two small islets separated by a deep cut and tied alongside a steep man-grove bank. Sectioned trunks of thatch palm trees were placed under the hull to serve as fenders, and the vessel was hauled over with heavy tackle secured to the masts. A certain amount of ballast had to be removed dur-ing the operation to lighten the ship and to facilitate cleaning the interior of the hull. The stones were dumped overboard on the landward side, creating an artificial slope over the years that aided subsequent careening endeavors. As the outboard area of the hull was exposed, the crew com-menced scraping and breaming (searing with fire) the fouled planks, re-pairing rotten timbers, or refastening loose sheathing, known as "planking copper." The careening process normally took several days, during which the crew fed on part of the salted turtle catch and drank whatever spirits were available. Trash, worn-out equipment, and broken tools and utensils

Fig. 25. The process of careening was essential for Caymanian turtling schooners in between lengthy fishing voyages. Drawing by Sema Pulak.

were discarded overboard in a general attempt to clean the ship before the next voyage. When the operation was completed, the schooner was reballasted, towed into open water, and sailed to a convenient anchorage to take on additional crew and provisions for sea.

Hurricanes

During particularly severe weather conditions, North Sound was, and still is, the haven most frequently sought by small island craft and other vessels that happen to be in the vicinity of the Cayman Islands. Ultimate safety, of course, could not be insured, and the Caymanian people have learned from centuries of dwelling on the sea that their islands have never really been independent of the marine realm. Indeed, the Caymans are located in the path of greatest hurricane frequency in the West Indies. The storms generally enter the Caribbean Basin through the Windward Islands and move toward Jamaica, passing northwest near the Cayman Islands and on to the Yucatán Channel and the western end of Cuba. Scores of hurricanes have impacted the island group in the last five hundred years, since records of such storms have been kept. During the last two centuries, no fewer than twenty-five major tropical cyclones have caused significant damage in the Cayman Islands. According to climatic researchers, historians, and eyewitness accounts, hurricanes affecting the islands occurred at the times shown in table 2.1. The most recent, Hurricane Gilbert in 1988, was a category 5 storm that left serious damage in its wake.

Table 2.1. Hurricanes Affecting the Cayman Islands

Month/Day	Year	Source*
October	1527	M, T
unknown	1662?	B
July–August	1674	M
September 8–9	1722	M
September	1731	B
September	1735	B, D, H, M
August–September	1751	B, D, H, T
October	1756	M, T
August–September	1772	M
August 16	1780	M, T
August 27–29	1785	B, H, M, T
October	1812	B, D, H, T
unknown	1826	H, T
August	1835	B, D, T
June	1836	B, D, H
September 28	1838	B, D, H, T
October 25	1838	B, H
no month	1845	H
October 10	1846	B, D, H, T
September 29	1873	N, T
October 12	1876	B, H, N, T
November 17	1879	N
October 8–12	1882	T
October 8	1885	N, T

continued

Table 2.1—*continued*

October 9	1887	N
October 20	1893	N
September 26	1896	N, T
October 27	1899	N, T
August 11	1903	B, D, H, N, T
October 14	1904	N
November 7	1906	N
August 24	1909	B, H, N
October 12–13	1910	H
October 26	1911	N
November 21	1912	N
August	1914	B
September	1914	B
August 13	1915	B, D, N, T
September 2	1915	N
September	1917	B, D, T
October 18	1923	N
October 18	1927	N
November	1932	B, D, N, T
July	1933	B, D, T
September 27	1935	N
November 1	1939	N
October	1944	B, D, N
October 11	1945	N
September 19	1948	N
October 14	1951	N
September 14 (Hilda)**	1955	N
October (Hattie)	1961	N
September 19 (Eloise)	1975	N
August 6 (Allen)	1980	N
November (Katrina)	1980	B
September 13 (Gilbert)	1988	B, N

*Source abbreviations: B = Burton, "Climate and Tides," 58, 60. D = Doran, "Physical and Cultural Geography," 22. H = Hirst, *Notes,* 139, 177. M = Millás, *Hurricanes of the Caribbean,* 7–23. N = NOAA, *Tropical Cylcones.* T = Tannehill, *Hurricanes,* 140–228. **Hurricanes were not named until 1954.

The dominant role of the ocean over the ultimate destiny of the islands has been demonstrated numerous times during extreme marine conditions, and the lack of coastal elevation throughout the islands makes them vulnerable to any increase in sea activity. For example, a hurricane in 1751 temporarily altered the topography of Grand Cayman. George Gauld's

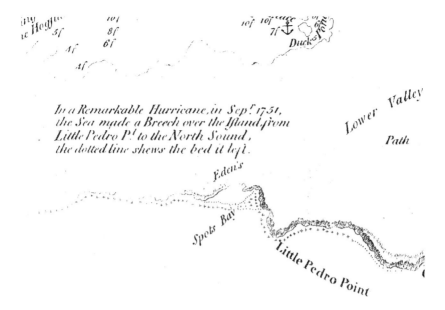

Fig. 26. On his 1773 survey chart of Grand Cayman, George Gauld noted the effects of a fierce hurricane in 1751. Courtesy of United Kingdom Hydrography Office and Cayman Islands National Archive.

map bore this notation: "In a Remarkable Hurricane, in Sep[r] 1751, the Sea made a Breech over the Island from Little Pedro P[t] to the North Sound, the dotted line shews the bed it left" (fig. 26). In effect, storm tides temporarily partitioned the land into separate sections at the lowest part of the island. Similar phenomena occurred in 1731, 1846, 1932, 1933, and 1988, as the sea flooded from south to north over the lower valley areas of Grand Cayman at Newlands, Prospect, Pedro, Spotts, Savannah, and Red Bay.[25]

Cayman Islanders have learned the hard way about their precarious position on the sea and often have suffered the consequences of its fury. A memorial addressed to the queen of England in 1838 by the custos, magistrates, and inhabitants of Grand Cayman reflects the unavoidable corollary to an insular environment:

> We suffering from two violent hurricanes on the 28th of September and the 25th of October, have now to entreat the sympathy and charitable consideration of your Majesty's Government. By these visitations St. George's Church . . . has been blown down, the other seriously injured; upwards of 100 dwellings have been totally destroyed, and not a single one has entirely escaped injury. Out of the

18 vessels belonging to the island and by which the inhabitants draw their principal means of support, 13 have been wrecked; every plantation and provision ground utterly destroyed; and unless Christian sympathy be awakened and Christian benevolence be extended many of the inhabitants will be involved in the deepest and bitterest distress.[26]

During the 1876 hurricane, all of the vessels in the different coves and anchorages were either driven ashore or broken up.[27] In an attempt to avoid similar damage to island shipping during the onslaught of another hurricane in 1903, all of Grand Cayman's schooners, except one that broke her moorings and disappeared, put to sea as the storm grew in intensity. Only two returned after the hurricane; the remaining five were never heard from again.[28]

The great hurricane of 1932 still is discussed by elderly survivors, since it was the worst natural disaster ever to befall the Cayman Islands. The tropical cyclone developed northeast of Barbados on October 31, then drifted to the southwest and west. On November 2, it began to move in a west-northwest direction, and by November 6 it turned gradually north and north-northeast, approximately a hundred miles south of Grand Cayman. The hurricane hit Grand Cayman with winds of about 150 miles per hour on the evening of November 7. The accompanying storm surge, estimated to be thirty feet high, flooded the southern portion of the island with salt water, destroying many homes, one of which was swept 157 feet inland.[29] The region of Prospect suffered extensive damage, and was to be badly hit again by a hurricane the following July.[30]

The hurricane reached the Lesser Caymans on the night of November 8, with a storm surge of thirty-two feet roaring in from the east-southeast and sweeping over Blossom Village on the south side of Little Cayman. Many of the seventy-odd residents fled into the interior; most of their homes along the coast were destroyed, but not a single life was lost. On Cayman Brac, the situation was different. As the eye of the storm passed over the island around midnight, an eerie calm set in, and many residents ventured from shelter, assuming that the worst was over. But others realized that the respite was only temporary. At four o'clock in the morning, the winds sprang up from the north-northwest and blew in at two hundred miles per hour, as the storm resumed from the opposite direction. Unprotected by a reef, the north shore was struck by the full force of the hurricane, which drove the sea up over the twenty-foot-high ridge on which the houses and road were located. A raging river of salt water poured through a section of land between the ridge and the bluff, killing whole families in their collapsed houses. Many saved themselves by swimming to the bluff and taking refuge in caves. Sixty-nine people lost their lives, more than one hundred were injured, and almost every structure on Cayman Brac was obliterated.[31]

Many personal and vivid stories of this catastrophe survive in oral histories. One tells how the wife of Ashlan Foster, who was at sea, managed to catch hold of her husband's catboat as it washed up the beach. She placed her children and parents aboard just before a wall of water pushed them onto the bluff where they could escape the fury of the sea.[32]

The Brac schooner *Carmena* was catching turtle off the Pedro Banks, located about 240 miles to the southeast, below Jamaica, when the hurricane occurred. She was lost with her master, Nelson Jackson, and twenty-six men on board.[33] The schooners *Fernwood* and *Melpomene* also were lost with their boats and crews. The storm had taken the lives of forty Brac mariners. Others were more fortunate; men of the schooner *Acme* had left Cayman Brac in late October to fish the Pedro Banks. After several days of good catches, the wind died and the barometer began to drop. A series of heavy swells preceded fierce squalls as the hurricane overtook the tiny schooner. For days, Captain Bernard Ryan and her crew fought the winds and waves, losing their boats, spars, and rudder and constantly in danger of capsizing in the storm. Miraculously, the boat held together. The men rigged a jury mast and steered *Acme* toward Jamaica, where they eventually drifted ashore near Bluefields.[34]

Caymanian Place Names

The cultural effects of maritime geography in the Cayman Islands are demonstrated most clearly by the names given to various locations and the manner in which they reflect specific nautical activities. The Watering Place on Cayman Brac and Anchorage Bay on Little Cayman are obvious examples of place names that explain their significance in everyday island life. Other, less transparent, examples include areas called Spotts on Grand Cayman and Spot Bay on Cayman Brac. Not only were these two locations good landing spots, but they also could be identified readily by sailors at sea because their sandy beaches appeared as white spots on the coastline.

A section of the northern shore of Grand Cayman called Bowse Bluff has an equally interesting etymology. *Bowse* is an old word that means "to haul by means of a tackle." This area was another landing place but, as it lacked a sandy beach, boats had to be hauled ashore over the rocks. Similarly, there is the curiously named Pull-and-Be-Damned Point near the entrance to South Sound on Grand Cayman. Even today, tacking under sail against wind and current past this point remains difficult in the narrow channel, although the aid of an outboard engine guarantees access to the sound. In the days before motorized propulsion, the continuously outflowing water from the channel entrance must have exhausted all but the most robust oarsmen seeking refuge in the sound.

An analogous place name is that given to the open-water channel between the two Lesser Islands, which locally is called the Bogue. The term may have been derived from the Spanish verb *bogar* (to row), but its English meaning is "to edge to leeward." This procedure is precisely the maneuver required to complete a safe passage from Cayman Brac to Little Cayman, given the often heavy seas and swift currents of the channel. According to local inhabitants, certain weather conditions in the Bogue create a small maelström, or whirlpool.

Other place names are more obvious, such as Anchor's Point on Grand Cayman or the Moorings and Cat Head Bay on Cayman Brac. Each was familiar to local pilots as a convenient temporary anchorage. Additionally, each of the Cayman Islands has a Crawl Bay, where captured turtles were confined in pens or "crawls" built in the shallow waters of lagoons. On Grand Cayman, turtle crawls were located in North Sound, West Bay, George Town, and South Sound. Taking its name from the Dutch word *kraal*, the enclosure was constructed of vertical stakes set in shallow water for the purpose of keeping fish, shellfish, or turtles until sale or slaughter. Port Royal, Jamaica, and Key West, Florida, major maritime entrepôts, had the largest turtle crawls in the New World. Those at Port Royal in 1692 were swallowed by the sea during an earthquake; those in Key West have been abandoned during the last half century owing to a decline in the turtle trade. Today, a commercial turtle farm on Grand Cayman breeds and raises sea turtles in cement tanks that are artificially flushed; the tradition of holding turtles remains, but the turtle crawls that once occupied a principal place in Caymanian economic life have vanished. Remains of one early crawl were discovered partially buried under the beach of South Hole Sound, Little Cayman, in the course of archaeological survey in 1979. Exposed during dredging of the area, the crawl site consisted of fragmentary wooden pickets, turtle bones, and what appeared to be parts of a small ballasted boat associated with the crawl.

To a large extent, the Cayman Islanders have their own designations for coastal features. Lagoons, for example, are called sounds, although they do not strictly adhere to dictionary definitions as "passages of water connecting two larger bodies of water" or "broad inlets of the ocean." However, it is precisely this usage of the term that reflects the Caymanian perspective of the lagoon as a passage to the open sea. Some sounds, especially North Sound, actually could be called bays, but in the Cayman Islands any indentation of the shoreline, however slight, is called a bay. There are at least forty-four "bays" in the three small islands, some of which are hardly distinguishable from the adjacent coastline. In some areas, small rocky coves, most only large enough for a boat, are called barcaderes, perhaps a derivation of *embarcadero,* the Spanish word for a wharf or quay (*barca* is a boat). In Central America, whence the term "embarcadere" may have been brought to the Caymans, an *embarcadero* was a place, usually on a river, where hardwood and dyewood were assembled on shore for stripping and loading into watercraft. Often located along exposed sections of the coast, Caymanian barcaderes usually were equipped with davits or derricks set into the rock for loading small cargoes or lifting boats from the water.

Thus, the seaward outlook of the Caymanian people has been and continues to be mirrored in their geographical terminology. A glance at the topographical maps of the Cayman Islands reveals more than twice as many designations for marine areas than for terrestrial landmarks.

Similarly, the daily vocabulary of Cayman Islanders always has contained a strong nautical lexicon. For example, distance on land often was measured in fathoms, and directions were indicated by nautical terms: "twenty fathoms down the road"; "she was gone leeward [west]"; "it was on the port [left] side."[35] The floor of a house often was called the deck, and a leaky metal container with holes in the bottom was said to be bilged. To go swimming is to go "in the sea," and the reef is referred to as "where the white water begin."[36]

This anecdote illustrates Caymanian maritime expression:

We saw an amusing incident one day when a nor'wester was blowing. A little boy came dashing out of a home, with his mother, clad in the more voluminous skirt of a generation ago, in hot pursuit. He had been raiding the pantry perhaps, and set off before the wind with his mother rapidly bearing down on him. A small boy, anxious for the safety of his friend, called out, "try her up on the wind!" The hint was at once taken. He luffed up sharp and went off to windward. The mother found her skirts too much of a handicap in the high wind, and was soon far astern.[37]

Shoal of Sea Turtles  3

Among West Indian cultures, the inhabitants of the Cayman Islands are a uniquely seafaring people. While the majority of Caribbean fishermen rarely ventured far from home, Caymanians always have been distinctly renowned for long-range nautical pursuits. Indeed, the evolution of the Caymanian culture contrasts sharply with that of other island peoples. This difference initially can be explained by the relatively limited, barren and dry topography of the three remote islands. Overlooked during the profit-motivated settlement of most West Indian regions, the Caymans, with their lack of terrestrial resources, were excluded from early mining, stock raising, or plantation endeavors. Instead a seaward perspective, both natural and necessary, provided inhabitants of the Cayman Islands with a means of subsistence. Unlike other West Indian islanders, who remained tied to the land even in postslavery times and who viewed their coastlines as boundaries or barriers, Caymanians always have depended on the sea as a resource and an avenue to survival. The official motto displayed on the flag of the Cayman Islands, "He hath founded it upon the seas," states unequivocally the nature of their inherited destiny.

Fig. 27. The coat of arms of the Cayman Islands prominently depicts the sea turtle, along with three stars on a field of waves.

Discovery of the Cayman Islands

Another glance at the Crown Colony's flag reveals the prominent figure of a sea turtle, a creature inextricably bound to the heritage of the islands, the predominant thread in the cultural fabric of their inhabitants. From the moment of their recorded discovery, the Cayman Islands were recognized for their abundance of marine turtles. During his fourth and final voyage to America, Christopher Columbus passed between the Lesser Caymans in May 1503 and accidentally discovered what was to become the New World's largest sea turtle fishery. Ferdinand Columbus, who accompanied his father on the voyage, saw so many of the swimming reptiles that their shells looked to him like a reef around the islands:

> On Monday 1 May 1503, we stood to the northward with winds and currents from the east, because of which we struggled continually to lay up as close to the winds as we could. And although all the pilots said that we would pass to the eastward to the Caribbe islands, the Admiral feared he could not make Hispaniola. And this proved to be correct. For on Wednesday 10 May we were in sight of two very small and low islands, full of turtles, all the sea about there was so full of them that they looked like little rocks, and for this reason those islands were called Las Tortugas.[1]

When the Admiral imparted the name Las Tortugas to the Cayman Islands, he did not realize that he was among the first Europeans to witness the yearly gathering of the creatures to breed and to lay eggs. But from that day it was the sea turtle that had put the Cayman Islands on the map and would determine their destiny.

The Sea Turtle

Europeans arriving in the New World found the sea turtle an unfamiliar and remarkable creature. Grazing among beds of sea grass and massing to converge on quiet, uninhabited beaches, the free-swimming reptiles were large, easy to spot, and abundant. Like the North American bison, the sea turtle quickly was recognized as a novel source of fresh meat by people accustomed to a diet based on domesticated animals.

Even more curious to European explorers was the extraordinary native custom of capturing turtles with the aid of a fish, the remora (*Echeneis remora*). This practice first was observed by Christopher Columbus during his second voyage in 1494 among the islands of the Jardinella de la Reina on the south coast of Cuba. An account from his journal was published in 1501 by Peter Martyr and later translated into English:

> Nowe shall you heare of a new kind of fishing. Like as wee with Greyhoundes do hunt Hares in the playne fieldes, so doo they, as it were with a hunting fishe, take other fishes: this fishe was of shape or fourme unknown to us, but the body thereof not much unlike a greate yeele, having on the hinder parte of the head a very tough skinne, like unto a great bagge or purse: this fishe is tyed by the side of the boate with a corde, let downe so farre into the water that the fish may lie close hid by the keele or bottom of the same, for shee may in no case abide the sight of the ayre. Thus when they espie any great fish, Tortoyse (where of there is a great abundance, bigger than great targettes) they let the corde at length, but when she feeleth herself loosed, she invadeth the fish or Tortoyse as swiftly as an arrowe, and where she hath fastened her hold, she casteth the purse of skinne, whereof we spake before, and by drawing the same together, so graspeth her pray, that no mans strength is sufficient to unloose the same, except by little and little drawing the lyne, she bee lifted somewhat above the brimme of the water, for then, as soone as she seeth the brightnesse of the ayre, shee leteth goe her hold. The

pray therefore beeing nowe drawen neare to the brimme of the water, there leapeth sodenly out of the boate into the sea, so many
fishers as may suffice to hold fast the pray, untill the rest of the
company have taken it into the boate. Which thing done, they loose
so much of the corde, that the hunting fish may againe returne to her
place within the water, whereby another corde, they let down to her
a peece of the pray, as we use to rewarde greyhoundes after they have
killed their game. This fish they call Guaicanum, but our men call it
Reuersum.[2]

This unusual Amerindian method of employing a semidomesticated
sucker fish as an angling device has long interested naturalists, who recorded the practice in the Indian Ocean, South China Sea, and northern
Australia.[3] It was still in use in the waters south of Cuba as late as 1932.[4]

Among the various species of marine turtles, the green sea turtle (*Che-
lonia mydas*) has historically been an important food source in tropical
latitudes, and became a natural factor in the colonization of the Americas.
It was large and easy to catch, and could be kept alive in a space no bigger
than itself. Its lean, high-protein meat and rich, gelatinous undershell
would feed many mouths, from those of common sailors to those of roy-
alty. The hawksbill turtle (*Eretmochelys imbricata*) has been prized for its
shell since Roman times, but usually was not eaten by Europeans. The
loggerhead (*Caretta caretta*), leatherback (*Dermochelys coriacea*), and ridley (*Lepidochelys* sp.) generally have not been eaten at all.

The green turtle (named for the greenish color of its body fat) usually
is the largest of these species. In the past, wild males might weigh a thousand pounds. Today the largest are around four feet in length and weigh
some five hundred pounds, while most are under a hundred pounds.[5] The
green is a nonconformist among sea turtles, generally being herbivorous
rather than carnivorous like the others. Feeding on the ubiquitous marine
plant *Thalassia testudinum*, commonly called turtle grass, adults supple-
ment this primary diet with a small species of jellyfish (*Linuche* sp.) called
sea thimbles. This may explain the turtles' curious habit of closing their
eyes while biting and chewing, since the jellyfish contain stinging cells, or
nematocysts.[6] Green turtles have also been known to feed on algae, mollusks, and small crustaceans.[7]

These great reptile relics from the age of the dinosaurs are wanderers
of the sea, known to migrate long distances—in some cases a thousand
miles or more. They are strong swimmers and divers; physiological studies

Fig. 28. A contemporary account of Sir Francis Drake's West Indian voyage of 1585–86 includes this image of a sea turtle on a map of Santo Domingo. From Bigges, *Drake's West Indian Voyage.*

have found that a green turtle can survive up to five hours with no measurable oxygen in its system and that its heartbeats can be as far apart as nine minutes.[8] With powers of navigation that surpass even those of birds, green turtles have a long-range reproductive homing sense that allows them to return to the same breeding grounds and nesting beaches year after year. Although this pathfinding process is not well understood, turtles are able to navigate across the deepest ocean water between feeding and breeding locations, locate the general region of the far-off home shore, and crawl up onto a beach close to where they have nested before, and most likely were born.[9]

The remote and undisturbed coasts of the Cayman Islands were ideal nesting beaches for the free-swimming reptiles. The eighteenth-century historian Edward Long observed that the "shore of the Caymanas, being very low and sandy, is perfectly well adapted to receive and hatch their eggs; and the rich submarine pastures around the larger islands afford a sufficient plenty of nourishing herbage, to repair the waste they have necessarily undergone."[10] Long believed that the turtles found in the Caymans came from the Gulf of Honduras. The buccaneer-author William Dampier took for granted that they came from the nearby cays of southern Cuba.[11] Regardless of their migratory ambit, the creatures congregated in abundance in the islands during the months of May to October—so much so that it was claimed that "vessels, which have lost their latitude in hazy weather, have steered entirely by the noise these creatures make in swimming, to attain the Caymana isles."[12]

Early descriptions of natural fauna in the West Indies classified sea turtles with fish, although they often were compared with their more familiar terrestrial counterparts, the land tortoises. Indeed, when egg-bearing females came ashore at night, they easily could be incapacitated by turning them onto their backs. The Spanish historian Gonzalo Fernández de Oviedo y Valdes mentioned this procedure as early as 1526, claiming that a long staff was required to overturn nesting turtles.[13] It was further noted that turtles often were netted by the native fishermen of Cuba along with other fish, and that some were so large that six men had difficulty pulling one out of the sea.

Fig. 29. An eighteenth-century sailor turns a sea turtle on its back. From Pierre Labat, *Nouveau Voyage aux Iles de l'Amérique,* Paris, 1727. Courtesy of the John Carter Brown Library at Brown University.

Whereas collecting turtles from beaches during their nocturnal visits was extremely simple and profitable, European mariners found that they also could harpoon the swimming creatures from small boats. One method, adopted in Bermuda and elsewhere, involved the use of a bright fire carried aboard a fishing boat at night.[14] Transfixed by the light, a turtle could be approached while still on the surface and lanced with an iron-tipped harpoon attached to a length of line. As in whaling, the animal was caught when it grew tired of swimming against the drag of the boat and its crew.

Regardless of the astonishing numbers of sea turtles that frequented their shores, the Caymans were ignored by the architects of Spain's colonization scheme in the West Indies. The absence of precious metals, native aborigines, and arable land caused the islands to be viewed as insignificant. In the words of an eighteenth-century Spanish captain, Don Juan Tirri, Grand Cayman's "diminutive size, in comparison with the vast territories which ever since the age of discoveries have claimed the attention of our Government, doubtless explains why it has been entirely neglected. In fact so far as its productive value is concerned it does not merit the slightest attention."[15] Located on charts of the region but never permanently settled by the Spaniards, the island group instead served the annual treasure convoy system as a maritime landmark along the route to Veracruz from Spain.

Although they apparently did not utilize the Cayman Islands as a food resource, Spaniards recognized the protein value of sea turtles. Archaeological investigations of the early sixteenth-century pearl fishing colony of Nueva Cádiz, located on the island of Cubagua off the coast of Venezuela, produced numerous turtle bones among other food remains.[16] However, it is unclear whether turtles were eaten regularly by New World Spaniards or were fed to pearl-diving slaves brought from South America, the Bahamas, and Africa. Certainly the colonizers of Cuba became familiar with sea turtles and were shown by indigenous Indian fishermen how to catch them. An account of a Dutch reconnaissance mission into the harbor of Havana in 1628 described the discovery of small boats laden with hides, fish, and turtle that subsequently were seized by the fleet of Admiral Pieter Ita.[17] Thomas Gage, an English Jesuit who traveled in disguise to Spanish America from 1625 to 1637, noted that mariners and passengers in the convoy system were provided with turtle meat to augment their shipboard diets. On his arrival in the West Indies aboard a ship from Spain, Gage recounted that "we fed the first week almost upon nothing but tortoise;

which seemed likewise to us, that had never before seen it, one of the sea monsters. . . . Our Spaniards made with them an excellent broth with all sorts of spices. The meat seemed rather flesh than sea fish, which being corned with salt, and hung up two or three days in the air, tasted like veal."[18] Similarly, Gage observed that ships departing from Havana on the homeward voyage commonly were provisioned with dried and salted turtle meat.

However, the Spaniards had mixed feelings about turtles as a primary dish. Spanish friars arriving in the New World had misgivings about eating turtle on Friday because the flesh looked and tasted like veal.[19] Many colonists seem to have avoided the meat entirely. William Dampier's somewhat biased English reasoning on the topic provides an amusing insight into contemporary cultural opinions: "The Reason that is commonly given in the West-Indies for the Spaniards not caring to eat of them [turtles], is the Fear they have lest, being usually foul-bodied, and many of them pox'd (lying as they do, so promiscuously with their Negrines and other She-slaves) they should break out loathsomely like Lepers; which this sort of Food, 'tis said, does much incline men to do, searching the Body, and driving out any such gross Humours."[20]

The Turtle Hunters

If the Spaniards failed to exploit the real resource of the Cayman Islands, their European neighbors, the English, Dutch, and French—early interlopers in Spain's overseas empire—recognized the great turtle fishery and made good use of it. The first published description of English sailors taking turtles in the Cayman Islands is in an account of Sir Francis Drake's voyage of 1585–86: "The Tortoise in the night comming up to lay egges as is aforesaid, is watched by us, who purposely walking along the seaside, as soone as we can espie them on land either going up or comming downe, we runne to take holde of them, who runnth but slowly, and so overturne them by the side of the backe shell, and lay them on their backs, and so leaving them go on to seeke more until the morning, and then gather them all together, for they can not possibly turne themselves on their belly againe."[21]

Another English privateer, William King, who cruised in 1592 aboard the two-hundred-ton *Salomon* to the West Indies, also stopped at the Caymans to revictual and to refresh his men, noting that on the largest island "we found no people, but a good river of fresh water; and there turned up threescore great tortoises; and of them we tooke our choice, to wit, fifteen of the females, which are the best and fullest of egges, whereof two served an hundred men a day."[22]

In the days before refrigeration, mariners normally fed on salted or pickled beef or pork, which often became rotten before a voyage was completed. The sea turtle offered the prospect of fresh meat daily because the reptile could be kept alive aboard a ship for weeks without difficulty. According to the eighteenth-century historian Oldmixon, "they may be kept out of the Water twenty days or more, yet they will be so fat as to be fitting Meat, provided about a half a Pint of salt Water is given them every Day."[23]

Dutch mariners soon recognized the value of fresh turtle meat at sea, stopping at the Cayman Islands on several occasions during the early seventeenth century while en route to Cuba, where Dutch West India Company ships gathered to harass the Spaniards. The fleet of Commander Pieter Schouten anchored briefly at Little Cayman in 1624 to procure turtles.[24] Two years later, the ships of Boudewijn Hendricksz, cruising from Jamaica for the Yucatán Channel, anchored overnight along the west end of Grand Cayman, where Dutch sailors found "many turtles and crocodiles, from which the name of these islands comes."[25] A year later, during the height of the breeding season, West Indiamen again reached the Caymans and took advantage of the fact that "there were at night many turtles eager for the land, [because] it was the right time for them to lay their eggs on the beach."[26] In 1630, ships of Dirk Ruyters and Pieter Ita approached the Caymans in June intending to take turtles, as was becoming the custom for Dutch fleets. Three vessels, sailing in the vanguard of the fleet, were dispatched to the Lesser Islands to turn turtles at night.[27]

By this time the Dutch appear to have become quite familiar with the Cayman Islands, each of which was described in what amounts to the first sailing directions pertaining to the island group. In a section entitled *Bescrijving van de Caymans,* the seventeenth-century Dutch historian Johann de Laet gives this description of the Lesser Islands:

These Caymans are three low islands, so that not over four or five miles [of the coastline] can be seen from the sea. The easternmost [Cayman Brac] is very steep on the eastern end, with sharp cliffs which are very barren without rubble; they stretch WSW about three miles in length. The west end is a long point; one can lie to behind the roadstead in about six, seven, and ten fathoms of water, but one can come to lose cable and anchor there. The second [Little Cayman] lies NNW about two miles from there and has the form of a triangle. Those mariners who would sail near the east cliff of the island will find that a bad reef awaits them, which from the cliff lies a great distance off; once past that, traveling near the northwest corner situated next to a sandy beach, many tasty turtles come from May to October to bury their eggs in the sand, which in the course of ten days hatch; they are mostly on the westernmost island, so that men can often come by one or two thousand and some so large that twenty or thirty men have enough to eat; they taste like calf flesh. Here are also many Caimans, which the islands take their name from; there are also many seabirds, good to eat. The islands are nothing more than stony sand, without fresh water or any fruit.[28]

Dutch ships continued to frequent the Caymans, arriving on one occasion in 1653 to discover a group of marooned French women and children. Part of Levasseur's colony that had fled the island of Tortuga during a Spanish attack, the unfortunate group was abandoned in the Cayman Islands when shipboard provisions ran low. According to the French historian DuTertre, the women and children certainly would have perished had they not been rescued by the Dutch.[29]

By the mid-seventeenth century, the French were spending six weeks or more during the turtling season turning, butchering, and salting their catch at the Cayman Islands. The fishery proved to be an ideal food source for the colonists arriving in growing numbers in the French West Indies. In fact, the French were among the first Europeans to distinguish the various species of West Indian marine turtles and to enumerate the useful properties of each. John Esquemeling, who accompanied many of the buccaneers on their voyages in the West Indies, returned to Europe to publish his version of their various exploits in 1681. He noted four varieties of turtles in the Cayman Islands: one with a soft shell (probably the leatherback); the green turtle; one called *cavana* (hawksbill or ridley, which the French called *caouannes*); and *caret* (probably the loggerhead). Esquemeling almost certainly copied his descriptions of the species from Charles de Rochefort's natural history of the West Indies, which had been published in France several years earlier.[30]

Translation of an obscure Spanish document suggests that the French established perhaps the earliest seasonal settlement in the Caymans during the middle of the seventeenth century. Interrogation in 1670 of several

Frenchmen captured by Spaniards and brought to Cartagena included the testimony of Jean Pixon, a twenty-five-year-old sailor. Upon being questioned by the Spanish governor's men, Pixon declared that he had been sent from Paris to the Cayman Islands, where he lived in a French village for four years before going to Tortuga, off the north coast of Hispaniola.[31] While it is not clear on which of the islands he settled, further archival or archaeological research might clarify the French presence in the Caymans during this formative period.

That the Cayman Islands increasingly were visited by English, Dutch, and French vessels seeking turtles is specifically noted in an account by Captain William Jackson describing his privateering activities among the Spanish-American colonies in 1642: "This place is low land & all rockye, & there bee two Islands of ye same name & Quallitie, being by ye Spanyards called Chimanos, from ye multitude of Alligators here found which are Serpents, if not resembling ye Crocodiles of Egypt. Hither doe infinitt numbers of Sea Tortoises yearly resorte to lay their Eggs upon ye Sandy Bay, which at this time swarmed so thicke. The Island is much frequented by English, Dutch & French ships, that come purposely to salt up ye flesh of these Tortoises."[32]

However, among European mariners, it was the English who ultimately took over the Cayman turtle fishery for their own. With the invasion of Spanish Jamaica by Cromwell's English forces in 1655, Anglo domination of the nearby Cayman Islands began. When occupation troops quickly exhausted local food supplies in Jamaica by the wholesale slaughter of livestock along the south coast of that island, they were forced to follow the French example by turning toward the Cayman Islands for provisions. Within weeks of the May 11 attack on Jamaica, the ships *Arms of Holland, Falmouth,* and *Dove* were dispatched to the Caymans to collect turtle meat for the famished soldiers. They apparently met up with French ships gathered for the start of the turtle migration and brought a good supply of meat back to Jamaica.[33] A few weeks later, they were sent back to the islands, but the French had gone, and the English were left to gather the reptiles on their own.[34]

English Turtle Fishing

The extent to which the English conquerors depended on the turtle fishery in the Caymans to provide sustenance and to retain their hold on Jamaica during the first year of occupation is reflected prominently in historical records of the period. In July 1656, a Council of War resolved to purchase turtle meat from a private ship that had been in the Cayman Islands for that purpose.[35] With more than 2,700 hungry men to feed, commander in chief Colonel Edward D'Oyley issued a General Order to his troops:

> Whereas there is a great scarcity of provisions at this time in ye army and ye allowance given of turtle is very short, though as much as we can give, and yet notwithstanding some officers and most quarter-masters of the army do make it less by carelessness in receaving and keeping the same, so that the allowance of ye turtle is much less than intended them and ye quartermasters do defraud them under color and pretense that it waisteth more than can well do, these are there-fore to require all officers, especially quartermasters that they take special care in receaving and keeping ye turtle to be next receaved as they will given an account upon oath what they receave and give, so that we may not want, whilst we have it not, here I expect a perfect performance as they will answer contrarywise at their utmost peril.[36]

Despite these strict measures, soldiers found their rations dwindling from fifteen pounds of turtle and fifteen pounds of "flower" for each man every three weeks at the beginning of August to only one pound of turtle, twelve pounds of flour, and one "pottle pease" (half-gallon of peas) at the end of the month. By October the supply of turtle had been exhausted, and each man had to make do with twelve pounds of flour and three quarts of oatmeal, which was reduced further to twelve pounds of flour and one quart of oatmeal at the end of the month.[37]

Although Cromwell's troops initially found a convenient source of staple protein in the Cayman Islands, they learned from experience that the fishery was a seasonal phenomenon and that the source declined at the onset of autumn. The following year was no different, but turtle meat still was relied on heavily to sustain not only the soldiers but also the mariners who had joined the occupation forces in Jamaica. Lieutenant-General William Brayne wrote to the treasurer of the navy on August 8, 1657, that "the fleet and land forces being in imminent danger of starving for want of provisions, I was forced to agree with Captain James for as much salt turtle as his ship could bring." James landed an astonishing 50,603 pounds of salt turtle in Jamaica that summer, valued at three pence a pound.[38]

It became increasingly clear that the Cayman Islands represented one of the basic sources of sustenance for the growing English stronghold in the Caribbean and would continue to do so in the future. The newly appointed governor of Jamaica, Thomas Windsor, was issued a series of instructions in 1662 that included orders to take charge of the Cayman Islands:

> And foreasmuch as there are severall little Islands adjacent to the said Island of Jamaica, and belonging to the Territories thereof, as the Caimanes Islands, Salt Island, Goate Island, Pidgeon Island, and diverse others, although they be not particularly nominated in the Commission granted you for the Government of our said Island of Jamaica, which by the Planting and raising Fortifications upon them, may be of great concern and Advantage, towards the security and well setting of our Island of Jamaica.
>
> These are therefore to authorize you to pass and consign the Lands belonging to these other Isles, or any of them, and any part or parts thereof to any person or persons by grant under our public Seal of Jamaica, according to the tenure and Custom of the rest of our Plantations in Jamaica, and also raise forts therein, as to yourself, by advice of the Council, shall deem necessary and expedient for the carrying on of our Interest and affairs in those parts. And in doing so you have hereby as full power, to all Intents and Purposes, as if the said Islands were particularly by name expressed to be continued under your Government, in the Commission and Letters Patent given to you by us for the Government of Jamaica aforesaid under our great Seal of England.[39]

Although there is no evidence that Governor Windsor implemented the fortification of the Cayman Islands on his arrival in Jamaica, turtlers from that island continued to fish in the Caymans, supplying the growing harbor town of Port Royal with provisions. A fishing station with at least twenty houses eventually was established on Little Cayman, under the command of a "governor" appointed by the authorities in Jamaica. The persistent importance of this fishing pursuit is reflected in a letter written by Colonel Hender Molesworth to William Blathwayt in London describing how French and Spanish corsairs drove the English turtling sloops from the Caymans and the south coast of Cuba in 1684:

The turtling trade being thus lost for a while, Port Royal willl suffer greatly. It is what masters of ships chiefly feed their men in port, and I believe that nearly 2,000 people, black and white, feed on it daily at this point, to say nothing of what is sent inland. Altogether it cannot be easily imagined how prejudiced is this interruption of the turtle trade. We must inevitably set ourselves to remove the existing obstructions; it maybe difficult, but our own galley must be the chief engine, with two or three small vessels to attend her.[40]

Sir Hans Sloane, a physician and naturalist who visited Jamaica in the late seventeenth century, wrote that there were at least forty sloops from Port Royal engaged in the turtle trade. He observed with some disdain that the reptiles "infect the blood of those feeding on them, whence their shirts are yellow, their skin and faces the same colour, and their shirts under the armpits stained prodigiously."[41] A contemporaneous but opposite view was expressed by John Fryer, who claimed that turtle meat "restores vigor to the body, giving it a grace and lustre as elegant as viper wine does consumptive persons and worn out prostitutes."[42] Whether eaten fresh, boucaned (grilled over an open fire), or dried and salted, turtle meat had assumed a vital niche as the staple fare of mariners, common people, and slaves. Despite Sloane's unsavory remarks, turtle began to attract the palates of the higher class in the latter half of the century and became "esteemed the best and wholesomest Food in the Indies."[43] While sailors had long considered the meat to be a cure for scurvy, landed gentry began to insist on it as a health potion. William Dampier noted that "many of our English Valetudinarians have gone from Jamaica (tho' there they have also turtle) to the I. Caimanes, at the Laying-time, to live wholly upon Turtle that then abound there; purposely to have their Bodies scour'd by this Food, and their Distempers driven out; and have been said to have found good Success in it."[44]

Dampier and other English privateers who cruised the western Caribbean in the seventeenth century normally employed Indians of the Miskito Coast of Central America, who were adept at harpooning turtles and were said to possess a knack for finding them (fig. 30). These "strikers" were to maintain a supply of fresh meat for the men on board, who arranged their voyages so that "when we careen our ships we choose commonly such places where there is plenty of turtle or manatee for these Miskito men to strike."[45]

Fig. 30. Indians of the Miskito Coast of Nicaragua fished for turtles from a small boat. From Squier, *Waikna*.

Turtle eggs, either dug from the sand or collected from butchered females, were also a prized source of nourishment. Likewise, oil from turtle fat was utilized, sometimes as a substitute for butter although more often as a lamp fuel or lubricant. An account of a ship stranded in Bermuda in 1594 described how the survivors used turtle oil to caulk their leaky vessel and to continue a voyage to Newfoundland.[46]

A primitive attempt at ecological utilization of the sea turtle was practiced on the Miskito Coast. Live turtles, probably hawksbills captured at sea or on the beach, were held down on the sand, and dry brush was placed over their carapaces. The brush was set on fire to loosen the shell plates, which were then removed from the carapace with a sharp knife or machete. This "shelling" of live turtles often caused them to expire, but those that survived the process were released into the sea on the assumption that their shells would grow back.[47]

It is not clear how widespread this practice of shelling was; however, English turtlers supplying the crawls of Port Royal in the seventeenth century developed various methods of turning, striking, and netting their catch to a remarkably skilled degree. Throughout the eighteenth and nineteenth

Fig. 31. Under the false assumption that the shells would regenerate, turtle hunters removed portions of the carapace from sea turtles along the Miskito Coast. From Squier, *Waikna*.

centuries, the increasingly long-range pursuits of Caymanian turtlers were a culmination of these early methods, ultimately involving the highly specialized use of small nets to catch individual turtles.

Caymanian Turtlers

In the early 1700s, land grants were issued by the authorities in Jamaica to individuals who sought to occupy the Cayman Islands on a permanent basis. Settlement occurred on the island of Grand Cayman, the Lesser Islands being left uninhabited except for camps of seasonal fishermen. The French still came to the smaller islands to take turtle. However, it was the English in Jamaica who continued to dominate the trade. A note of concern was expressed in a formal complaint to the duke of Newcastle, written in 1738 by a Jamaican merchant: "By the 16th article of the treaty of 1686, the French have the liberty to fish for turtle at both the islands of the Caimanas whilst by the 5th article the English are restrained from fishing on any French Islands etc. The English should have the same liberty of fishing for turtle on the south and west ends of St. Domingue [Haiti] and the French should be restrained from fishing at the Caimanas."[48]

By the latter half of the eighteenth century, the establishment of a distinct culture had taken place on Grand Cayman. Amounting to only 160 white men, women, and children, the islanders elected their own governor and abided by regulations of their own choosing, ignoring those of Jamaica, such as a law enacted in 1711 that stated that "no person shall destroy any turtle-eggs upon any island or quays belonging to Jamaica."[49] Limited cultivation in the center of the island provided enough corn and vegetables to feed the populace. Hogs and poultry brought from Jamaica were bred to augment the staple diet of turtle meat. Sugarcane was grown, but no mill had been constructed, and the cane was used primarily as hog fodder and in the distillation of crude spirits.

Turtling, however, remained the paramount occupation of the early Caymanian settlers, who took over the Jamaican trade by furnishing the meat of green turtles and the shell of hawksbills directly to Jamaica, as well as supplying Europe-bound shipping, which began to stop periodically at Grand Cayman to take on turtle meat and water. Thus, the first economic system in the islands was a basic one derived from the sea, but dispersed externally. Turtles and turtle products were bartered to outside customers, who in turn supplied British wares and manufactured goods such as clothing, tools, fishing apparatus, and other necessities. These subsequently were traded internally among Caymanian families for island-grown produce and local products.

Like the turtlers from Jamaica before them, Caymanians not only fished their own waters but also regularly sailed to the southern coast of Cuba to take turtles. In the latter half of the eighteenth century, the waters around Cayman began to become depleted of turtles, a result of over-fishing and the use of nets to take reptiles of all sizes, including juveniles. By 1800, nine island vessels, between twenty and thirty tons burthen, were turtling exclusively off Cuba, returning to Grand Cayman with their catch to stock the island crawls.[50]

However, like the Jamaican turtlers of a century before, Caymanians were not welcomed by the Spaniards of Cuba, who viewed them with disdain if not outright enmity. A letter sent by an English missionary, Mr. E. Lockyer, to his principals in London in 1841 described the hostilities of the Cubans:

A Militia was first organized in the years of 1787 or 8 for the protection of themselves and families from invasion of the Spaniards who frequently made descents upon the west-end of the island burning and destroying their houses and other property and carrying the inhabitants captives to Cuba. The people here have suffered a great deal from the Spaniards from Cuba who appear to entertain feelings of animosity and revenge which they take every opportunity to execute. The people have been basely murdered, their vessels burnt and destroyed or taken into their ports and crews imprisoned and vessels confiscated even in times of peace and without preferring any charges against them. They have frequently applied to the Government for a redress of these repeated injuries but somehow or the other no notice has yet been taken of their application.[51]

Tensions between Cuba and Grand Cayman never were formally resolved.

In the late 1830s the turtling grounds on the south coast of Cuba began to deteriorate as had those in local waters. With the serious depletion of its single vital resource, Caymanian society might have been expected to adjust its subsistence base and to seek other sources of livelihood. However, the strong nautical tradition ingrained in the Caymanian consciousness for more than a century prevailed. Turtlers of Grand Cayman simply shifted fishing operations south to the Miskito Bank, a vast complex of cays, reefs, and shallow fishing grounds off the Central American coast, where turtles were plentiful. The change in geography apparently was made with little hardship; the fishermen were accustomed to being away at sea during the turtling seasons.

Turtling voyages normally were planned for two seasons, one from January to March and the other from July to September. Fleets of fifteen to twenty schooners and several small boats set sail from Grand Cayman for the Nicaraguan fishing grounds and were gone approximately ten weeks. These vessels typically carried three officers (a captain and two mates) and ten to twelve seamen.

When the fishing grounds were reached after a voyage of several days, each schooner carefully sailed among the shoals, selecting lone coral outcroppings on the seabed, narrow reef channels, or round depressions of white sand ("white holes") ringed by coral—places that were likely to harbor turtles at night. After feeding all day in submerged pastures of grass, the turtle generally sought these sheltered locations to avoid shark

Fig. 32. Turtlers from the schooner *A. M. Adams* set their nets on the Miskito Bank in 1961. Photo copyright Wright Langley.

attacks while they slept. The fishermen marked their chosen spots with floats of light "bob wood" anchored to big chunks of fossil coral, or "kellecks," for later identification.

Before nightfall, the schooner anchored safely in the lee of the reefs, and the business of setting turtle nets commenced. The fishermen separated into three or more catboat crews, each with a "captain" in charge. Their boats were lowered into the water in the quiet hours of the evening and sailed to the marked fishing designations as the sun dipped low on the horizon and the turtles prepared to roost under the rocks. Each wooden float was quietly approached upwind under oars, and a net was paid out from the bow of the boat over the selected "set" spot.

Two sorts of nets were employed by the turtlers of Grand Cayman. The "swing net," normally ten to thirteen fathoms in length, was anchored to the bottom at one end to allow it to swing with the current. The "long net" was anchored at both ends and was much larger, measuring either four by twelve or eight by thirty fathoms.[52] The nets were attached to a hand rope buoyed with floats so that they hung parallel to the surface of the water. Sometimes a decoy, fashioned of wood in the shape of a turtle, also was attached. Initially made of thatch line and later of cotton line, turtling nets typically were woven into ten-inch-square mesh.

Between ten and thirty nets were set horizontally over coral heads each evening. As sleeping turtles slowly rose to the surface to breathe during the night, they would strike the overhead net, struggle, and become entangled. The wide mesh encouraged tangling, but permitted turtles to haul the net to the surface in order to breathe and not drown. As the sky lightened at dawn, the turtles grew restless and struggled to reach the open sea. But the turtlers soon were back over their nets, pulling them into the boats. Haste was necessary to prevent the struggling catch from tearing the nets across the coral and escaping, or from being depleted by sharks, a sometimes unavoidable occurrence. Empty nets, or "water sets," meant additional days on the turtling grounds. During the full moon, rising turtles could see the white mesh and often managed to avoid the nets. The most difficult part of the entire voyage, the task of hauling an ensnared turtle aboard a small boat, was complicated by the size, weight, and clumsy thrashing of the entangled creature. Pulled over the gunwale

Fig. 33. Caymanian turtlers aboard a catboat haul in an ensnared turtle, circa 1950. Photo by Ivor O. Smith, Cayman Islands National Archive collections.

Fig. 34. A catboat filled with captured turtles returns to the *Adams* during the 1961 turtling season. Photo copyright Wright Langley.

by its front flippers ("hooves") and positioned on its back in the bilge, each turtle was carefully disengaged from the net. When first taken aboard, the turtles slapped their flippers on their bellies, then subsided and lay still. After the catboat crews collected their catches, they made their way back to the schooner.

As the boats came alongside the schooner, a cable ending in double nooses was lowered from tackle on the foremast boom. With a noose around each fore flipper, the turtles were swung inboard over the rails (fig. 35). To avoid excess commotion on deck, the turtles sometimes were "spancelled" by piercing their flippers with a hot poker from the galley fire, then tying them together with thatch string, forelimb to rear limb. Often the men cut the initials of their schooner's name into the bottom plate of each turtle as a brand that would distinguish their catches later at market (fig. 36).[53] Left right-side-up out of the water, a green turtle would suffer

Fig. 35. One by one, the turtles are hoisted by their front flippers aboard *Adams*. Photo copyright Wright Langley.

lung collapse from the pressure of its top shell and body weight against its soft bottom shell, so the turtles were placed upside down on deck. Wedges were kicked under the shells of the upturned reptiles to keep them from sliding in rough seas, and wooden pillows placed beneath their heads for support.[54]

The captured turtles were taken to a central cay, where they were confined in a crawl under the supervision of two "crawl minders" for the duration of the season or until a sufficient number, usually around two hundred, were obtained to warrant returning home to the Caymans. The crawls were fashioned of long mangrove saplings stuck into the soft seabed in five feet of water and lashed together by thatch rope into pens twenty feet square. Each crawl had a gate at one side that could be lowered to admit or retrieve turtles (fig. 37).[55] Those turtles taken dead or killed for meat were used by the fishing crews to augment the ship's meager provisions, which included plantains or flour that was made into "johnny cakes." The penned reptiles were fed turtle grass or other greens, such as bay vines or bean vines, for the duration of their confinement.

When a sufficient number of turtles had been gathered in the crawls, they were rounded up, lassoed, wrestled from the water amid much commotion, and loaded into the hold of the schooner for the passage home. In Grand Cayman, the catch was crawled again until the turtles were bartered or sold, either live or butchered. Turtles also were taken to Kingston, Jamaica; in later years they were marketed at Key West or Tampa, Florida, at the end of each season. The traditional arrangement for division of the catch was quite similar to that used by whalers. Proceeds of the season

Fig. 36. Their flippers tied together, these sea turtles have been marked with the symbol "AD" to show they have been caught by men of *Adams.* Photo copyright Wright Langley.

Fig. 37. A green turtle is hauled aboard a catboat from the turtle crawl at Miskito Cay. Photo copyright Wright Langley.

were split into two parts, half given to the owner of the turtling schooner and half to the captain and crew.[56] The latter half was divided into shares, with the captain receiving one and three-quarters, each mate one and one-quarter, and the men one share apiece.[57]

As Caymanian turtlers became familiar with the Miskito Cays, many elected to stay camped in huts on the cays for several months to fish turtles, several kinds of sharks, and other fin fish. Crews of "rangers" were delivered early in the season by the schooners, their catches were collected regularly, and at the end of the season they caught passage back home. Often, Miskito Indians visited the cays in small *cayucas*, or dugout canoes, to trade for dried fish and turtle meat. For the rangers, this arrangement offered an independent occupation with a low cost of living and an opportunity for a longer harvest period with a greater catch.

Caymanian turtlers developed a unique maritime folklore based on the swimming reptiles. Over seasons of hunting, catching, and crawling, they became intimate with the ways and wiles of turtles. To make good sets, the fishermen studied the animals' routine behavior in combination with the topography of the sea bottom, viewing both through their water glasses. They learned the subtle underwater signs to locate the best turtle roosting rocks and reefs; they spent years watching and waiting for the right combination of water and weather in order to outwit their quarry. Captains and crews swapped stories about famous turtle catches, storms at sea, and adventures ashore on the Central American cays. Dr. Archie Carr, the late dean of sea turtle preservationists, related a story told to him by Captain Allie Ebanks of West Bay, one of the most famous of the Caymanian turtle captains.[58]

In 1942 Captain Allie was working the turtling grounds northeast of Miskito Cay aboard his schooner *A. M. Adams*. A man in a catboat laden with green turtles approached him and asked his help in selecting five of the best greens out of the catch to send home for his family's own use. Once the men had agreed, the five were marked on their bellies with the man's recognition symbol, and three days later they were loaded on the schooner *Lydia E. Wilson*, homeward bound for Grand Cayman.

On reaching George Town, the turtles were placed in a small rock crawl to await their owner's return. But soon a storm struck, and the seas dashed over the shoreline and washed the turtles away. Meanwhile on the Miskito Bank, Captain Allie waited out the same stormy weather for three days, then returned to his grounds.

On the twelfth day after the storms had started, the same catboat man approached *Adams*, calling for Captain Allie in a low, worried voice. He

Fig. 38. The Caymanian schooner *Rainbow* discharges a catch of sea turtles at Kingston, Jamaica, circa 1910. From Vaquero, *Life and Adventure in the West Indies.*

Fig. 39. The schooner *A. M. Adams* under sail, circa 1938. Photo by Gilbert Sayward, Cayman Islands National Archive collections, reprinted with permission from *Motor Boating and Sailing.*

was concerned about *Wilson,* confiding that at daybreak that day he had caught one of the same turtles that he had sent back to his family, under the same rock where the turtle had slept before *Wilson* had carried it away. He showed Captain Allie the turtle; it was one that they both had selected, with the unmistakable mark on its belly. The two men decided that either *Wilson* had been lost, or somehow the turtle had escaped en route and returned to its home. Word of the returned reptile spread across the banks, and the turtling men, most of whom had kin or friends aboard *Wilson,* also grew worried.

One morning a schooner from Grand Cayman came sailing onto the banks. Its crew, when asked if they had seen *Wilson,* replied that she was safe at anchor in West Bay and relayed the news about the flooded crawl. The turtlers concluded that the green in question had covered almost four hundred miles of the open western Caribbean Sea in only twelve days—a remarkable feat of determined navigation.

The basic pattern of the early turtling trade of the Cayman Islands with Jamaica, and later the United States, was affected little by the move of the fishing grounds from Cuba to Central America. However, a subtle but lasting change did take place in the economic and cultural systems within the Cayman Islands. The longer voyages to the Miskito Cays meant that larger schooners and sloops were needed, and the islanders responded with increased shipbuilding activity. Still, the lack of a market system based on monetary exchange prevented most islanders from building their own craft, as few had accumulated sufficient capital. Profits from turtling mostly went to merchants in Jamaica, England, or the United States, who controlled the market price and grew wealthy from the trade. Although the turtlers from Cayman continued to operate on a barter arrangement for their catch, an elite class of Caymanian shipowners and merchants began to develop on Grand Cayman as the system gradually shifted from external to internal economics. In 1909 a local justice of the peace, Edmund Parsons, described this exchange system as "a very pernicious custom," in that

> during the absence of the vessel on the Turtling Ground the wives and families of the crew draw on the owner (who in most cases keeps a store) goods such as rice, flour, salt beef and in many cases hats, ribbons, fancy dress fabrics, etc. the cost of which (together with the owner's profit) are debted against the man who is away turtling. On his return he receives his account which in many instances exceeds the value of his share [of the catch]. Thrift and any attempt on the man's part to keep his "head above water" are thus ruthlessly discouraged. In the turtling trade, as in most other insular industries, "truck" is the order of the day, the labourer gradually descends whilst the employer gradually ascends.[59]

Thus the growing minority merchant class dealt in a monetary market with the outside world, while the turtling crewmen continued to operate in an internal exchange system, dependent on the former for livelihood.[60]

In the Lesser Caymans, inhabitants also gradually began turtling outside the islands. First permanently settled as late as 1833 by three families from Grand Cayman (the Fosters, Ritches, and Scotts), Cayman Brac had remained extremely isolated, relying on trade from the larger island until 1850, when Brackers were able to build a vessel of their own.[61] Shipbuilding became a necessity on the Brac, and boats were constructed to fish the remote southern banks of Serrana, Quita Sueño, Serranilla, and Pedro. Brackers fished primarily for the hawksbill turtle, preferring to trade in turtle shell rather than meat. Using specialized methods that were somewhat different from those of their neighbors on Grand Cayman, Brac schooners and sloops of fifty to sixty tons served as transport vessels for small fishing boats. As many as ten boats could be carried on the deck of a fifty-ton schooner, arranged on edge between the hatches and the wheel-house.[62]

The boats figured prominently in the hunt for turtles, each carrying two men and a single net. The "puller" manned the oars, propelling the boat toward a turtle spotted on the surface of the water. He was directed by the "trapper," who sat in the bow and, if the turtle dived and swam away, followed its progress with the aid of a water glass. Usually a square wooden box with an open top and a clear pane of glass inserted into a groove at the bottom, the water glass was held on the surface of the water to act as a portable window into the sea. This enabled the trapper to guide the puller, who maneuvered the boat directly over the turtle. A conical-shaped "trap net," fashioned from six-inch mesh, was lowered quietly into the water. Weighted at the base by an iron ring five to seven feet in diameter, the net was open at the bottom and attached to a line at the top, which was controlled by the trapper so that the net could be dropped over the turtle at the appropriate moment. Once encompassed by the trap net, the turtle would attempt to rise, would become entangled, and then quickly would be pulled to the surface of the water and heaved into the boat. A coordi-nated pair of Brac turtlers, sighting a turtle floating on the ocean or lazily swimming under water, could stalk their prey and drop a net over it with quiet and efficient ease.

As many as sixty boats were employed by Brackers during the turtling season.[63] Sometimes crews and boats would be left on the remote cays for several weeks, operating from land until the larger vessel returned for them. Occasionally the schooners remained on station with a cook on board during the day, the boats returning at nightfall with their catch. Most of the hawksbill turtles were slaughtered soon after they were net-ted, rather than being kept alive in a crawl. As one Caymanian turtler declared in 1928, "We don't keep the Hawk's-bills alive at all. We kills 'em right off, hand runnin,' dries the meat an' sacks the shell for the Kingston market. A good Hawk's-bill gives us four to seven pound o' shell, worth mebbe twenty-five shillin's a pound. And there's the water-white shell, worth eight pounds a pound. That's rare though. We has to give them Nicaraguans two shillin's a head. Tortles is gettin' scarce now and business ain't what it used to be—not in that, nor no other way for Cayman. Nor, sor, not by a long chaulk."[64] The meat was scored with a knife, rubbed with salt, and hung in the sun to dry. Sometimes it was "corned," or pickled in brine. Salt was obtained from the Turks and Caicos Islands via Jamaica, where hawksbill shell was sold. On occasion, small amounts of salt were taken from limestone depressions in the ironshore of Cayman Brac, where seawater evaporated in the heat of the sun.

Unlike that of the green turtle, the meat of the hawksbill was not exported because it generally was not considered edible on the foreign market. However, the inhabitants of the Lesser Caymans seem always to have regarded the hawksbill's flesh as the best among the various species. Turtle eggs also were consumed by the islanders. Undeveloped or "red" eggs, taken from butchered females, were dried, salted, and stored in bags by the turtlers for the return home, where they were sold or distributed locally among friends and neighbors, along with the preserved meat. Collected from nests, "white" eggs, which did not keep, were boiled and eaten by the fishermen during the turtling venture.[65]

Hawksbill turtle shells were marketed primarily in Jamaica, where they were fashioned into decorative items or shipped directly to North America or Europe. As with the turtling pursuits of the seamen of Grand Cayman, the proceeds of the voyage, both shell and meat, were divided among the fishermen at the end of the voyage. In this case, the owner of the large vessel received only one-third of the catch. The remainder was shared among the owners of the small boats and their partners, both of whom played a more active role in the fishing.

Brac fishermen also collected seabird eggs and phosphate-rich guano, particularly on the larger of the Serrana Cays, Southwest Cay. Big Cay, as they called it, was a nesting area for thousands of noddy terns, whose eggs and droppings brought additional income to the hawksbill fishermen, who often camped in small huts on the remote, windswept islet for weeks until sufficient amounts of these products were collected for market in Jamaica.[66]

A class of wealthy merchants associated with shipbuilding and shopkeeping, similar to that on Grand Cayman, soon developed on the Brac and established a trend of marked contrast between the living standards and income of this small group and those of the seaman class—a distinction that remains apparent in the islands today.

This change in Caymanian society was only one of the factors that heralded the ultimate decline in the turtling traditions of the Cayman Islands. At first, the turtlers had free access to the Miskito Cays, but the question of sovereignty over the offshore territory was disputed between Great Britain and Nicaragua. The government of the latter country at-

Fig. 40. Captured sea turtles in a Cayman yard await slaughter or shipment, circa 1955. Photo by Dorothy Minchin Comm, Cayman Islands National Archive collections.

tempted to tax each turtle taken by Caymanian schooners; however, it allowed nesting beaches to be leased to the highest bidder with little or no control over practices in which females were taken before they had laid their eggs.[67] The dispute over turtling rights thus placed an added strain on traditional fishing pursuits and accelerated the depletion of the resource.

Additionally, in the early years of the twentieth century, Caymanian seamen found that they could market their nautical skills directly for money. A gradual shift from turtling to professional merchant marine service took place. This new occupation, easily undertaken by a society well suited to adapting its seafaring pursuits, brought hard cash into the hands of those who traditionally had been confined to the exchange system. However, as one study of Caymanian social structure has pointed out, while the wages accumulated by seamen and sent to their families at home allowed a certain amount of capital to be built, the system of local indebtedness to merchants continued, especially when earnings were received irregularly.[68] Nevertheless, the standard of living in the Cayman Islands gradually began to increase through the introduction of currency from the merchant marine, and Caymanian seafaring men broadened their once-insular perspectives by voyaging worldwide. These factors further sapped the incentive to sail for the old turtling grounds on the far horizon.

Between the years 1929 and 1939, the value of turtles dropped from an average of forty shillings per head to twenty shillings. During the same years, the export of turtle shell declined by almost half, the value of each shell falling from an average of twenty-six shillings to seven shillings, six pence.[69] The depreciation of the latter reflected the gradual replacement of "tortoise shell" by synthetic products such as plastics. By 1948 the price of shell had dropped to six shillings a pound, and the industry no longer could operate at a profit.[70] As green turtles approached extinction in the Caribbean, Caymanian turtling entered a sharp decline; in 1950 the annual fleet sailing to Nicaragua numbered only ten vessels, whereas not long before there had been twenty-five. By 1970 the government of Nicaragua had severely limited the number of fishing permits issued, and not a single registered turtler sailed from Cayman.[71]

Farming Turtles

Early attempts in the 1940s and 1950s to establish turtle ranches in the Cayman Islands were initially unsuccessful because of limited knowledge of the reptile's biology and reproductive behavior. A turtle soup cannery was built by the Colonial Development Corporation in 1952, but it closed a year later because of marketing difficulties.[72] However, in 1968 an ambitious attempt at commercial breeding of turtles was started on Grand Cayman by a group of British investors, who were attracted by the historical market for green turtle products. Incorporated as Mariculture Ltd., the project hatched eggs collected on Costa Rican beaches, kept the hatchlings for a year in floating tanks, then released them into Salt Creek, an estuary of North Sound, to feed on sea grasses. A mile-long pipe was installed to flush the creek with ocean water, but it was insufficient to keep the habitat clean. Besides, the yearling turtles had begun to wander from the feeding grounds. In 1971 the operation moved to its present land base, Goat Rock, which is close to clear ocean water. On sixteen waterfront acres north of Seven Mile Beach, a large rectangular breeding pond was built with an artificial nesting beach. An additional series of fiberglass and cement tanks was constructed to hold turtles, all of which were kept in circulating water pumped at a high rate from the sea.[73] Eggs were also collected from Surinam and Ascension Island in hopes that a captive breeding herd could be established in the Cayman Islands and that the release of young turtles might help to reestablish wild herds.[74]

Marketing of frozen meat and turtle products began in 1972. Virtually all parts of the green turtle are marketable: the lean meat, which constitutes almost half of the products by weight and is used for steaks and stew meat; white calipee (the unhardened undershell) and calipash (the greenish gelatin that lines the shell), which are used for soup; and eggs. Other products include oil, used in soap, cosmetics, and folk medicine; shell, made into jewelry and other ornaments; and skins, used as leather.[75] Since it is a cold-blooded creature that uses no food energy to maintain body heat, the green turtle has a food-to-meat conversion ratio of approximately 2:1, which is half that of chicken or pork and less than one-eighth of beef.[76]

The turtles breed between April and July. Nesting begins thirty days after mating. Females crawl up from the pond onto the artificial beach at night to dig a pit in which they lay approximately a hundred eggs. Fertile females will lay five to seven clutches of eggs at ten-day intervals during one reproductive season.[77] Before the female buries them, the eggs are collected and placed in incubation boxes in a warmed room for sixty days until they hatch. Shortly thereafter, they are transferred to water tanks and fed specially formulated feed. As they grow larger, they are transferred through a series of larger tanks until they are either butchered, kept for breeding purposes, or tagged and released.

The enterprise had difficulties with domesticating wild marine reptiles and with marketing an endangered species. In 1974 Mariculture Ltd. went into receivership. The business was purchased in 1976 by a German family, who changed its name to Cayman Turtle Farm, Ltd., and in 1983 the Cayman Islands government took over the venture.[78] In the mid-1970s, the farm was processing between 12,000 and 15,000 animals a year. But difficulties in marketing still resulted from conservation efforts to protect the dwindling population of wild turtles. The Convention on International Trade in Endangered Species (CITES) was formed in 1973, and by 1975 enough countries had signed to create an international treaty. The same year, the United States proposed regulations listing the green turtle as a threatened species, prohibiting its importation into that country. Although an exemption was to be provided for products of mariculture projects, the final regulations in 1978 did not permit the importation of farmed products or access to Miami as a transshipment point. The Cayman Turtle Farm filed suit against the U.S. Department of Commerce, but lost its case in 1979.[79] Sales of turtle products dropped by more than eighty percent, and without a U.S. market, the farm reduced its population of turtles.

The argument between those who believed that farming would stimulate demand, further endangering wild populations, and those who felt that mariculture could help in the struggle to save the ancient species continued during a World Turtle Conference attended by representatives from forty nations. In 1980 the Turtle Farm released nearly two thousand young turtles into the sea at Rum Point on the northwestern coast of Grand Cayman, and hatchling releases became a new mission, along with a recognition of the tourist value of the unique enterprise.[80] Husbandry research at the farm continued, and the operation became self-sufficient in egg production. A colony of ridley turtles was established in hopes of breeding them to bolster the severely depressed wild population. The farm's tagging and release program continues to be an important priority.[81] Since 1980, more than 27,000 green turtles have been released into the Caribbean Sea off the coast of Grand Cayman. Hundreds of thousands of tourists visit the turtle farm each year, where they can learn about the unique reptiles and perhaps sponsor a turtle's release for a small fee. Aside from the farm's collection of green, ridley, loggerhead, and hawksbill turtles, there are freshwater turtles, iguanas, parrots, agouti, and a crocodile.

Today, many Europeans and most Americans have never tasted the unique flavor of sea turtle. Turtle soup, if one can find it at all on the shelves of markets or in expensive restaurants, has ceased to capture the fancy of gourmets. Jewelry and eyeglasses made from the shell of this marine reptile are now uncommon relics found in antique shops. No longer is turtle stew or corned turtle a staple West Indian dish; few islanders remember how best to capture and to slaughter the reptiles, except perhaps the Cayman Islanders, many of whom grew up on a diet based on protein from this animal source.

Caymanians no longer set sail on turtling voyages. Although there are many elderly seamen who were raised out on the turtling grounds, they are the last of the generations of Caymanian turtlers. Their offspring have taken up pursuits that are more relevant to the modern world and that provide more income with less labor. Today, sea turtles are protected in the islands by a strict marine conservation law, and the once-busy crawls and slaughterhouses have long been abandoned. Visitors to the islands still can taste turtle meat, prepared as traditional island dishes from turtles bred in captivity at the Turtle Farm, although it is said that the farmed turtles lack the taste of those caught in the wild.

Crocodiles and Pirates

 4

Avast belay, yo ho, heave to,
A-pirating we go,
And if we're parted by a shot
We're sure to meet below!

"Most of all," Hook was saying passion-
ately, "I want their captain, Peter Pan. 'Twas
he cut off my arm." He brandished his hook
threateningly. "I've waited long to shake his
hand with this. Oh, I'll tear him." . . . "Peter
flung my arm," he said, wincing, "to a crocodile that happened to be passing by."

"I have often," said Smee, "noticed your
strange dread of crocodiles."

"Not of crocodiles," Hook corrected him,
"but of that one crocodile." He lowered his
voice. "It liked my arm so much, Smee, that
is has followed me ever since, from sea to sea
and from land to land, licking its lips for the
rest of me."

Yo ho, yo ho, the pirate life,
The flag o' skull and bones,
A merry hour, a hempen rope,
And hey for Davy Jones.

JAMES M. BARRIE

To some, the Cayman Islands are reminiscent of the children's fabled Never-Never-Land, which always was "more or less an island, with astonishing splashes of color here and there, and coral reefs and rakish-looking craft in the offing. . . . Of all delectable islands the Neverland is the snuggest and most compact; not large and sprawly, you know, with tedious distances between one adventure and another, but nicely crammed."[1] However, this Neverland existed, not in the heads of sleepy boys and girls, but on the far horizon between other ports of call. It was and is a real place where, once upon a time, crocodiles and pirates did coexist.

"An Abundance of Monstrous Crocodiles"

Mariners sailing in the vicinity of the Caymans soon discovered that the islands contained not only congregating fleets of sea turtles but also numerous large, dark gray lizards, up to nine feet in length. Larger than the iguanas that also inhabited the three islands, these crocodilians provided another source of fresh meat for passing sailors, second only to that of the

Fig. 41. A contemporary account of Sir Francis Drake's West Indian voyage of 1585–86 includes this image of a crocodile on a map of Santo Domingo. From Bigges, *Drake's West Indian Voyage.*

sea turtle. An early reference to these large reptiles in the Cayman Islands occurs in conjunction with the West Indian voyage of Sir Francis Drake. While putting into the islands early in 1586 after successfully sacking Santo Domingo and Cartagena, Drake's hungry veterans searched the shores for fresh water and victuals. After sunset, they noticed a series of shadows creeping stealthily out of the jungle toward the water's edge. They watched in the darkness as giant reptiles clawed in the sand and devoured buried clutches of eggs laid by female sea turtles. Drake's privateers set upon the crocodiles with muskets and pikes, killing more than twenty in two nights, which they in turn devoured. A chronicle of the expedition includes one of the first descriptions of this curious Caymanian creature:

> [This] strange beast . . . is called by our English mariners *Aligarta*, by the Spaniards *Caiman*, which liveth both at sea and land, he watcheth the Tortoise when she laieth egges, & when the Tortoise is done from them he will hunt them out, & devour them all that he findeth. He hath bene seene by the Spaniards to take hold of an oxe or cow by the taile and so to draw them forcibly into the sea, and there devour them: & so likewise a man whom he hath surprised a sleepe or otherwise at unwares: for if he be in time espied a man may well escape by flight, for he runeth not so fast as a man, but with pieces & pikes we killed many in desolate Islands and eate them, whose flesh is most like to veale in sight, but the olde are somewhat rammish in taste: the young of half growth are very speciall good meate, his back is well armed with a strong scale, but his belly soft, and betwene the forlegge and the body is the best place to strike him with a pike, they are of eight or nine foot long and some lesse, his backe of a darkish gray collour, his belly whitish yeallow. . . . In the *Island of Caimanes* . . . we killed also many *Aligartas* aforsaid, & therwith refreshed our people greatly.[2]

French mariners also found the large reptiles while frequenting the Cayman Islands on a seasonal basis to capture turtles. Charles de Rochefort noted in 1667 that the crocodiles became much bolder when the slaughter of turtles took place on the beach:

> There are . . . an abundance of monstrous crocodiles in the islands that are thereby named *les Iles du Cayeman,* and these are not frequented except in the season when the turtles are turned: because

after the best flesh of the turtles is taken, the crocodiles come in groups during the night to feed on the intestines and carcasses that are left on the sand. Those [turtlers] that are supposed to watch for turtles to turn are obliged to carry a large wooden club to fend against these *Cayemans,* which they frequently overpower, and subsequently break their backs with the clubs.

These animals have a white fat that sometimes serves as medicine to dissolve the flux that arises from cold humors; because it [the fat] is hot and composed of soft parts. And for the same reason, these maladies are rubbed [with the fat] during the approach of the fever, in order to provoke perspiration. Pliny recited a thousand other virtues he knew about the crocodile, in order to fight each malady.[3]

Captain William Jackson, armed with a privateering commission from the Earl of Warwick, arrived in the West Indies in 1642 and had no difficulty signing on more than a thousand men, mostly from St. Kitts and Barbados, for a plunder cruise along the Spanish Main from Venezuela to Honduras. When he and his men sailed west from Jamaica, they reached Grand Cayman, noting, "This place is low land and all rockye, and there bee other two islands of ye same name and Quallitie [Little Cayman and Cayman Brac], being by ye Spanyards called Chimanos, from ye multitude of Alligators here found which are Serpents, if not resembling ye Crocodiles of Egypt."[4] More than thirty years later, when William Dampier and his men anchored at the west end of Grand Cayman, Dampier noted that they "saw many Crocodiles on the Bay, some of which would scarce stir out of the way for us. We kill'd none of them (which we might easily have done) though Food began to be short with us."[5]

As both marine and terrestrial reptiles became prey to passing sailors in need of food, their numbers began to decline. However, the free-swimming turtles swarmed the islands only seasonally, while the crocodiles were relatively landlocked and less numerous. Consequently, the latter food resource dwindled earlier through overhunting.

There has been some confusion as to what sort of crocodiles roamed the Caymans in the past. By the time the islands were settled, only rare sightings of the reptiles occurred in the remote interior. It has been suggested that these sightings may have been of large land iguanas (*Cyclura nubila*), several captured examples of which have measured up to five feet in length. Apparently reliable reports of actual crocodiles captured on Grand Cayman and Cayman Brac early in this century could not be verified by scientists.[6] However, in 1939 Captain James Banks of Little Cayman sent to the Institute of Jamaica the head and feet of one of two crocodiles that he had captured at Charles Bay on the south side of the island. The teeth of the Little Cayman specimen closely resembled those of *Crocodylus acutus,* which is a widespread species occurring in South Florida, the Greater Antilles, Mexico, and northern South America. This American crocodile is associated with marine or brackish-water environments where mangrove lagoons and tidal marshes occur.[7]

More recent recoveries of crocodile remains from Grand Cayman have been identified as a freshwater species (*Crocodylus rhombifer*), associated with the freshwater marshes and swamps of Cuba. In 1976 a single fossil tooth was discovered with other animal remains in a cave near East End.[8] Since that time, four nearly complete skulls, many incomplete skulls,

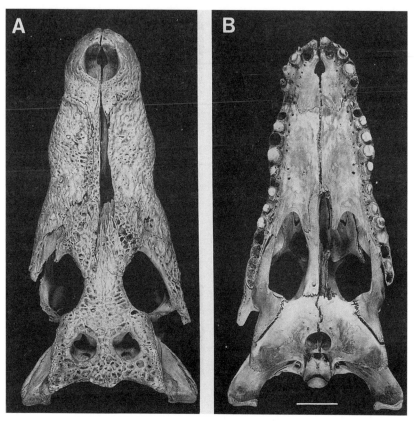

Fig. 42. Fossil skull of *Crocodylus rhombifer* from Conally Cow Well, Grand Cayman, in (A) dorsal and (B) ventral views. Scale bar equals 25 mm. Courtesy of Gary Morgan.

teeth, and other bones have been found in caves, limestone sinkholes ("cow wells" to local residents), and in a man-made canal.[9] Although rare in Cuba today because of overhunting, this freshwater crocodile may have grown to be more than fifteen feet in length, accounting for Captain Jackson's comparison with the crocodiles of Egypt. The fossil examples from Grand Cayman, while much smaller, probably do not represent the remains of fully adult reptiles.[10] The presence of this species in the Cayman Islands suggests that it developed a tolerance for the marine environment, since it would have had to cross more than a hundred miles of open sea to reach Grand Cayman from southern Cuba. As additional field and laboratory research on Cayman's extinct crocodile population is undertaken, we may come to understand more about this unusual aspect of the islands' natural history.

Buccaneers

In the wake of early privateers, who sailed under royal commission and legal protection, came the outlaws of the sea, for whom the West Indies was an ocean of opportunity. Along Spanish trade routes these maritime highwaymen established bases on islands where there was a promise of fresh water and victuals and a place to careen their vessels. Hardwood forests and secluded coves allowed them to hide between raids on Spanish settlements and hijackings of unlucky ships. Variously called *flibustiers* (a French corruption of "freebooters") or buccaneers (from *boucan*, a barbecue on which long strips of meat were cured over a slow fire of dung and wood chips), the loosely knit bands of desperadoes began as renegades from French and English colonies. They roamed the northern coast of Hispaniola, hunting large herds of wild cattle and pigs descended from Spanish domestic stock. These *boucaniers* lived a life of utter freedom from authority, selling their smoked meat to passing ships until, in the middle of the seventeenth century, the Spaniards drove them out by force. Harmless butchers of cattle were transformed into butchers of men, as they retreated to the island of Tortuga a few miles off the north coast of Hispaniola and established a small republic defended by a fort.[11] For a while, the band of buccaneers was left to its own devices, but then it was attacked again by the Spaniards and the colony was wiped out. After the Spanish force left, some of the band drifted back to Tortuga and formed the nucleus of a new settlement under a French Calvinist named Levasseur.

Tortuga soon became a major haven for French and English adventurers, disaffected planters, and runaway sailors throughout the Caribbean. Meat and hides from neighboring Hispaniola and plunder from Spanish vessels were traded for liquor, guns, and cloth from English and Dutch ships that called at the outlaw outpost. A sinister school of piracy called the Brotherhood of the Coast branched out into the frontiers of the Caribbean Sea, with such notorious pirates as Pierre Legrand, François Lolonois, and Rock Brasiliano leading groups of ruthless fortune hunters against the vulnerable Spaniards. But Tortuga became too well known for it to be left unmolested; again and again the pirates' headquarters was attacked by Spanish forces. The buccaneers searched for a new center of operations and found an ideal retreat on the island of Jamaica, where Port Royal, at the end of a sandy spit on the south coast, offered a strategic base for their seaborne enterprises and a haven for their drunken revelries and debaucheries.

Captured in 1655 from the Spaniards by English forces carrying out Oliver Cromwell's Western Design, Jamaica began as a colony occupied by troops that ultimately were left to feed and defend themselves in the middle of a Spanish sea. Joined by would-be planters, the new residents were given sections of land to cultivate, although they were not provided with a permanent naval defense to prevent the Spaniards from retaking the island. On the seaward side of Kingston harbor, seamen began to collect at Port Royal, which soon became the English hub of the Caribbean. As we have seen, many of these mariners ventured to the Cayman Islands, where they learned from the French how to collect turtles; others assaulted passing Spanish ships and returned with money and merchandise, which began to pour into Port Royal.

Charged with the security and successful colonization of the newly won Jamaica, Thomas Modyford, a planter from Barbados who was appointed governor in 1664, was faced with two options. Mitigation of the continuing Spanish threat required either a strong local maritime defense network, not yet provided by the English crown, or peaceful trade relationships with Spanish-American colonies. Overtures to establish mercantile ties were ignored or rebuffed by Spanish authorities responsible for upholding Spain's monopolistic trade policy with the Indies. Moreover, the self-styled privateers in Port Royal, whose numbers had grown steadily since the 1660s, threatened to move their ships and base of operations to Tortuga and to combine forces with the French, leaving Jamaica undefended and vulnerable to attack by Spaniards or buccaneers.

Modyford soon found himself treading a thin line, lending tacit approval to unauthorized privateering in order to secure the English stronghold against invasion by the Spaniards. His subtle encouragement of the privateers in Port Royal resulted in raids against Campeche in Mexico, Isla de Providencia off Nicaragua, and Puerto Príncipe in Cuba. Intelligence reports of levies being collected in Cuba and Panama for an expedition against Jamaica, and the arrival in the West Indies of the *armada de barlovento,* the Spanish windward fleet, prompted an attack on Portobelo, Panama, by Henry Morgan in 1668 and the sacking of Maracaibo, Venezuela, a year later. Confronted by the armada at the bottleneck exit of Lake Maracaibo, Morgan ingeniously managed to escape, learning as well that the fleet had intended to attack Jamaica and the Cayman Islands.[12]

Morgan's seizure of Portobelo stirred Spain's queen regent to issue a royal *cédula* dated April 20, 1669, instructing the governors of Cuba, Panama, and Colombia to grant reprisal commissions against the English in Jamaica—a decree that amounted to a declaration of war in the West Indies. Several commissions were issued to one Captain Manuel Rivero Pardal, a braggart and poet whose fourteen-gun frigate *San Pedro y La Fama,* crewed by eighty-six men, captured the Jamaican vessel *Mary and Jane* and killed her popular privateer commander, Captain Bernard, in February 1670. According to a survivor, purser Cornelius Carstens, Rivero boasted that he had a commission valid for five years throughout the West Indies for the "satisfaction" of the English attack on Portobelo.[13] When news of Bernard's death and the capture of his ship reached Port Royal, it "so incensed the whole body of privateers," wrote Governor Modyford to Lord Arlington in England, "that I hear they meditate revenge and have appointed a general rendezvous at Caimanos next month, where I will send to divert them or moderate their councils."[14]

A Corsair Raid on Cayman

But Rivero already had visited the Cayman Islands several months earlier. The deposition of Samuel Hutchinson, unfortunate captain of the ship *Hopewell* that had been stationed at the turtle fishery on Little Cayman, provided an account of the first recorded battle in the Cayman Islands.[15]

On April 14, 1669, *Hopewell* was at anchor in Hudson's Hole (South Hole Sound) when four ships and a small lateen-rigged vessel called a tartan appeared off the island and anchored up "within a Muskett Shott" of the fringing reef. The mysterious vessels were flying English flags, but

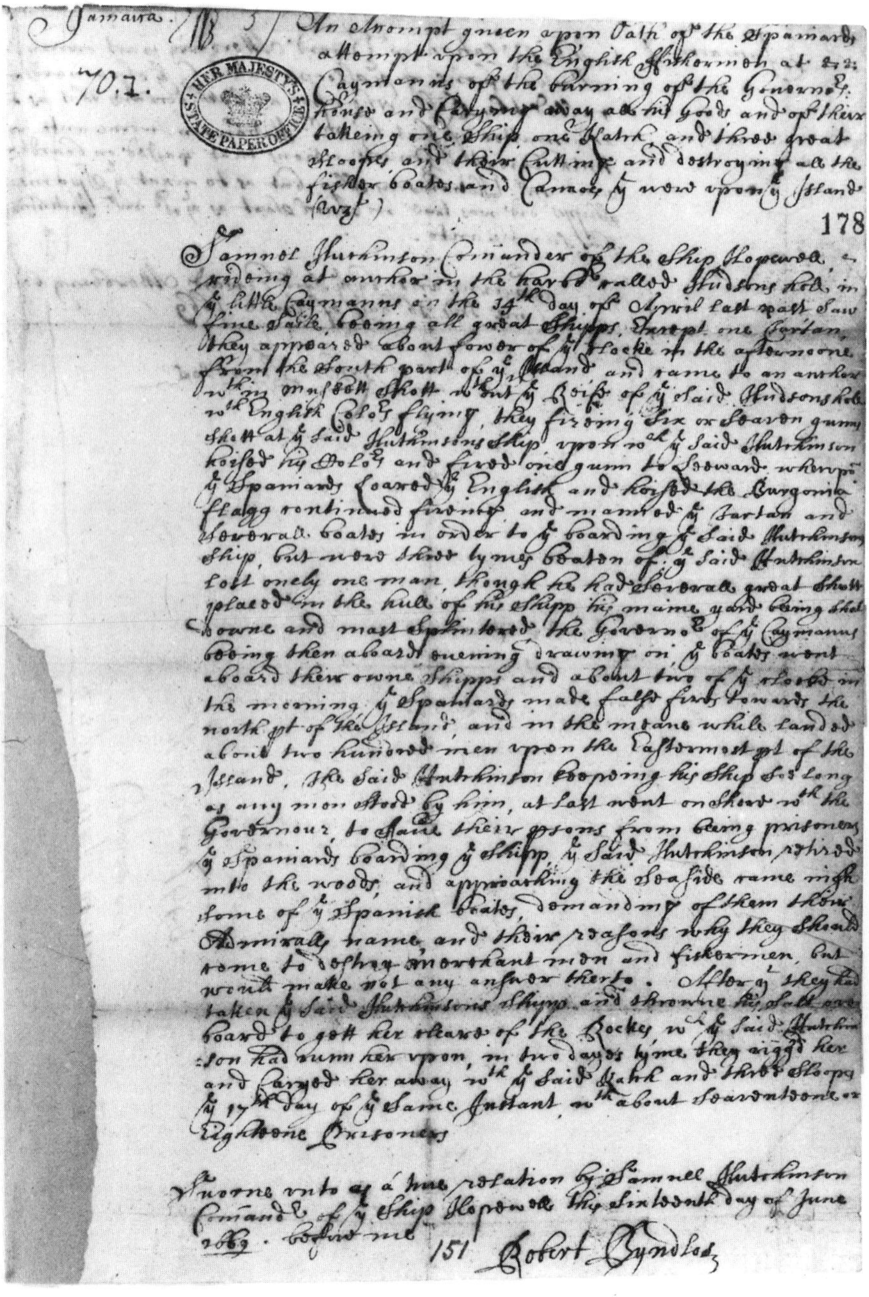

151

Fig. 43. The deposition of Samuel Hutchinson, captain of the *Hopewell*, describes the Spanish privateer attack on Little Cayman in 1669. Public Record Office.

to Hutchinson's surprise they opened fire on his ships, which had no colors showing. Hutchinson ordered his standard raised and fired a return signal to leeward, upon which "ye Spaniards loared ye English and hoisted ye Burgonia flagg"—the royal standard of Spain, which Rivero was entitled to display under his commission.[16] Determined to attack *Hopewell*, the shallow-draft tartan and several small boats entered the sound through the channel in the reef. Despite repeated attempts, the Spaniards failed to board *Hopewell*, but the ship sustained damage to her rigging and hull.

At dusk the Spanish vessels weighed anchor and sailed around the island to create a diversion on the north coast while secretly landing some two hundred men on the eastern point of the coastline in the middle of the night. They succeeded in destroying the fishing village and all of the small boats and canoes on the island. Captain Hutchinson and the "Governour of ye Caymannes," who were aboard *Hopewell* when the attack occurred, both abandoned the ship after running her onto the reef, and fled into the bush. A Dutch prisoner aboard the Spanish vessels, who managed to escape, claimed that "hee heard the Spaniards bragg that they put the English in the Hold of the Friggot, Nayled downe the Hatches, sett her on fire, and burnt the English men alive in it."[17] But according to Hutchinson, after being relieved of her cargo of salt, *Hopewell* was refloated by the attackers and taken prize along with a ketch, three sloops, and their crews.

Not three months after this deceitful incident, authorities at the colonial capital of Jamaica received the alarming news that Spanish raiding parties were landing on the north coast of the island, burning houses and taking prisoners. Several days later, the attacks were repeated on the southern coast. The marauders were identified when a piece of sailcloth was discovered nailed to a tree near the scene of the most recent raids. A handwritten challenge to Henry Morgan was scrawled on the canvas, signed by Manuel Rivero Pardal, who claimed responsibility for the attack on the Cayman Islands. Apparently it had been Rivero's intention all along to go ashore in Jamaica; two prisoners who escaped in Little Cayman in April claimed that he planned then to land at Port Morant, on the southeastern coast, steal fifty or sixty slaves, and sell them in Havana to fit out his squadron for further assaults on the English.[18] But contrary winds prevented his reaching Jamaica, and he settled for an attack on the Caymans.

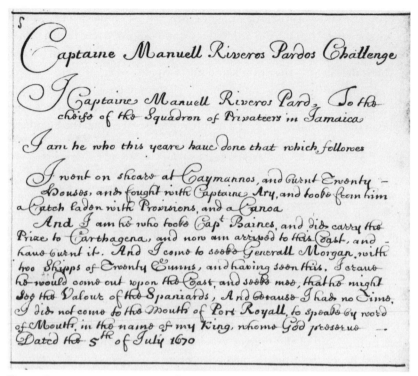

Fig. 44. Portuguese privateer Manuel Rivero Pardal's challenge to Henry Morgan, written on a piece of sailcloth and posted at night on the south coast of Jamaica, was transcribed for the Colonial Office records. Public Record Office.

The battle at Little Cayman may have been inevitable, given the hostilities that existed between the Spaniards and the English during this crucial period. The fishing station was comprised of only twenty houses, according to Rivero. Although it was protected by at least one armed ship, *Hopewell*, the outpost was remote and vulnerable to attack by an organized squadron such as Rivero's. Moreover, the fishery may have been occupied only seasonally and the houses merely huts built of thatch palm. The governor of Cartagena, where *Hopewell* and the other prizes were taken, claimed in a letter to the king of Spain that Rivero had attacked and burned fifty houses.[19] His report may have been an exaggeration designed to enhance the governor's standing with the Crown, a not uncommon gesture in correspondence of this sort. When Rivero himself wrote a brief account of his corsairing expeditions in a stylistic and boastful poem, he did not include any details about the English turtling station.

Rivero's papers, including his commission, were captured along with his frigate a few months after his swaggering challenge to Morgan. Rivero was shot through the neck and killed, but his poetic penmanship survived in a curious handwritten letter. The captured papers were sent to England, where they still exist in the archives. A brief extract deals with his raid on Cayman:

Las velas al mar hundoso,	[Setting] sails and ploughing
Y surcando hasta el caiman,	the deep sea to Cayman,
hize de fuego un destrozo,	I made a destruction of fire,
queme Casas y a Ruine,	burned houses and caused ruin,
Con mi Pecho Baleroso,	with my valorous breast,
a que toda la Canalla,	until all the multitude,
terrible de mi nombre solo . . .	[was terrified] by my name alone . . .[20]

Evidence from the Past

Archaeological survey in the waters of South Hole Sound, Little Cayman, in 1979 revealed several sites buried for centuries under the seabed that are thought to be associated with the conflagration that took place when Rivero's fleet arrived to show the fishermen "the valour of the Spaniards." Discovery of the remains of two wrecksites led to a systematic magnetometry search that revealed more than forty magnetic anomalies under the sand and turtle grass covering the floor of the lagoon. When a magnetometer detects a sudden change in the magnetic field of the earth at a given location, the anomaly suggests the presence of some cultural material. Two important anomalies were localized in the vicinity of one of the wrecksites, the Turtle Wreck, which is thought to be the remains of one of the small vessels destroyed by Rivero in 1669 (discussed in the next chapter). Test excavations of these two areas produced similar archaeological evidence of the conflict.

The first anomaly was caused by an assortment of iron fastenings and encrusted metal objects. A test pit nearly two meters across was excavated to a depth of one meter below the seabed, exposing ballast stones, turtle bones, and other objects resting on a layer of dead coral. Clay tobacco pipe fragments were found, some of which were decorated with rouletting and fleur-de-lis patterns. Measurements of the pipe stem diameters suggested a mid-seventeenth-century date for the materials. Small bits of wood and earthenware sherds were also encountered among the ballast stones, al-

Fig. 45. Fragments of clay tobacco pipes found near the Turtle Wreck in South Hole Sound, Little Cayman. Photo by KC Smith.

though no evidence of timbers or ship structure suggesting a distinctive wrecksite was found in the tested area.

The association of these materials with the battle in 1669 was further indicated by the discovery of a lead musket ball, flattened by impact. Additionally, a length of encrusted cordage was recovered that consisted of two small strands of hemp wound loosely together, coated with a calcareous amalgam of sand, sediments, and minerals (fig. 46). This object was determined to be a section of "slow match," commonly used to ignite firearms and heavy ordnance during the colonial period. Ordinarily, organic matter such as hemp rope does not become encrusted in the same way that metal objects do under water. However, hemp cordage used for slow match was soaked in a solution of sulfur and nitrates that allowed the ignited hemp to burn slowly for a long time. Residue from this mineral solution probably precipitated the encrustation.

In addition, a small cylinder of lead was found. One end of the cylinder appeared to have been partially cut with a knife and then broken off, suggesting a lead plug that could be sectioned as needed, possibly for ammunition. Finally, a delicate brass sewing thimble was recovered during the test excavation (fig. 47). Fashioned from thin metal worked into a

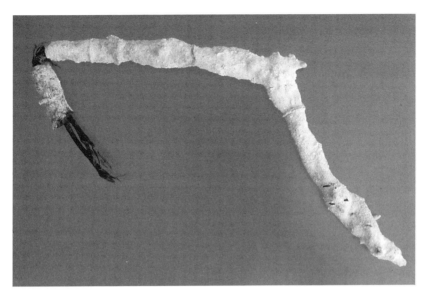

Fig. 46. A length of slow match, such as was used to ignite cannons and shoulder arms, recovered during test excavations in South Hole Sound, Little Cayman. Photo by KC Smith.

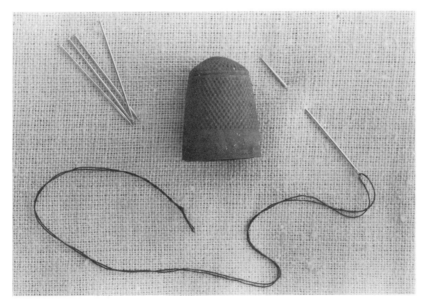

Fig. 47. A brass sewing thimble recovered from the sediments adjacent to the Turtle Wreck at Little Cayman. Photo by KC Smith.

crosshatched pattern, the thimble may have been part of a sailor's sewing kit.

The second anomaly that revealed evidence for the battle in South Hole Sound was discovered nearly a hundred meters from the first, with magnetic readings centered over a thick bed of turtle grass that was difficult to penetrate during test excavation. The dense root structure of the grass was removed until the outline of an encrusted iron object appeared in a layer of silt and dark sand. Careful excavation revealed a long, thin tubular shape, concreted with sand and shell. As the test pit was widened, the distinctive shape of a Spanish olive jar neck also was uncovered. The feature was dug progressively until bedrock was reached. At this point, the iron object was identified as a gun barrel that looked as though it had fallen onto the jar and broken it (fig. 48).

Both the barrel and the jar were removed from context, and the test area was expanded to search for the remaining pieces of the ceramic vessel, but these were not found. However, an encrusted section of an iron barrel hoop and a ballast stone were discovered lying adjacent to the jar.

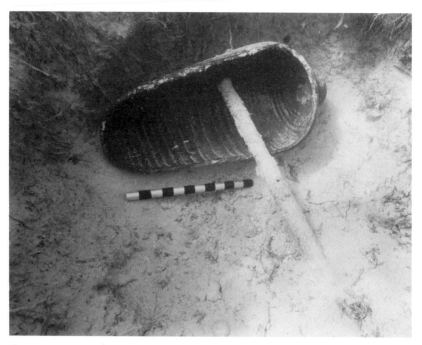

Fig. 48. Discovery of this matchlock musket in association with a broken Spanish olive jar provided clues to the seventeenth-century attack on the English turtle fishing station on Little Cayman. Photo by KC Smith.

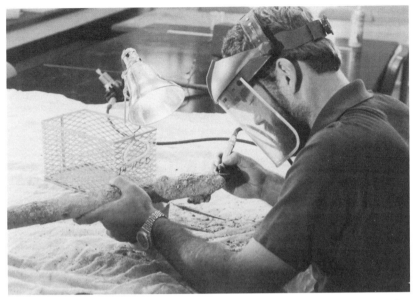

Fig. 49. The author uses a pneumatic scribe to mechanically clean a matchlock musket in the laboratory prior to electrochemical treatments. Photo by KC Smith.

Subsequent cleaning of the gun barrel revealed that it was from a matchlock musket, a common firearm of the sixteenth and seventeenth centuries (fig. 49).

The matchlock musket was the first firearm with a self-contained ignition system; earlier hand weapons had consisted simply of an iron tube set in a wooden stock. The musket, which required two separate movements for aiming and firing, was ignited by applying a lighted slow match to the touchhole, much the same way cannons were fired. The burning match was set in a cock, or "serpentine," connected to a lever projecting under the gun butt; when the lever was pressed upward, the serpentine brought the match down into a pan containing powder and ignited the charge in the barrel. The weight of a matchlock musket necessitated the use of a forked barrel rest to support the weapon as it was aimed and fired. Undoubtedly, the barrel rest would have been dispensed with aboard ship and the barrel positioned on the gunwale or some other solid structure. For all its advantages, the matchlock was not an ideal device. The difficulty of keeping the match lit (especially in the rain), the need to adjust it constantly as it burned down, and the danger that a glowing match might reveal a gunner's position to the enemy at night all contributed to the development of other, more efficient firearms. To the perils inherent in the operation of a matchlock, further disadvantages would have been added at sea. Lighted matches represented an extreme fire hazard, especially during engagements with other ships, when employed by musketeers perched in the highly flammable rigging.

The associated olive jar, typical of larger containers of this type manufactured throughout the seventeenth century, was nearly three-quarters intact, affording examination of its form and method of production and the taking of detailed measurements. Invariably found on archaeological sites associated with Spanish occupation, the widely distributed ceramic vessel known as the olive jar, or *botija,* was one of the most common containers for liquids and certain foodstuffs throughout Hispanic America.[21] Examples also have been found on Amerindian and English sites— a testimony to the practicality and durability of the form. Undoubtedly derived from the wine jars, or *amphorae,* of classical antiquity, the vessels had distinctively rounded or pointed bases that allowed convenient and compact storage when placed atop the shoulders of other jars aboard a ship.

The jar from Little Cayman had been thrown on a potter's wheel, probably in Spain, where mass manufacture of the jars supplied vast numbers to the shipping trade. Before the piece was fired in a kiln, a thick, squat, collared mouth was attached to the neck of the jar. Although the jar was adequately fired, a distinct bulge near the base indicated that as the pot had been thrown a small quantity of air became trapped in the layers of clay. When fired, the air expanded and caused the side of the jar's body to bulge outward. This imperfection is a reflection of the haste in production of this utilitarian ceramic industry. A carbon-darkened discoloration of the middle layers of paste suggested that the jar had been fired in a reducing atmosphere lacking oxygen for a long period of time under slow heat.

The materials found at the anomalies and the nearby Turtle Wreck strongly suggest that the maritime remains of Little Cayman's disrupted turtling station have been discovered. Clues to this little-known episode, such as spent ammunition, a lost firearm, turtle bones, and charred ship's timbers on the seabed of this remote lagoon have brought a battle that occurred long ago into the light of the present day.

Rivero's opportunistic attack on the Cayman Islands and his subsequent taunting of the authorities in Jamaica ultimately caused his demise and opened renewed and unrestrained warfare against the Spaniards, resulting in the total destruction of the city of Panama at the hands of

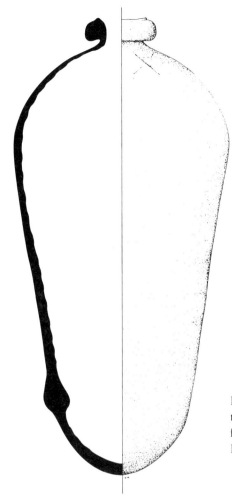

Fig. 50. A reconstruction drawing reveals the original shape of the buried olive jar from South Hole Sound, Little Cayman. Drawing by Sheli Smith.

Morgan's privateers. Rivero and his men were discovered lying at anchor in a secluded harbor on the south coast of Cuba by John Morris, captain of *Dolphin*. Although Rivero's frigate had superior firepower, having on board "eight good guns, six petareos [swivel cannons] and a Good store of ammunition with Granadoes and stinck potts," Morris's men caused the Spaniards to panic, and Rivero was shot dead while attempting to prevent his men from fleeing.[22] Surgeon Browne of *Dolphin* related how the Spaniards leapt overboard into the water and were killed by Morris's men. Only four or five of Rivero's crew survived by hiding in the hold of the Spanish frigate; they were captured when the ship was taken. Claiming *San Pedro y La Fama* as a prize, Morris discovered among Rivero's papers three reprisal commissions, which were taken to Port Royal with the frigate and Spanish prisoners. Governor Modyford sent the commissions of "that same Vapouring Captain that so much annoyed Jamaica" to England as proof of the Spaniard's organized intentions, pointing out that Rivero had been "a person of great value amongst them and empowered to carry the royal standard at the maintop."[23]

Thus ended corsair Rivero's adventurous career, along with a unique chapter of West Indian rivalry in which the turtle fishery at the Cayman Islands played a central role in the struggle for power. The Treaty of Madrid, ratified late in 1670, proclaimed peace between the colonies of the two countries and revoked all reprisal commissions and licenses to take prize ships. More important, the agreement specified that the king of England was to "have, hold, keep and enjoy for ever, with plenary right of sovereignty . . . all those lands, islands, colonies and places whatsoever situated in the West Indies, or in any part of America, which he and his subjects at present hold."[24] Spain at last had recognized England's possession of Jamaica, the Cayman Islands, and other satellites in a legally binding compromise.

Although the fishing station had been destroyed, the Cayman Islands still hosted groups of "divers soldiers, planters, privateers, and other late inhabitants of this island [Jamaica]," who were ordered to return to Jamaica in a proclamation issued by the new governor, Thomas Lynch. The proclamation was recorded in the minutes of the Council of Jamaica on August 12, 1671:

> Present, Sir Thomas Lynch, Knt., Lt.-Governor and four of the Council. Ordered that, whereas there are divers soldiers, planters, privateers, and other late inhabitants of this island now at Caimanos, Musphitos [Miskito] Keys and other remote places, who made scruple of returning, either fearing his Majesty's displeasure for their past irregular actions, or doubting their being prosecuted by their creditors, the Governor sends forth to declare his Majesty's pardon and promise of freedom from all arrests and debts to said creditors &c., for a term of one year, provided they return within eight months after the date hereof and enter their names in the Secretary's Office, from which time their impunity shall commence; and that this be proclaimed a-fixed on some convenient place at Port Royal.[25]

Either considering the islands too remote for continued protection or the individuals inhabiting them too dangerous to leave alone, Lynch offered amnesty to those who would repatriate. It is not clear how many persons took advantage of the governor's offer; however, outlaws from society, and particularly the Brethren of the Coast, continued to frequent the Cayman Islands.

A Pirates' Lair

Formal hostilities in Europe continued to spill across the Atlantic with the Anglo-French Nine Years' War ("King William's War" in the colonies) and the War of Spanish Succession ("Queen Anne's War"), which ended with the Treaty of Utrecht in 1713. England at last was at peace with Spain and France, ending legitimate privateer activities in the Americas. However, many of the younger sailors on the privateering ships had known no business other than the legal plundering of enemy vessels. Corsairs continued to roam throughout the Caribbean, as well as along the eastern coast of North America. A proclamation in 1717 offered the king's pardon to any pirate who surrendered within a stated time. Some gave themselves up in Jamaica and Bermuda, but others refused to abandon piracy. Some took advantage of the pardon, then slipped back into their old occupation.

The Cayman Islands, long known by buccaneers for their protecting reefs and secluded harbors, continued to provide a haven for renegades who sought to live outside the rule of law. It is not known exactly how many pirates made their way to the Caymans over the years; indeed, modern outlaws of the ocean still occasionally come ashore with stolen or smuggled goods, as they do on many West Indian islands. However, among those historically notorious freebooters, the exploits of several are tied to Caymanian history.

Perhaps the most legendary and archetypal of the pirates was Edward Teach, or Thatch, alias Blackbeard. Allegedly born in Bristol, Teach served in a privateer vessel during the wars against Spain, but never was given a command. Then in 1716 the pirate Benjamin Hornigold offered him command of a captured sloop and the following year command of a French merchantman taken in the West Indies. Teach renamed the prize *Queen Anne's Revenge,* placed forty guns aboard, and went cruising on his own account. Presently he joined up with a Barbadian pirate named Major Stede Bonnet aboard the ten-gun sloop *Revenge* and persuaded Bonnet's men to favor him as their new commander. Teach's "large Quantity of Hair, which like a frightful Meteor, covered his whole Face," gave him the name of Blackbeard:

> His Beard was black, which he suffered to grow of an extravagant Length; as to Breadth, it came up to his Eyes; he was accustomed to twist it with Ribbons, in small Tails, after the Manner of our Ramellies Wigs, and turn them about his Ears: In Time of Action, he wore a Sling over his Shoulders, with three braces of Pistols, hanging in Holsters like Bandaliers; he wore a Fur-Cap, and struck a lighted Match on each Side, under it, which appearing on each side his Face, his Eyes naturally looking Fierce and Wild, that Imagination cannot form an Idea of a Fury, from Hell, to look more frightful.[26]

Blackbeard's "Frolicks of Wickedness" became legendary among pirates; he wanted his own men to think that he was the devil incarnate. One day at sea, and being not a little flushed with drink, he suggested to his crew, "Come, let us make a Hell of our own, and try how long we can bear it." Whereupon he and one or two others went down into the ship's hold, closed up all the hatches, filled several pots full of brimstone and other combustible matter, and set them on fire. They continued until they were almost suffocated and some of the men cried out for air. After a while Blackbeard opened the hatches, pleased that he had held out the longest.

Queen Anne's Revenge and the sloop *Revenge,* flying a black flag with a death's head in the middle, managed to capture and plunder another ship and several sloops in the Gulf of Honduras in the spring of 1717. They then sailed for Grand Cayman to repair and refit the ships. The pirates captured a small turtling vessel lying off the island, and it may have been here that Blackbeard demonstrated his savage humor one evening. Drinking with the ship's master and pilot in the cabin by candlelight, he secretly drew a small pair of pistols and cocked them under the table. Suddenly Blackbeard blew out the candle and discharged the pistols at his companions, wounding Israel Hands, the master, in the knee and laming him for life. When asked the reason, Blackbeard cursed his drinking partners, saying that if he did not now and then kill one of his men, they soon would forget who he was.

Ranging off the Carolinas, Teach and his pirate sloops continued their thievery, violence, and extortion. Gradually he began to think about breaking up his company, taking the captured money and cargos, and cheating the others of their shares. Under the pretext of running into Topsail Inlet,

Fig. 51. Edward Teach, also known as Blackbeard, was one of the most notorious pirates to visit the Cayman Islands. Courtesy of the Library of Congress.

North Carolina, to refit, he grounded *Queen Anne's Revenge*. When the sloop *Revenge* came to assist, she too was grounded and both vessels were lost. Teach took forty hands in one of other sloops and marooned the rest of the men on a small sand island off the coast.

Eventually Blackbeard met his match. In November 1718, Lieutenant Maynard of HMS *Pearl* caught and killed him in the James River. Blackbeard's head was taken to Bath Town, North Carolina, and his men were tried and condemned to death.

Still other pirates continued to show up in the Cayman Islands. George Bradley and Thomas Anstis broke away from the pirate band of Bartholomew Roberts off the coast of Africa in 1721 and sailed for the West Indies with seventy men aboard the brigantine *Good Fortune* under the command of Anstis. They cruised between Jamaica and Hispaniola and soon plundered several ships of their cargoes. Off Bermuda they took a vessel named *Morning Star*, which was bound from Guinea to Carolina. Taking guns and tackle from another captured ship, they mounted thirty-two cannons on *Morning Star*, manned her with a hundred men, and headed again for the Caribbean. Things did not go well for the roving band. Some of the men began to fear capture and punishment, since they knew that the governor of Jamaica had declared war on piracy in the Caribbean. They drew up an anonymous petition to the king of England, claiming that they had been forced into serving under Roberts but had run away hoping to obtain clemency and a pardon. Circulating copies of the petition aboard several ships heading for Jamaica, the pirates then retired to the south coast of Cuba. In late summer 1722 they made ready for sea, having learned that nothing had been done in England for them. They sailed southward and one night, "through intolerable neglect, they ran *Morning Star* upon the Grand Caymans and wrecked her."[27] Most of the crew made it safely ashore on the island. The brigantine weathered the storm but retreated to Honduras when warships from Jamaica showed up to capture *Morning Star*'s survivors. The older pirates fled to the interior of the island, but the younger ones chose to surrender, claiming as they had in their petition that they had been forced to become accomplices. Most were later tried and imprisoned for their crimes.

Another renegade who frequented the Cayman Islands was Edward Low. He began his criminal career while a schoolboy, raising "contributions" from his classmates by force, though he never learned to read and write. His brother shared his propensity for thievery, by age seven riding around in a basket on a porter's back through London's crowds, snatching hats and wigs. The boys graduated to picking pockets, then housebreaking. Young Edward became well known at the House of Commons, where he gamed with the footmen in the lobby. The Low brothers went to sea, and Edward worked for a while as a rigger in New England before joining the company of a sloop bound for the Gulf of Honduras to cut logwood. There he was assigned to command a small boat that ferried the woodcutters upriver. As the boat returned for dinner one evening, the sloop's captain ordered them back out again for one more cutting trip. Low took up a musket and fired at the captain, but missed and shot another man through the head. The next day, Low and his crew left the sloop and captured a small ship, declaring themselves "at war against all the world."

Fig. 52. A career criminal, Edward Low took up piracy in the Caribbean, where he became noted for his cruelty and greed. Courtesy of the John Carter Brown Library at Brown University.

The men soon found themselves retreating to the Cayman Islands, where they fell into company with another pirate, George Lowther, who also had come to the Gulf of Honduras, aboard the ship *Delivery*. Lowther had been mate on the vessel, which had belonged to the Royal African Company under the name *Gambia Castle*. While waiting for cargo on the Gambia River in 1721, Lowther roused the anger of the ship's captain, who ordered him punished. But his fellow shipmates took up handspikes and threatened to knock down the first man to carry out the captain's order. Eventually Lowther took control of the ship, and the crew "were all of his Mind, [that] they should seek their Fortunes upon the Seas, as other Adventurers had done before them." They drew up and signed articles of piracy, sworn to on the Bible, and agreed on shares of future plunder. The

Fig. 53. George Lowther became an outlaw when he and his shipmates mutinied and seized control of their ship and headed for the West Indies to follow the path of piracy. Courtesy of the John Carter Brown Library at Brown University.

last article stated "he that sees a Sail first, shall have the best Pistol, or Small-Arm, on Board her."[28] *Gambia Castle* was modified into a pirate vessel and renamed *Delivery*, and Lowther set a course for the West Indies under a black flag.

At West Bay on Grand Cayman, they met up with Edward Low and his thirteen men, who agreed to join forces with Lowther's group to increase their chances of successful plunder. Low stripped and scuttled his ship and became second in command aboard *Delivery*. He soon gained a reputation for inhumanity and "grew wanton in his Cruelties, putting Men to the most exquisite Tortures, if their Behaviour, or even Looks displeased him."[29] On one occasion, Low and his men captured an English ship from Jamaica. After punishing the crew, he cut off the captain's ears, slit his nose, and plundered the ship before letting it proceed on its voyage.

Low grew bolder and bolder, until one day he attacked the wrong ship, HMS *Greyhound*. The twenty-gun man-of-war was on patrol when, on June 10, 1723, the two pirate sloops *Fancy*, commanded by Low, and *Ranger*, under a rogue named Harris, met up with the smaller *Greyhound* and gave chase. The warship's captain let them pursue him for two hours, until he was ready for combat. Suddenly he tacked and stood down toward the pirates, coming within a musket shot before opening fire on the sloops. For two more hours the ships maneuvered around each other, cannons blazing away, but when the wind began to die, the pirates slipped away from the warship under oars. *Greyhound*'s crewmen took up their own oars and managed to catch *Ranger* late in the afternoon, shooting her main yard to pieces. As the navy vessel closed in on *Ranger*, Low in *Fancy* bore away, leaving his consort as a sacrifice while he escaped. Harris and his crew surrendered and were brought to trial at Newport, Rhode Island. Twenty-five men were executed, two were given reprieves, and eight were found not guilty of piracy.

Low went on to further depredations, capturing a sloop that was whaling off Nantucket. The unfortunate captain was whipped naked around the deck and his ears were cut off before he was shot through the head. After the crew was set adrift in a whaleboat with a compass, a little water, and a few biscuits, their sloop was plundered and sunk. Ranging north to Newfoundland, Low took several French vessels and manned them with pirates with the intention of raiding nearby harbors, but during the voyage he fell ill and died. Some said that he actually was cut down by his own men, who had grown weary of his cruel and tyrannical command.

At about the same time, a Welsh mariner named John Evans was employed as mate on a merchant ship out of Jamaica. Dissatisfied with the wages and unable to get better-paying berths on another vessel, Evans and his shipmates decided to quit and go abroad for adventure. Paddling a canoe that they had stolen from Port Royal, they came ashore one night on the north coast of Jamaica and robbed some houses. From this petty introduction to piracy, they proceeded up the coast and chanced upon a small Bermuda sloop at anchor. Evans went on board and informed her crew that he was the new captain, "which was a Piece of News they knew not before."[30] Now Evans and his men had a proper pirate vessel, complete with four cannons. They renamed her *Scourer* and set sail for Hispaniola, where they captured a rich Spanish ship that netted £150 per man. Gaining additional vessels and men, Evans's group scoured the Windward Islands, but soon returned to its earlier hunting grounds for fear of discovery and arrest. After taking a small vessel laden with sugar, the men decided to hide in the Cayman Islands, where they could careen and repair their ships. But an unhappy incident was to put an abrupt end to their roving enterprise.

The boatswain of *Scourer* was a surly man, with whom Evans had quarreled often. After an exchange of threats and curses, he had challenged the captain to fight with pistols and swords in the customary pirate manner on the next shore they came to. When they reached Cayman, Evans declared himself ready, but the boatswain refused to fight and would not go ashore for fear of being forced into the duel. Thereupon Evans took out his cane and gave the cowardly man a severe beating, so much so that the boatswain drew a pistol, shot Evans through the head, jumped overboard, and swam toward shore.

Evans's men decided that the death of their leader could not go unpunished. They sent a boat after the boatswain, brought him back on board *Scourer,* and began to consider the most exquisite means of torture to avenge the murder of Evans. Before they could decide, a hot-headed gunner took up a pistol and shot the boatswain in the chest. The wounded man pleaded with his shipmates to allow him a week to repent before being put to death, but one of the crew stepped up to him, saying "that he should repent and be damned to him," and without waiting for a reply, shot him dead. Thus in 1723 Evans's career and that of his subordinate ended in gunfire at a place thought by some to be Boatswain Bay, Grand Cayman, named after the mutinous officer.

Scourer's mate was the only man aboard who understood navigation, but he declined to assume command in place of their late leader, perhaps not wishing to share the same fate one day. The pirates dissolved their company and left the vessel in possession of the mate, who sailed off to Port Royal. The remainder of the men, some thirty in number, went ashore carrying about £9,000 worth of booty with the intention of dividing it and going their separate ways. It is reported that four of them, who were pirates not by choice but by force, decided to stay on the island and make honest livings; their names were William Porter, Joseph Hyndes, James Moore, and Robert Saunders.[31]

The last known episode of piracy on the high seas involving the Cayman Islands occurred in 1922, when the crew of a yacht out of Cuba murdered the vessel's owners and seized the craft. The three men involved were a Cuban named Pablo and two Caymanians, Evans Rivers and Gideon Ebanks. According to oral history, Pablo shot the yacht's owner and his wife in cold blood, and Rivers threw their child overboard. The vessel's cook was shot by Ebanks. After they landed in Grand Cayman, Pablo escaped in a small boat and eluded capture. Rivers, who confessed to his family, was seized by local constables at his home and sent to prison in Cuba for ten years, returning to Cayman in 1933. Ebanks managed to take passage on a schooner to the Miskito Cays, where he hid for years. Thinking that he might no longer be wanted, he returned to Grand Cayman, where he was apprehended and put in jail. Somehow he managed to escape, but constables soon caught up with him at George Town Barcadere, where he was shot and killed.[32]

The maritime legacy of the Cayman Islands always will be associated with pirates and other frontiersmen of the sea. Of crocodiles long vanished, only a few fossils remain to mark the territory that they once roamed. Of buccaneers who made the islands their haunt, other kinds of evidence turn up now and then. Near Driftwood Village, a hoard of pieces-of-eight was found buried under the beach in a copper pot, perhaps a long-lost trove of Spanish plunder left on a barren shore and never retrieved. Similarly, on Cayman Brac, Spanish silver coins have been found. In the mangroves of Little North Sound on Grand Cayman, a nested cluster of cutlasses was discovered wrapped in oiled leather. Two of the blades now adorn the wall above a bar in one of the island's larger hotels. Fragments of other cutlass blades have been found on the beaches of Little Cayman after storms; perhaps they are reminders of the age of piracy. Occasionally, curious objects are found in caves. Years ago a resident of Cayman Brac discovered a clock in a cave while searching for shipbuilding compass timber on the southern side of the island.[33] Disguised by algae and mineral deposits, the clock was perched on a rock inside the cave. When cleaned, the timepiece was found to have been fashioned from pewter with gold plating. Engraved with the legend BARCELONA 1729, the clock perhaps may represent pirate booty hidden between seagoing forays against the Spaniards.

Catboats and Schooners  5

An intrepid and independent island society that developed on the frontier of the sea, Caymanians depended on their watercraft and nautical skills for communication and transportation, not only between the islands, but with the outside world. Specialized craft evolved in form and function to meet their maritime needs, from local fishing activities along fringing reefs to organized voyages hundreds of miles from home. Blessed with native hardwoods for timber and palms for rope, the outward-looking islanders used the sea as an avenue of subsistence, rather than viewing it as a barrier. They learned its seasonal moods, both good and bad, and how to construct by hand vehicles that were swift, efficient, and durable in the offshore elements. Passing these nautical secrets down through generations, Caymanians forged a unique legacy that carried them not only throughout the Caribbean but eventually around the globe.

Early Caribbean Small Craft

During the sixteenth and seventeenth centuries, ships of exploration and trade usually were outfitted with small boats employed for a variety of uses. Either carried on deck or towed astern, these boats assisted in anchoring maneuvers, loading and unloading provisions, fetching fresh water from shore, coastal reconnaissance, and fishing. In the small-craft terminology of the period, such vessels were called skiffs, barks, shallops, longboats, *bateles,* and *barcas,* according to size and function. They normally were propelled by oars and various sailing rigs, depending on their characteristics and usage.

Mariners stopping at the Cayman Islands for turtles or fresh water during the early colonial period most likely dispatched ship's boats to enter shallow lagoons or land on shore. During the first recorded Dutch visit to the Caymans in 1624, Commander Pieter Schouten sent a *chaloupe* ashore on the evening the islands were sighted, to collect turtles on the beach.[1] The next morning, as the ships lay at anchor on the northeast side of Little Cayman, the boat was hoisted on board with her catch.

Chaloupes, chalupas, or shallops were commonly mentioned in nautical writings of the early seventeenth century. Aside from their function as auxiliary boats, the small craft became widely used for coastal fishing and trading.[2] Somewhat lighter than a ship's longboat, the shallop appears to have been a single-masted, double-ended, undecked craft. One reconstruction of a Dutch *chaloupe,* circa 1650, suggests that her dimensions were twenty-six feet in overall length, eight feet four inches in breadth, and three feet three inches in depth.[3] The Dutch craft would have been beamier than boats of the same type from other European countries. On the other hand, shallops built in the American colonies seem to have been larger and were equipped with two masts and partial decks.

A similar transition in small craft occurred in Jamaica subsequent to the English invasion of 1655. When Admiral Penn's naval forces returned to England after taking part in the Western Design, they left behind in Jamaica twelve frigates and a number of small craft to be used for gathering turtles at the Cayman Islands and for other duties.[4] No doubt these smaller vessels, as well as the ship's boats, were found to be ideal for turtling in shallow water.

Within a few years, construction of small fishing boats began in Jamaica. A proposal to acquire a plantation on the island for King Charles II in 1664 suggested that "ship's carpenters could be employed in felling and squaring timbers and building shallops for his Majesty's service. The plantation should be near a harbour, and three shallops would be needed, which could be employed to go aturtling and in carrying dispatches and provisions."[5] Such vessels may have been comparable in size to a shallop that was ordered built in 1667 to defend the Isle of Wight in Great Britain.

The craft was to be forty feet in length, nine feet in breadth, three and one-half feet deep, and fitted out with masts, yards, sails, rigging, a grapnel and rope, and ten oars.[6]

As the seventeenth century progressed, shallops gave way to small craft called sloops, which were mentioned with increasing frequency in West Indian contexts. Although some confusion between shallops and early sloops exists today among nautical historians, it has been suggested that, as the rig and decking of shallops expanded, they became known as double shallops and ultimately were called sloops.[7] The origin of the term "sloop" is thought to be Dutch, but the design most likely was brought to the English colonies via New Netherlands (New York) or directly from England.[8]

Although proper categorization of the vessel during this evolutionary period remains difficult, it is clear that sloops began to assume a major role in West Indian affairs as the need arose for lightly built, nimble sailing craft. The use of these vessels for turtling and other activities is recorded soon after their appearance in Jamaica. Three such sloops were engaged at the turtle fishing station in the Cayman Islands when it was attacked by the corsair Rivero in 1669.[9] The size of these vessels, their crews, and their armaments can be gauged by descriptions of contemporary sloops participating in privateering raids against the Spanish. At least five vessels of meager tonnage were designated "sloops" in a list of English and French ships under the command of Henry Morgan prior to his raid on Panama in 1670. These smaller ships in Morgan's fleet included:

> The sloop *William,* Captain Thomas Woodriff, twelve tons, thirty men; The *Betty Sloope,* Captain Thomas Curson, twelve tons, twenty-five men; The *Lambe Sloope,* Captain Richard Powell, thirty tons, four guns, thirty men; *Le Serfe* sloop, Captain Joseph, twenty-five tons, two guns, forty men; *Le Lyon* sloop, Captain Charles, thirty tons, four guns, thirty men.[10]

Nine sloops of between eight and twenty tons appeared among vessels registered at Port Royal as trading in "Campeachy Logwood" during the same year.[11]

Turtling Boats

Sloops from Jamaica soon began to range farther afield, as turtling operations expanded from the Cayman Islands to the southern cays of Cuba.

However, the latter fishing ground was far from secure, as turtlers often ran into difficulties with Spaniards or Frenchmen, who also fished there. The year 1684 was an especially tempestuous time for turtling because the Spaniards were guarding the southern shores with two oared galleys, each carrying 80 to 120 men, and seven "periagos," carrying 50 to 70 men. A periago, periagua, piragua, or pirogue was a large Caribbean canoe, fashioned from two hollowed logs rather than one, as was the case with the ordinary dugout canoe. *Piraguas dobles* had two hulls with a connecting platform for heavy cargos. Within just a few months, two turtle sloops were captured by the Spaniards.[12] Three others managed to escape imprisonment by repelling the assaults of a galley and periago, but six sloops were taken by armed French vessels, which also included two sloops.[13]

William Dampier, commenting on "such villanies," corroborated the dangers of Cuban waters.[14] His descriptions of the turtling and trading pursuits of Port Royal mentioned vessels that he called Jamaica sloops, which may have been an emerging vessel type as opposed to sloops that simply came from Jamaica. To be sure, Jamaica, as an English stronghold in the Caribbean, became a center for the construction of small craft suitable for her growing maritime needs. An account of the island written in 1676 cites "about 60 or 70 vessels belonging to the Islands and wholly employed in fetching logwood and salt, turtling and striking manatee . . . small vessels, built in the Island, pay[ing] no tonnage or any duties. . . . [It is] best to encourage them for they employ an abundance of men, bring trade, [and] prevent surprise."[15]

Modern naval architects have classed the Jamaica sloop as a distinct vessel type for the West Indies, with an evolution adapted to the unpredictable and dangerous maritime period of the seventeenth century. The Jamaican type was notoriously fast, with considerable rise in the hull, low freeboard, raking ends, and a raked mast. It had such a reputation for speed and weatherliness that orders for new sloops depleted the supplies of suitable timber on the island of Jamaica.[16] Large numbers of the shipbuilders moved to Bermuda, where abundant growths of light red cedar proved eminently suitable for the continued building of their specialty, which then became known as the Bermuda sloop. Whether Jamaican shipwrights actually moved to Bermuda or Bermudans adopted the Jamaican precedent (which is more likely), the Jamaica sloop remains vague as a distinct type. Virtually no contemporary plans or illustrations exist of such a vessel in the seventeenth century. Indeed, the only known set of lines for the Bermuda sloop was published as late as 1768.[17] It has been

Fig. 54. Eighteenth-century sloops, like this one depicted in *Falconer's Marine Dictionary* (1780), were favored vessels for Caribbean trade and fishing activities. By permission of Augustus M. Kelley, Publishers.

suggested the design was an antecedent of the famous Baltimore clippers of later generations.[18]

References to sloops such as Morgan's do not supply any details of construction or rigging. However, as typical small fishing boats, turtling sloops undoubtedly employed a minimal crew, retaining optimum space for a good catch (fig. 54). As Sir Hans Sloane observed in 1707, "it may be [that] four men in a Sloop may bring in 30, 40, or 50 turtles."[19]

The Turtle Wreck

During an archaeological survey of Little Cayman in 1979, the remains of a small sailing vessel were discovered in the shallow waters of South Hole Sound (fig. 55). Outlines of timbers and ballast stones were visible along the edge of a low mound of turtle grass, which extended into a large depression in the sandy floor of the lagoon. Uneven bottom terrain and disarticulated frames and planks strewn around the periphery of the wreckage suggested that the site had experienced modern disturbance despite its sheltered location inside the reef. Local fishermen confirmed this observation, recounting visits to the island by treasure hunters in recent years. Close examination of the area revealed that only portions of the wrecksite had been disturbed by the looters and that much of the ballast had been left in place.

To evaluate the site, exposed wooden components were dusted off and their principal dimensions recorded. An exploratory trench was excavated perpendicular to the long axis of the wreckage, near a grouping of associated frames at the northern extremity of the site. As digging commenced, evidence of fire damage to the upper surfaces of buried planking and frames was immediately apparent. Small bits of burned wood were encountered among the ballast stones, many of which displayed discoloration from heat and smoke. As the trench grew larger, countless turtle bones, some of which were charred around the edges, began to emerge from the sand. The deposit included a profusion of long bones, vertebral elements, pectoral girdle fragments, and carapace plates. Consequently, the site was named the Turtle Wreck.

Although sediments over the site were minimal, consisting of sand and shell above a layer of dead coral fragments that covered the limestone

Fig. 55. The remains of a small, armed colonial vessel, which had been engaged in gathering turtles at Little Cayman, were found buried under sand in South Hole Sound. Photo by KC Smith.

bedrock, a compacted grass root structure had provided a protective mantle preserving the buried remnants of the wrecked vessel. Less than one meter below the seabed, the garboard strakes (lowermost planks) and keel at the bottom of the ship's hull were uncovered. A segment of hemp line and a worm-eaten pulley sheave were discovered beneath one of the planks. The bitter end of the line had been served (whipped) to prevent fraying, and close scrutiny revealed that the rope had been "cable-laid." This method of laying line consists of twisting together three "hawser-laid" (right-handed) strands in a left-handed direction.[20] Cable-laid line was sometimes used in a ship's running rigging because it would not kink as it ran through the tackle. The association of the line with the pulley sheave indicated a clear example of this use.

Careful recording of the Turtle Wreck produced plans and detailed photographs of its general arrangement and individual features. Although the site was quite small and only partially exposed on the seabed, more than seventy photographic frames were required to produce a photo-mosaic, which aided in the formulation of a site plan. The size, shape, and association of surviving timbers in relation to the amount of visible ballast made possible a preliminary evaluation of the original vessel lost at Litle Cayman: a small sailing ship, approximately sixty feet in length, solidly framed and fastened with iron. The craft's narrow beam and shallow draft had allowed her to enter the sound with ease.

Like many large and small ships venturing into remote waters during colonial times, the vessel was armed. The discovery of a cannon carriage truck (wheel) during test excavation indicated that she was carrying at least one piece of heavy ordnance to protect her crew and cargo. The vessel's armament and ground tackle, such as anchors, were not found despite careful searching; cannons and anchors may have been salvaged shortly after the vessel's sinking, or in subsequent years.

Diagnostic artifacts encountered on the site yielded glimpses of the wreck's historical significance. Bits and pieces of evidence suggested a crew of simple, unrefined seamen engaged in turtling at the island. Limited provisions for a small number of men during short voyages were stored aboard the ship in wooden barrels and earthenware jars. Two iron barrel hoop fragments and ten earthenware sherds were recovered during test excavation. Eight of the sherds were of the Spanish olive jar variety, a common ceramic form in the Caribbean region. The men smoked tobacco in clay pipes and ate fish, dried fruit, and probably turtle. Clay smoking pipe fragments, fish bones, and the pit of a plum or prune were recovered

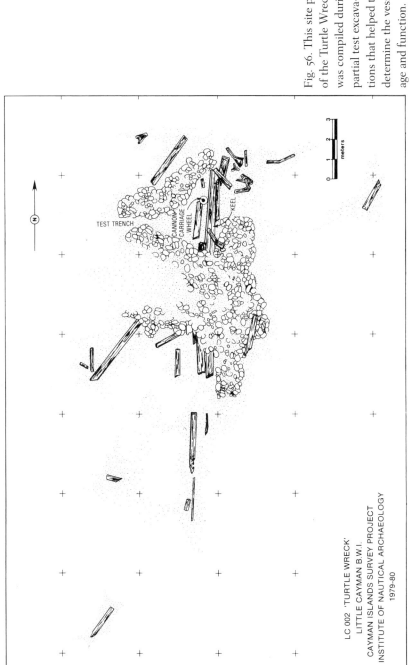

TEST TRENCH

CANNON
CARRIAGE
WHEEL

KEEL

N

0 1 2 3
meters

LC 002 'TURTLE WRECK'
LITTLE CAYMAN B.W.I.
CAYMAN ISLANDS SURVEY PROJECT
INSTITUTE OF NAUTICAL ARCHAEOLOGY
1979-80

Fig. 56. This site plan of the Turtle Wreck was compiled during partial test excavations that helped to determine the vessel's age and function.

from the test area. Cooking was occasionally done in a small firebox, perhaps situated on deck. A firebox was suggested by the discovery of a hand-molded brick with heat discoloration apparent on the surface; however, the brick may have been part of the vessel's ballast. The vessel's cargo of turtles probably were stored in the hold, on their backs with flippers lashed together. The conclusion that the turtles were live is supported by the presence of carapace fragments and vertebral bones, which normally were discarded during the slaughter of the reptiles. Furthermore, no butchering marks were found on any of the bone samples.

The ship appeared to have been destroyed by fire, given the absence of upper hull remains and the charred condition of timbers that survived. Her demise can be placed tentatively in the mid-seventeenth century by analysis of the clay smoking pipe and ceramic fragments.[21] Measurements of the internal diameters of pipe stem fragments ranged from 7/64 to 8/64 inches, suggesting a chronological range of 1620 to 1680. One distinctive fragment displayed alternating fleur-de-lis diamond-bordered impressions and rouletted banding, which compares closely with a Dutch example from a site dated to 1630–50.[22] A box of clay pipes with the same design was recovered from the Dutch East Indiaman *Vergulde Draeck,* wrecked in Western Australia in 1656.[23]

Although further excavation of the wreckage might provide particulars offering a fuller understanding of the historical context to which this vessel belonged, it is likely that the Turtle Wreck was among those craft destroyed during Manuel Rivero Pardal's raid on the fishery at Little Cayman. Aside from any historical association, the remains of this small ship, more than any other recorded site in the Cayman Islands or Jamaica, offer an example of the typical fishing craft of the seventeenth century discussed above.

The Caymanian Canoe

While European-designed vessels were being adapted for fishing and trade in the West Indies, the merits of native-built canoes did not go unnoticed. Hewn from a single tree, with its hollow expanded by gradual use of fire or boiling water, the dugout canoe appears in mariners' reports as early as the first European discovery voyage. In his description of native Americans on the day following his first landfall in the New World, Columbus noted that "they came to the ship in dugouts which are fashioned like a long-boat from the trunk of a tree, and all in one piece, and wonderfully made (considering the country), and so big that in some came 40 or 50 men, and the others smaller, down to some in which but a single man came."[24]

While Spaniards appear to have adopted the use of canoes early on along with other native products, the relatively late establishment of Anglo control in the West Indies, by which time the Indian populations had been decimated, prevented the English from absorbing native customs in the islands. Along the Central American coast, however, seventeenth-century Jamaican logwood cutters learned to appreciate native canoes, used traditionally for river navigation and also in the deeper waters of the Gulf of Honduras and the Bay of Campeche.[25] Although the uses to which sloops were put had increased with their size and capabilities, turtle fishing still required relatively small craft to approach nesting beaches or to set traps among coral reefs. The canoe was an ideal vessel for these purposes. The simplicity of design and practicality of production made it inevitable that the dugout canoe would be incorporated into the turtle fishery.

Canoes were recorded among the vessels destroyed at the turtle fishing station on Little Cayman in 1669, and they appear to have been part of the primary watercraft in the Caymans soon after the islands were settled permanently in the eighteenth century. The crews of the ten ships that ran aground simultaneously on Grand Cayman in 1794 were rescued by island canoes.[26] A schooner wrecked on the same reef in 1845 was approached by a fleet of local canoes, the occupants of which were eager to negotiate rescue and salvage.[27]

It is not clear whether fishing canoes were built in the Cayman Islands during the early settlement period. While stands of hardwood certainly grew on each island, the size of the trees would have precluded the construction of larger canoes like those of Central America. As ties were established with the Bay Islands of Honduras and the fishing grounds of the Miskito Coast in the first part of the eighteenth century, canoes were imported to the Cayman Islands.[28]

Dugout canoes of Central America were of two types: the dorey and the pitpan.[29] The dorey usually was fashioned from a single trunk of mahogany or cedar and was from twenty-five to fifty feet in length. Thomas Young, who was sent to Honduras by the British Central American Land Company in 1839, recorded his experiences and observations for the benefit of prospective settlers. Explaining the differences between native watercraft, Young claimed that "doreys built of cedar, are liable to split from stem to stern on beaching, even although protected by knees, but they do not take the worm so much as mahogany doreys, which if kept in the water for a short time, will soon be spoilt; mahogany doreys however do not split. Doreys made from tuberose for sea service, are decidedly best, and are used by Caribs."[30] A relatively large craft, the dorey was known for its seaworthiness in deep water as long as it was handled by an experienced crew. The pitpan was somewhat smaller; built of the same materials, this canoe was considered faster than the dorey as it had a relatively flat bottom. Miskito Indians, famous for their ability to harpoon turtles, preferred the pitpan as their primary fishing craft.

The Caymanian turtling canoe may have been an adaptation of the double-ended pitpan. The craft's weatherliness was increased by the addition of two planks on each side of the hull to gain more freeboard. Internal strength was insured by the insertion of thwarts and occasional framing of the hull. In pursuit of turtle, the canoe was either rowed or sailed. Rigging traditionally was comprised of rope made from the thatch palm, which grows in abundance in the Cayman Islands.

Canoes acquired in Central America and adapted for turtling were considered too long by some Caymanians. A craft of typical dimensions— for example, twenty-two feet in length, six feet in breadth, and equipped with four oars and a mast eighteen feet tall that supported a mainsail and a jib—ordinarily might have been suitable for netting green turtles. Drawing only eighteen inches of water when fully loaded, a canoe of this size certainly could have carried a large catch. But Cayman Brackers, who stalked the hawksbill turtle with drop nets, found the long canoe much too unwieldy to turn on short notice when attempting to center their nets over the unpredictable reptiles.[31]

The Caymanian Catboat

In 1904 Daniel Jervis, a turtling captain from Cayman Brac, decided to build a shorter and wider boat that would be easier to maneuver than a canoe.[32] The resulting vessel, which he named *Terror*, was to be the prototype of the traditional Caymanian catboat, an ultimate adaptation of small craft designed especially for turtling. Only fourteen feet in length and three feet eight inches in breadth, the new vessel was constructed by attaching four temporary frames to the keel, planking the entire boat, and then inserting permanent framing and thwarts. Equipped with sails and oars, the design was so successful that it soon was adopted by the islanders of Grand Cayman. Unfortunately, Jervis's *Terror* was lost at sea on a schooner that went down with all hands in the hurricane of 1932.[33]

The double-ended catboat's features soon became standardized. Typical dimensions were sixteen feet in length and four feet in breadth, although some boats were slightly larger. The first step in catboat construction was to carve a half-model of the intended shape of the boat. The model usually was scaled 1:10 or 1:12. No plans or drawings were considered necessary, since the builder invariably knew exactly the desired shape and dimensions from long experience building or fishing in catboats. Framing shapes were taken directly from the half-model, which occasionally was cut into station sections to facilitate obtaining the desired curves.

Frames and compass (naturally curved) timbers for the keel, stem, and sternpost were carefully selected from local hardwood forests. Mahogany (*Swietenia mahagoni*), cedar (*Cedrela odorata*), pompero (*Hypelate trifoliata*), jasmine (*Pumieria obtusa*), whitewood (*Tabebuia heterophylla*), plopnut (*Thespesia populnea*), fiddlewood (*Petitia domingensis*), sea grape (*Coccoloba uvifera*), wild sapodilla (*Sideroxylon salicifolium*), and bitter plum (*Picrodendron baccatum*) were used, the first two woods being the most common.[34] Curved timbers needed for boat and schooner building were selected by "curve stalkers" searching the buttonwood swamps; the partially buried roots that buttress the mahogany tree were ideal. Occasionally a hardwood sapling was bent over to the lee of the prevailing wind and tied to the ground to be "trained" to the desired curvature. This practice demonstrated the foresight of Caymanian boatwrights because, with the slow growth rate of hardwoods, the timber could not be used for at least a generation.

Floor frames (called "dunnage") and half-frames, numbering from eleven to fifteen, were either sawn or steamed to fit the internal shape of the hull and were fastened to the keel, stem, and sternpost with treenails. Seven or sometimes eight strakes of white American pine were carvel-fastened to each side of the boat. Copper nails from Jamaica and, later, brass screws were used. The uppermost or sheer strake was slightly thicker than the others, which averaged 11/16 inches thick. A caprail and sometimes a rubrail were added to the gunwale. The sheer strake and rails reinforced the gunwale of the boat, which took the brunt of the action when a thrashing turtle was hauled aboard.

A longitudinal stringer was inserted on each side of the internal hull, serving to support the four thwarts. The forwardmost thwart—a heavy

member often made up of three or more planks fitted edge to edge—
supported the mast, which was passed through the thwart and into a
keyhole-shaped socket of the mast step atop the stem scarf. This forward
thwart also served as a breasthook, reinforcing the bow. As in the typical
catboat rig, the mast was stepped far forward in the vessel, but it had no
stays or shrouds; the boom and mast assembly commonly was unshipped
quickly and laid in the boat when the turtling grounds were reached. The
mast was rigged with a sprit or Marconi mainsail and had a distinctive rake
aft to distribute the weight of the sail toward the center of the shallow craft
(fig. 57). Sometimes the catboats used small jibs, which were useful when
sailing to windward. In high winds, boats from Grand Cayman used a
"weatherboard" set well outboard on the windward side, upon which one
of the crew could perch to add leverage and prevent the craft from capsizing (fig. 58). Sailors from Cayman Brac considered this apparatus a lub-
berly piece of gear and almost never used it.[35]

A deep keel or centerboard and standing rigging were not considered
necessary, since the boat operated only part of the time under sail. Rather
than a tiller that would become fouled by turtle nets, the catboat's rudder
head was fitted with a yoke bar with steering lines that could be dropped
quickly in the bilge. This arrangement also allowed the rudder to be unshipped and stored out of the way. With sailing rig and rudder removed,
the double-ended catboat became a highly maneuverable platform under
oars for netting turtles and catching fish.

Each catboat was equipped with two or four oars that were eight to ten
feet in length, and sometimes with a spare. Called sculls by the turtlers,
the oars were composite-built: the loom of Spanish elm and the blade of
white pine. On Grand Cayman, oars were also made of strawberry and red
mangrove. A long paddle, sometimes more than seven feet in length with
a curious notched grip for the upper hand, was carried for use as a steering
oar when the rudder was unshipped. On Cayman Brac, short paddles used
at the bow were fashioned from wild ginep (*Exothea paniculata*), which
grows on the bluff.[36] The paddle blades could be cut thin and still retain
strength. The boats usually were not equipped with oarlocks; instead, a
small piece of wood called a pallet or oarblock was fastened to the capral.
Two holes bored through the pallet were threaded with thatch rope, which
held the oars to the gunwale. As with an oarlock, this arrangement was a
highly functional one, for the boat quickly could be backed, changing
directions as the turtle chase required.

Fig. 57. Caymanians under sail in a catboat prepare their turtle catching equipment, 1938. Photo by C. Bernard Lewis, Cayman Islands National Archive collections.

Fig. 58. The crew of the catboat *Defiance* use a weatherboard extended to windward to balance their craft. Photo by Gilbert Sayward, Cayman Islands National Archive collections, reprinted with permission from *Motor Boating and Sailing*.

Caymanian catboats invariably were painted a distinctive bright blue color. The same traditional color, "catboat blue," also was applied to those articles of the boat's gear that were used in the water, such as the oar blades, the paddle, a long pole for maneuvering in shallow water, and the water glass. The blue paint was a functional part of the turtling lore because it acted as an effective marine camouflage, blending with the surrounding water and allowing the fishermen to approach their prey undetected.

The catboat's complement of equipment included a "calabash" bailer, made from the woody outer shell of fruit from the gourd tree (*Crescentia cujete*), to scoop water from the hull.[37] A long pole, for propulsion in shallow water, often had barbs fixed at one end to double as a harpoon. In addition, a wooden fish club, or "muntle," might be carried along with the usual hooks and line.

When not in use, catboats were unrigged, pulled up on the shore, and stored under low, thatch-roofed shelters that were open to the sea breeze. The idle boats became a shady location for children to play or an ideal place to take an afternoon nap.

Sadly, the Caymanian catboat now is extinct as a vessel type. The twilight of its existence occurred when the marine resource it was specially

Fig. 59. The catboat *Ajax*, built by Lee Jervis on Cayman Brac, is one of the few surviving examples of this specialized turtling vessel. Photo by KC Smith.

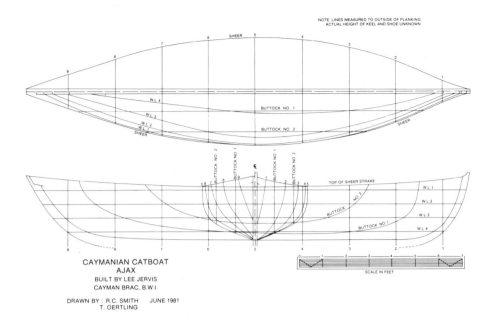

Fig. 60. The reconstructed lines of the catboat *Ajax* are based on offset measurements and detailed notes. Drawing by Roger C. Smith and Tom Oertling.

designed to capture dwindled, and restrictive legislation made turtling unprofitable. Fortunately, a surviving member of the catboat fleets was found stored in a shed behind a house on the north shore of Cayman Brac. Named *Ajax,* the boat was a veteran of sun-bleached shoals and countless struggling turtles, but it and its associated equipment were well preserved, ensuring that this craft would not go to its demise unrecorded. The half-model from which the boat had been constructed was kindly loaned for examination by Lee Jervis, the vessel's builder. Offset measurements were taken from both the model and the boat to establish the catboat's hull shape and characteristics.

Somewhat similar in form and construction to the New England whaleboat and the Newfoundland dory, the Caymanian catboat was their small Caribbean cousin. Each of these double-ended fishing craft was lightly built to be carried on larger craft and lowered into the sea when the fishing grounds were reached. As highly versatile vehicles under oars or sail, each was well adapted to the task required of it, without frills or nonfunctional features.[38]

The reconstructed lines of the Caymanian catboat *Ajax* (fig. 60) provide an interesting comparison with those of a typical New England whaleboat, such as the one built by boatwright Charles Beetle in 1933.[39] The whaleboat generally was larger than the catboat; pursuing and harpooning a cetacean required more oarsmen and equipment than setting nets or stalking turtles on the seabed. Beetle's boat measured twenty-nine feet five and three-quarter inches in overall length with a beam of six feet five inches, while Jervis's boat is nineteen feet overall and four feet four inches in breadth. However, the length-to-beam ratios of the two are similar, the whaleboat being 4.59 and the catboat 4.38.

The whaleboat was perhaps the better sailer; it usually had a retractable centerboard which, when lowered through the hull, would balance the sail area and give the craft more grip on the water when sailing to windward. The catboat had no centerboard or even a sailing keel. But the catboat's keel was slightly deeper than the whaleboat's, and its hull displayed a more pronounced deadrise, compensating to a slight degree for its shallow draft.

The Caymanian Schooner

As the turtle fisheries of the Cayman Islands and Cuba increasingly became depleted, Caymanians began to build larger craft for the seven-hundred-mile round trip voyages to the Central American fishing grounds. By necessity, the islanders became their own naval architects, shipwrights, carpenters, sailmakers, and blacksmiths. The first recorded ships to be built in the Cayman Islands were *Two Friends,* a 60-ton vessel, and perhaps another vessel built in 1793.[40] *Polly and Betsy,* a 36-ton schooner owned by John Drayton, was constructed in 1801 in Cayman but registered in Montego Bay, the closest Jamaican port.[41] Schooners were built primarily for the turtling industry, but many also began to carry passengers and freight, especially lumber. By 1850, the largest vessel built in the islands was not more than 45 tons.[42] Later, schooners used in the lumber trade, to haul hardwoods to the mainland and to return with pine for shipbuilding, tended to be larger, averaging 80, 90, or 100 tons.[43] The largest Caymanian schooner to be built was a vessel of 250 tons, constructed during the early 1900s; however, most turtling schooners were between 40 and 50 tons.[44]

Sloops occasionally were built in the Cayman Islands for use on the fishing grounds. Although some were as large as the schooners, built to 60-ton dimensions, the majority were around 20 tons.[45] Sloops needed less hardware, rigging, and maintenance, but they also were not as fast or efficient as the turtling schooners, and therefore were less popular.

As with catboats, schooners were designed and built from a half-model. Usually scaled at three-quarters of an inch to the foot, models were carved from cedar, sometimes with sharp pieces of glass.[46] The finished model was cut into sections, from which the progressive shape of the principal frames of the hull was obtained. A typical 76-ton turtling schooner of later years was seventy feet in length. Stem and sternpost were sawn or adzed from mahogany. Frames and knees were fashioned from either mahogany or other local hardwoods such as pompero, jasmine, fiddlewood, or sapodilla. Keel, planking, and decking were of pine, imported from the United States (Tampa or Mobile) or Nicaragua. Masts and spars usually were of Pacific yellow pine or Douglas fir. Sailcloth, fasteners, and tackle came from the United States, but anchors and cable ordinarily came from Great Britain via Jamaica. Some of the special fittings were obtained from Nova Scotia, where the schooner also was a principal fishing craft.

On Grand Cayman, the family names traditionally associated with shipbuilding were Arch, Bodden, and Ebanks; on Cayman Brac, the industry was headed by the Bodden, Foster, Scott, and Tibbetts families.

Fig. 61. George Town was the scene of a local shipbuilding tradition in Grand Cayman that produced turtling schooners, circa 1910. From Vaquero, *Life and Adventure in the West Indies.*

Fig. 62. A vessel under construction in Grand Cayman, circa 1942, demonstrates the intricate framing required for these seagoing craft. Photo by George Roy, Cayman Islands National Archive collections.

Their seaworthy schooners usually were designed, laid down, timbered, planked, and launched on the rocky shore in front of the family house (fig. 61). Although the progress of building a ship often was slower than contemporary yard-times of New England or Nova Scotia, Caymanian schooners typically were fashioned in nine or ten months by eight or ten men, working from scratch without plans.

A suitably level location on the ironshore was selected to lay down the keel, which, as with most West Indian craft, had a worm-shoe to protect the keel from shipworms. Stem and sternpost were attached at either end, and primary floors corresponding to half-model sections were fastened to the keel, usually at six-foot intervals. Compatible futtocks and half-timbers were added to each side of the floors to complete the framing shape of the hull. Then the vessel was fully framed with additional timbers between the originals (fig. 62).

The schooner next was planked, caulked with imported oakum, and decked. At first, treenails or "trunnels" of bastard mahogany (*Trichilia glabra*) were used to join timbers and planks.[47] However, shipwrights soon found that treenails of pine were more suitable because, when wet, they swelled to make a tighter fit. In the 1920s, galvanized iron fasteners replaced treenails.[48]

Masts were fitted by hand, utilizing a system of sheerlegs, blocks, and tackles. Originally, Caymanian vessels were stepped and rigged after they had been launched, but once it was discovered that they were stable enough without ballast and would not immediately tip over, masts were inserted prior to launching.

The launching of a Caymanian schooner, such as *Goldfield, Adams, Wilson,* or *Majestic,* was an island-wide event. The atmosphere was festive, complete with food and music and drink. Families, friends, neighbors, acquaintances, and everyone else took the day off to assemble for the task of moving the finished vessel from the shore into the sea by hand. A strong bridle was secured around the ship's hull and rove through a heavy block, which was attached to a large coral head or a stout anchor firmly embedded offshore. The bridle line ran from the anchor back to the beach, where the crowd waited in anticipation. Meanwhile, the schooner was eased down on her side by gradually cutting away shoring under the hull. Thatch palm logs were placed under the vessel to serve as rollers— a system less complicated and expensive than the use of a cradle. When most of the shoring had been eliminated, the signal was given. Men, women, and children all took up the bridle line (it was considered good luck to have the women pull), and the ship slowly was hauled and rolled into the water amid much encouragement and excitement.[49] The last traditional launching of a Caymanian-built ship, *Trial,* occurred on January 3, 1967, on Cayman Brac.

Originally, the typical turtling schooner was quite similar in design to the Gloucester fishing schooner; the shape of Caymanian hulls and especially the bows of the vessels corresponded to those of the Gloucestermen until the 1920s, when Cayman's shipwrights adopted the longer-hulled bow of the Nova Scotia schooner.[50] This shift in design seemed to produce a faster and more manageable sailing craft, ideal for the passage to the fishing banks and subsequent maneuvers through the coral reefs (fig. 63).

In the 1930s, Grand Cayman boasted a fleet of twenty-three schooners and about three hundred catboats. Rivalry among turtling captains was kept on a social basis through regularly scheduled regattas and races lasting five days. Inaugurated in 1935 by Commissioner Sir Allen Cardinall, the events usually were held the last week in January between the shark and turtling seasons, when most of the island vessels were back in their home port refitting.[51] Only commercial vessels raced, with cash prizes for the winning boats and small stipends to various captains for meals aboard their schooners during the races. Competition was keen among the mari-

Fig. 63. The classic lines and sail pattern of a Caymanian schooner are revealed in this photograph of *Goldfield* under sail in 1938. Photo by C. Bernard Lewis, Cayman Islands National Archive collections.

ners, especially those from West Bay, who were cheered from shore by their kinfolk. In addition to the regular regattas off the harbor area, there were "round-the-island" races (fig. 65). Senior class sailing vessels included *Adams*, *Wilson*, *Arbutus*, *Ziroma*, and *Goldfield*. The latter schooner won the Class A prize three years in succession—1936, 1937, and 1938.[52] Other Cayman schooners participating in the regattas included *Wembley*, *Alsons*, *Laguna*, *Armistice*, *Chamberlain*, *Blake*, *E. A. Henning*, *Village Belle*, *Rembro*, *Woodlark*, *Dreadnought*, *Gleaner*, and *Franklin*.[53]

Thatch Rope

Concurrent with Caymanian turtling and boat-building, a cottage industry of rope making and weaving developed in the islands. Leaves of the silver thatch palm (*Coccothrinax proctoril*) were used widely as roofing material, but use of the unopened "tops," or center shoots, for rope and string became a nautical tradition and then a national industry. The unique palm, referred to as "tatch," thrives in almost every habitat on all three islands, and is found nowhere else in the world. Women and children collected tops from woodland thickets and laid them tied in pairs in

Fig. 64. The annual Yacht and Sailing Club regatta drew a fleet of catboats competing against each other for prizes. Photo courtesy of Cayman Islands Yacht and Sailing Club.

the sun to dry. After two days, the dried tops were cut at the head, split with the thumbnail into single strips, and twisted into "pegs," strands about one-quarter of an inch in diameter and roughly thirty fathoms in length.[54]

The rope was manufactured outdoors, usually on the beach or in a cleared area where a "rope walk" made of hardwoods was erected to turn the strands into a finished product. Three pegs were "treaded" into a hand-

Fig. 65. The schooner *Rembro* competed in 1935 in the annual Cayman Islands Yacht and Sailing Club regatta. Photo by Reginald Parsons, Cayman Islands National Archive collections.

carved, triple-grooved "cob" that fed and combined them into a single line. The "bitter ends" of the pegs each were attached to a fixed frame with three crank handles, called a winch. A crankcase, made from a slat of wood with three holes, was inserted over the crank handles so that they could twist the three strands simultaneously. The other single end of the line was attached to a "cart" with a single crank, positioned some distance away. As the crank was turned, the cob was moved (along with the cart) toward the winch, combining three strands into one rope. Normally, three people were required to lay rope—one to operate the crankcase on the winch (usually in a clockwise direction), another to turn the crank on the cart in the opposite direction, and one to stabilize the cob as it moved toward the winch. Tension ("hardness" or "softness") of the finished rope was controlled by the degree to which the cob was pushed against the progressing lay, since forcing the strands apart created a tighter weave. After a rope was laid, it was taken off the rope walk, knotted at each end, trimmed of errant fibers, and coiled into twenty-five-fathom lengths, each slightly greater than half an inch in diameter. On average, three "twenty-five fathoms ropes" could be turned out on a rope walk each day.[55] Sometimes a smaller quarter-inch, two-strand rope was made for domestic use.

Fig. 66. A "rope walk" was used to produce rope from the tops of the silver thatch palm tree. Cayman Islands National Archive collections.

Fig. 67. Coils of "twenty-five fathoms ropes" ready for market in Jamaica are loaded into a catboat. Cayman Islands National Archive collections.

Thatch rope at first was sufficient for the needs of turtlers and fishermen. Although not as strong as sisal rope, thatch was resistant to damage by salt water. When its durability in the marine environment became recognized abroad, a "string" industry developed to meet a market in Jamaica and elsewhere, despite the small return for such a labor-intensive product. Although the practice has dwindled, hats and brooms and baskets still are made by hand in the islands and are used by residents today.

Lost at Sea

Caymanian-built craft were extremely seaworthy, and their crews were among the most sea-hardened mariners in the West Indies. But the deep blue waters of the Caribbean can become a cruel environment during periods of tropical depressions and sudden storms. A delicate balance exists for those who live and work in the marine realm, between wind and water and at the mercy of the weather.

On November 6, 1912, Captain Edwin Walton and crew departed Cayman Brac aboard the sloop *Fred Lowrie* for Southwest Cay, Serrana Bank, to collect rangers whom he had left there to fish. Contrary weather forced him to seek shelter on the Serranilla Bank at Beacon Cay, where he anchored six days later. As weather conditions deteriorated, the men decided to leave their boat for the protection of the cay. They carried only a few provisions ashore, since they expected the vessel to ride out the storm secured by two anchors with heavy chains. However, three hours after they went ashore, the sloop foundered and broke up, washing their turtles and a ship's lantern up on the cay.

The twenty-eight marooned mariners were on the cay for eleven days, eating birds and fish and drinking salty water, before another Brac turtler, the schooner *Bloomfield,* passed by along the bank and picked them up. Within three days they were home on the Brac. More than a month passed, then a cable from Bluefields, Nicaragua, arrived in Jamaica relaying a message in a water cask that had been found by Miskito Indians south of Cape Gracias on December 24. The message, dated November 15, had been written by Captain Walton and set adrift from Beacon Cay. It read:

> The sloop Fred Lowrie is foundered at Beacon, Cay Sarnellas, 28 men are in a perishing condition. Who ever finds this letter, try to come to our assistance for God's sake. I have been ashore here since the 13th instant with very little food and on a very small allowance, eating birds or anything else that we can obtain. If this message is picked up too far to reach us in a vessel, if there is cable or wireless communication at hand please send a message to A. D. Jacobs, Montege Bay, Jamaica, to hurry to our assistance. Hoping that the great God will give this message to someone who will take interest in it and come to our rescue by the grace of God.[56]

Other Brackers were not so fortunate that year. The schooner *Georgiana,* a veteran turtler built in the 1890s by G. R. Scott of West End, Cayman Brac, set sail for Montego Bay, Jamaica, in November. Under the command of a young skipper, Haman Bodden of Little Cayman, the vessel arrived safely and loaded a return cargo, which included what was to be the Brac's Christmas provisions and gifts. Reports of a storm could not dissuade Captain Bodden from setting out for home. But the old schooner never made port; she went down with her entire crew, along with the young captain's wife and child.[57]

A tragic example of how the sea can turn against those who are most familiar with its character occurred in 1941. The turtling season had been brief that year for the rangers of Grand Cayman, who had returned from the Miskito Cays by June with only a small catch. However, some of the crews decided to return for a short summer season, hoping to augment their catch of turtles with nurse sharks, which were in high demand for their skins. The schooner *Rembro,* one in a fleet owned by Dr. Roy McTaggart, transported three crews of rangers and their gear and provisions to different cays in late June and returned to Cayman.[58] Twenty-eight fishermen commenced to set their nets; for the next month, they made excellent catches, accumulating seventy-seven nurse shark hides, twenty-five to thirty pounds of hawksbill shell, and four hawksbill and three green turtles.[59] By the middle of August, they were anxiously scanning the horizon for a sail to take them home, since they knew that the weather likely would change around September 22, the autumnal equinox when the sun crosses the equator. At that time, winds would veer to the northeast and stay there for the rest of the year. Moreover, the hurricane season was upon them. By September, the men had to stop fishing because they had run out of salt to cure the skins.

Meanwhile on Grand Cayman, Dr. McTaggart managed to get his fifty-ton schooner *Majestic* ready with a crew partially made up of men from East End, some of whose kinfolk were on the cays. *Majestic* took four days to reach the cays and collect the rangers and their catch; however, as the schooner's crew began to prepare for the northward voyage home on September 27, a series of heavy squalls struck, intensifying from the north, and seas began to break over the anchored vessel's bow. Eddie Lou Dixon, a crewman from East End, expressed his concern about the weather to *Majestic*'s captain, eighty-two-year-old Steadman Bodden. When the weather worsened in the middle of the night and the wind increased to around fifty knots, Dixon helped to set another, heavier anchor and reef the standing jib sail.[60] The schooner fought hard at her moorings throughout the night as the barometer dropped. Captain Bodden finally realized that a dangerous hurricane was upon them.

At daybreak, heaven and earth looked as if they were coming together, and the men became alarmed. Differences of opinion arose over what to do. Dixon asked,

"Captain, what else you ga'an do?" He say, "See what I mean, Dixon, ain't nothing else for us to do now but stand by." I say to him, "Captain, I ain't ga'an by here, one tree holding on that cay, in there that God Almighty grow there, worth a thousand vessel mast standing on the water." He say, "Well, what you ga'an do?" I say, "I'm going 'shore." So all my men from East End, then, and some from West Bay, agreed to go 'shore with me. So I say, "Well, haul up that boat 'longside and get that load and go on first." It wasn't too bad then, the boat could make it then, under three oars to two oars.[61]

Nineteen men decided to abandon the schooner and make for the lee of the nearby cay in two catboats. The sea was so rough that to save the boats, the men dragged them up onto the cay. Seeking shelter in a creek, they tied the boats between mangrove trees, clinging to them as night fell and the sea flooded across the flat island. By next morning, the storm had passed and the sea subsided off the cay. The men had to cut the mangroves down to get their boats out of the trees. When they returned to the beach and looked out to where *Majestic* had been, the schooner was gone.[62]

Although the men weathered the hurricane, they faced further travails. Lacking water to drink, they sailed for another cay five miles away, where they knew rangers had stashed three drums of water and two boats. When they arrived, they found that the cay had been washed clean by the storm. In the afternoon, they saw a sail on the horizon, which turned out to be rangers from another cay, who also had been waiting for *Majestic* to pick them up. The crew had a little bread and a gallon of water, which they mixed with sea water and shared. The rangers suggested that they all return to their cay, on which they had left food and water. Rowing for hours against a strong current, the men finally reached their destination and consumed all but one of the drums of water.[63]

The following day, the survivors were picked by Captain McNeil Connolly on the schooner *Rembro*, which was searching for *Majestic*. They were transferred the next morning to *Lydia E. Wilson*, homeward bound for Grand Cayman after picking up all but five of her rangers in the storm. The sixty-three-ton schooner carried a total of forty-eight men home to George Town; sadness swept the island as *Wilson* docked and the survivors' story was told. Twenty-two lives, including one five-year-old boy, were lost with *Majestic* on the Miskito Bank. Counting *Wilson*'s lost rangers, mortality on the turtling grounds that year had been surpassed only by the deaths of sixty-seven rangers in an 1876 storm.[64]

The following year, the schooner *Hustler,* returning from Panama to Grand Cayman, was lost with all fourteen hands.[65] The Brac-built schooner *Alsons,* named for the Foster family of Alice, Lambert, and sons, was lost at sea with the entire family while returning home from Panama in 1939.[66] Another Caymanian schooner, *Merico,* disappeared carrying a cargo of oranges from the Colombian islands of San Andrés and Providencia.[67] She was the last schooner to be built in the East End district of Grand Cayman.

Aside from turtling schooners, small freight vessels also were built in the islands. The launching on Grand Cayman of *Cimboco* (Cayman Island Motor Boat Company) in 1927 was an especially festive event because the vessel was the first on the island to be fitted with an engine. A few years later, *Lady Slater* (named after the wife of the governor of Jamaica) became the second motorized ship built in Grand Cayman. Both vessels were constructed by Captain Rayal B. Bodden at his shipyard in George Town; they were employed to haul freight, passengers, and mail between Grand Cayman, Jamaica, and the United States.[68] *Lady Slater* was taken in 1940 by the British Admiralty and put into service at Port Royal, Jamaica, where she caught fire and sank.[69] Another motor vessel, *Nunoca* from Cayman Brac, carried passengers and freight between Cayman and Tampa. Her last voyage began on July 18, 1936; en route to Tampa, she vanished at sea without a trace.[70]

Fig. 68. The Cayman Island Motor Boat Company's *Cimboco* was launched on Grand Cayman in 1927. Cayman Islands National Archive collections.

As turtling declined and the hauling of freight became lucrative, some schooners were retrofitted as motor vessels. The 187-ton *Arbutus II*, built by James Arch's shipyard on Grand Cayman for Captain Warren Bodden and launched in 1940, was one of the largest two-masted schooners constructed on the island. A few days after launching, a storm cast her back on shore at the shipyard, damaging her hull. Once repaired, *Arbutus* set out for foreign ports to earn her living. Eventually she was refitted as a motor vessel and continued a lucrative trade in lumber to the United States and Caribbean ports, explosives to South and Central America, general cargo to Nicaragua for the gold mines, and occasional cargos of bananas.[71] Ironically, her last port of call was her original home port; *Arbutus* wrecked on the same rocks on which she had been built and launched. Today her remains lie in shallow water off the bustling waterfront of George Town.

Abandoned but Not Forgotten

The renowned schooner *Lydia E. Wilson* lies abandoned under the quiet waters of North Sound, Grand Cayman, where she spent many winters moored between turtling seasons. Archaeological survey of the sound in 1980 revealed two additional wrecksites that appear to be the remains of large vessels used in the turtling trade around the turn of the nineteenth century and eventually abandoned in shallow water adjacent to the Careening Place in North Sound. Each was stripped of its equipment, loose hardware, and fittings. However, the calm, silty bottom of the sound contributed to the preservation of lower hull timbers, allowing a study of each vessel to be made.

The first of these sites, nicknamed the North Sound Deep Wreck, consisted of a composite-built (partially reinforced with iron frames) sailing ship that had been either scuttled or sunk in a hurricane. Partially articulated remains of approximately ten percent of the hull were found buried under ballast, silt, and sand. Careful dusting of the wrecksite revealed the entire keel, which measured seventy-two feet six inches, as well as portions of the stem and sternpost. The stem was attached to the keel with a vertical flat scarf reinforced with bronze oval clamps. The sternpost attachment similarly was reinforced with bronze rectangular plates. The keelson had either eroded or been displaced, surviving only in areas where it had been fastened to the keel. Floors were bolted to the keel and to futtocks with iron nails. Occasional chisel- and spade-pointed bronze fas-

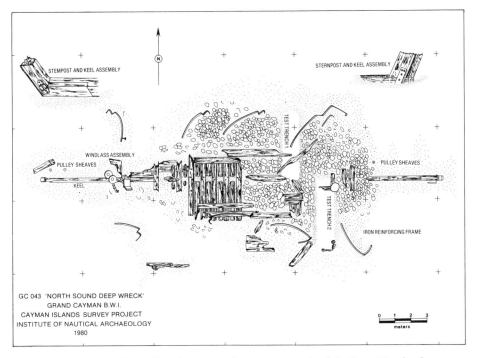

Fig. 69. After careful study and testing, a plan view was made of the Deep Wreck, a large composite-built sailing vessel abandoned in North Sound, Grand Cayman.

tenings were noted in association with the lower framing of the ship. Existing hull planking was fastened to the frames with treenails; ceiling planking, with square iron nails. At least eight large iron reinforcing knees or rider frames were splayed outboard of either side of the central keel area. Their curved shapes corresponded with the various stations of the hull, where they served to brace the ship internally. Evidence of copper sheathing and sheathing tacks were found on exposed portions of the hull in the bow and stern.

Other features of the site included a collapsed windlass assembly near the bow, several wooden pulley sheaves (some with bronze coaks, or axles), wire cable, a mooring bitt, and a timber with chain, which may have been a cathead piece. No ground tackle such as anchors or anchor chain was located on or near the wrecksite. Nor were major rigging assemblies found, except for two fragmentary sections of chainplates. Two shallow test trenches were excavated in order to investigate the site more comprehensively. Turtle bones and various fastenings were uncovered at the first location tested. The second test area, located near the stern on the port side, revealed sherds of ironstone ceramics, bottle glass fragments, and additional fastenings.

The iron-reinforced construction of this vessel, the clamps and plates at stem and stern, and the ironstone ware and bottle glass suggest that the vessel sank during the latter half of the nineteenth century or during the first quarter of the twentieth century. Numerous turtle bones found at the site suggest that the ship was engaged in the turtle trade. However, the amount of iron used in the construction of the vessel indicates that she probably was not built in the Cayman Islands, where hardwood normally was used.

Conversely, the second wreck that was examined may very well have been a locally built ship. Dubbed the Duck Pond Wreck, the site had narrowly escaped major damage during the modern dredging of an adjacent channel through North Sound. Lower timbers of the ship's hull were exposed sufficiently to enable easy examination of the manner in which the vessel had been constructed.

The hull of the ship had been fastened almost entirely with wood. Floors, half-frames, futtocks, and hull and ceiling planking all were connected with treenails. Infrequent iron bolts occasionally fastened floors to the keel. Futtocks sometimes were edge-joined to toptimbers by an iron staple driven into the inner face of the ends of the touching timbers. In fact, only two large iron fastenings were noted on the site: drift bolts eleven and one-half inches in length.

The vessel's keel was eighty-three feet seven inches long. Frame spacing averaged twenty inches center-to-center. Hull and ceiling planking were approximately three inches thick, and averaged nine to twelve inches in width. Both keel and frames had similar cross-sectional dimensions: eight inches sided and nine inches molded (the keel was slightly higher, measuring eleven inches).

A small test trench was excavated next to a pile of concreted stud-link chain. Recoveries consisted of nineteenth-century English ceramics such as annular and transfer wares and fragments of undecorated pearlware. Sherds of bottle glass, one from a Dutch case gin bottle, also were found. Again, numerous turtle bones were present on the site. A small lead fishing weight was recovered, as well as a profusion of copper sheathing tacks, all one inch in length.

From all indications, the Duck Pond Wreck appeared to date slightly earlier than the Deep Wreck. Situated in extremely shallow water that

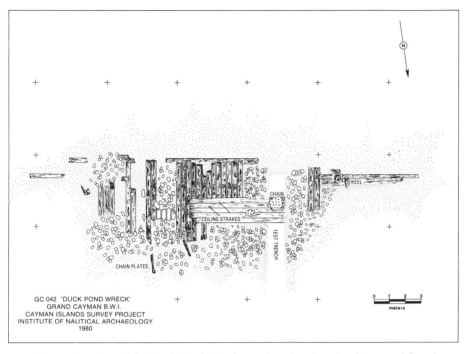

Fig. 70. Remains of the Duck Pond Wreck, another abandoned sailing vessel found near the Careening Place in North Sound, are shown in this site plan.

averaged six to eight feet in depth, the site was located on the edge of a small mangrove island adjacent to the Careening Place. It is highly probable, given the vessel's position perpendicular to shore, that it was run aground intentionally and left for a wreck. The paucity of artifacts and the accessible depth of the water suggest that the vessel was totally stripped of valuables just before it was abandoned. Of little profit to the salvor or relic hunter today, both sites still offer an archaeological insight into the nautical traditions of the Cayman Islands' turtling past and the types of vessels that were employed almost a century ago.

Perhaps the most notable remnant of the Caymanian turtling heritage is the schooner *Goldfield,* which was built for Conwell Watler by H. E. Arch and Sons on Grand Cayman in 1929. A classic example of the Caymanian turtling schooner, *Goldfield* had an overall length of 125 feet, a length on the waterline of 86 feet, a 22 1/2-foot beam, and a 7-foot draft. Her framework was constructed of Cayman hardwood, especially mahogany, and the planking was made of yellow pine. Launched in July 1930, the ninety-nine-ton vessel plied the turtling grounds of the Miskito Coast under a succession of masters, her first being Captain Reginald Parsons. Aside from turtling, the schooner also linked Grand Cayman with the United States, carrying vital merchandise to the island during World War II. Rayburn Farrington, son of one of her captains, Charles Farrington, recalled that *Goldfield* "was the telegraph, the plane, and the post. She brought food, and she brought people's loved ones home. She was everything."[72]

Goldfield arrived in George Town from Tampa early one morning in September 1937, laden with general cargo and passengers. After landing her passengers Captain Reginald Parsons became concerned about the weather but could not get permission to take the boat into the safer waters of North Sound. He anchored the schooner in the harbor, leaving his grandson to watch over the ship's contents. During the night, a storm dashed through the island, parting *Goldfield*'s moorings and carrying her out to sea. When her disappearance was discovered the next morning, concern swept across the island, not only for the fate of the vessel and her guard, but also for the badly needed provisions that she carried. Fortunately, the British warship HMS *Orion*, which had left Grand Cayman the previous day, was contacted by the wireless station, and returned to take aboard Captain Parsons and his crew for assistance in a search for *Goldfield*. *Orion*'s seaplane was launched in a westerly direction, although the schooner's crew suggested that their missing vessel had been carried off to the north. When the plane returned without finding anything, it was sent out again, but to the north. Within ten minutes, the pilot radioed back with a positive sighting, and *Orion* steamed out toward *Goldfield*, which was drifting in the open sea. Her crew reboarded the schooner, and she was returned to her legendary service.[73]

When the turtling trade began to decline, *Goldfield* was sold in 1958 to a Colombian, Alejandro Rankine, who put her into service as a cargo vessel, carrying coconuts from San Andrés to Barranquilla and returning with general supplies. Merchant mariner Ed Engemann bought the boat in 1967 for a private yacht and sailed her to the Pacific coast of Mexico, where he lived aboard her for ten years. Ultimately she found her way to Seattle under a new owner, Bradlee Johnson, who sold her in 1983 to the Cayman-based Goldfield Foundation, which began a fund-raising drive to bring the schooner home to Grand Cayman.[74] After lengthy restoration in the Bay Islands of Honduras, *Goldfield* finally returned in 1986 to the island where she was launched fifty-six years before. However, despite

Fig. 71. The famous schooner *Goldfield* returned to the Cayman Islands in 1986, where she had been launched fifty-six years before. Cayman Islands National Archive collections.

several years of efforts, sufficient funds to put her into service again could not be raised, and eventually the schooner was abandoned in North Sound at Canal Point.

Global Mariners

Although the need for schooners and catboats dwindled as the turtling tradition waned, Caymanian seamen continued to have the ocean in their blood. By 1906, as many as 1,500 islanders out of a total population of 5,000 were sailing on merchant vessels of the United States, Honduras, and Panama.[75] But the salt-soaked grain of weathered wood and the familiar smells of melting tar, thatch rope, and wet canvas gradually were replaced by walls of primered iron and the throbbing of oil-fired engines. At the beginning of World War II, hundreds of Caymanian mariners shipped out with the Royal Navy, the British Merchant Service, and the Trinidad Royal Navy Volunteer Reserve.[76] Their reputation for seamanship, courage, and hard work spread throughout the maritime world. After the war, many of these mariners obtained jobs on United States–owned banana and lumber boats. Others found opportunities at home on ships owned by the Kirkconnell brothers of Cayman Brac and by H. O. Merren of Grand Cayman, whose fleet included the vessels *Mizpah, Merco, Bodner,* and *Antares.*[77]

Foreign shipping companies soon sought out Caymanian seamen, who served on surplus tankers such as *Transpan, Transea, Trans Lake,* and *Transpar.*[78] The growth of the petroleum transport industry offered seagoing opportunities aboard fleets of tankers owned by Gulf Oil, Texas Oil, and Imperial Oil of Canada.[79] National Bulk Carriers of New York had discovered the seafaring talents of Cayman Brackers during crew recruitment in Jamaica. Soon they opened an office on Grand Cayman, signing up men to sail on ships such as *Bulk Trader, Bulk Star, Bulk Oil,* and *Bulk Oceanic.* As merchant ships grew larger, their crew lists continued to include names like Ebanks, Bodden, Webster, and Watler. Many islanders became officers, mastering some of the world's largest ships across the sea-lanes to the farthest corners of the globe. The Bulk fleet eventually was replaced by ships such as *Petro King, Petro Emperor,* and *Petro Sea,* and ultimately by the supertankers *Universe Leader, Commander, Defiance,* and others.[80] All carried, aside from their cargo, the maritime heritage of the Cayman Islands.

A Graveyard of Ships  6

The preponderant feature of the Caymanian seascape is the reefs that line the shores of each island. These undersea gardens have become famous worldwide for their breathtaking corals and fish situated in clear aquamarine waters. Yet before a diving visitor can swim very far, the reef reveals other curious and compelling secrets—the remains of countless unlucky seagoing vessels that have accumulated over centuries in the nooks and crannies of Cayman's submerged shoals. Some stick out like a sore thumb in stark relief above the waves, rusting in the West Indian trade winds. Others lie in the shadowy blue depths like ghost ships, harboring a nightly school of sleeping fish. Some have collapsed in twisted heaps, coated with corals that compete for living space in the soft, sunlit currents. Others have been ground to bits, camouflaged by time and tempests, invisible to the untrained eye. Captured by fate, each has its story to tell, and all belong to the maritime legacy of the Cayman Islands.

Landmarks in the Sea

The Cayman Islands are situated along the northern edge of the sailing track once used by ships exiting the Caribbean Sea through the Yucatán Channel bound for the Gulf of Mexico and beyond. This route was considered faster and smoother than beating up through the Windward Passage between Cuba and Hispaniola, especially by English mariners returning to Europe from Jamaica. Sailing against the prevailing trade winds was extremely difficult and time-consuming; it sometimes took ships a month or six weeks just to reach the Windward Passage.[1] Consequently, most English mariners preferred to navigate "downhill" with the trade winds and currents to the Yucatán Channel and into the Gulf of Mexico and the Florida Straits, where the Gulf Stream would carry them into the Atlantic.

Early Spanish convoys bound for Mexico from Spain entered the Caribbean Sea at the Lesser Antilles and ran with the trade winds along the southern coasts of the Greater Antilles. To avoid the treacherous cays and shoals of southern Cuba, they searched for the Cayman Islands as landmarks to guide their navigation. Sixteenth-century sailing directions for the West Indies specifically directed Spanish pilots entering the Caribbean basin from the Atlantic Ocean to "turn to the northwest continuing along the coast as far as Cape Tiburon [Haiti]. Having gone beyond it, you shall steer to the north in search of Los Alteres or Puerto de Cuba [southeast approach to Cuba] and, having recognized it, you shall steer west one-quarter southwest until you sight Cabo Cruz and Little Cayman Island. And from there you shall steer west and find Grand Cayman Island."[2] Likewise, treasure galleons of the South American fleet sailing north from Cartagena to Havana headed for the Cayman Islands to gain windward room and to keep off the Serranilla and Serrana Banks to the lee of the track.

A Trap for Ships

As landmarks, the low-lying Caymans were poor substitutes for the more mountainous headlands of the surrounding Antilles. Of the three islands, only Cayman Brac rises more than a few feet above the sea; Grand Cayman and Little Cayman both are difficult to distinguish on the horizon and almost impossible to see at night or in bad weather. In addition, it was difficult for a navigator to tell if his ship was approaching the islands by measuring the depth of water. Dropping a sounding lead over the side of the ship was useless because of the sudden rise of the seafloor from profound depths to the almost invisible reef line fringing the islands. Sailing at night, a captain might take a depth sounding that indicated that no bottom had been reached, but before he could take another reading, his ship would have run aground. George Gauld, who surveyed Grand Cayman for the Admiralty during the summer of 1773, remarked, "This Island, being in the track of all the homeward bound Jamaica Vessels, on the[i]r passage round the West end of Cuba, & through the Gulf of Florida, is frequently the cause of shipwrecks, It is low . . . & very dangerous in the night; being surrounded by reefs, beyond which the soundings do not generally extend more than a quarter of a mile."[3]

Moreover, before marine chronometers made precise reckoning of longitude possible, navigators could only guess how far east or west they had sailed. Thus, many early charts depicted various islands with distorted longitudinal dimensions or erroneous geographical locations. In fact, until the mid-nineteenth century, charts supplied by the British Royal Navy consistently placed the Cayman Islands farther to the west than they actually were. In 1820 Captain Lloyd of HMS *Parthian* passed by Grand Cayman and noted in his remark book that "the position of this Island as it is laid down in the Admiralty Chart furnished to the Ship, appears to be incorrect. When the *Onta[rio]* approached it from the Northwestward in September last, the Chronometer as well as Dead Reckoning, were for the first time very considerable out. And in the present instance where the Ships course is from the SE, the excess of Longitude corresponds with the observed in the former case which in both Tracks would have placed the Vessel in the body of the Island."[4] In addition, continual but shifting ocean currents flowing from the northeast and the southeast come together in the vicinity of the Cayman Islands to run through the Yucatán Channel. These unpredictable currents make dead reckoning (estimation of one's position) during a vessel's westward progress in the region unreliable. The combination of these factors—landmarks that are difficult to find, the abrupt change from deep to shoal water, incorrectly charted shorelines, and shifting ocean currents—has caused the Cayman Islands to be a virtual trap for ships.

A Close Call

Selected incidents from the historical record bear testimony to the hazards of navigation near the Cayman Islands. In 1545 a Spanish ship bound for Campeche on the Gulf of Mexico paid an unscheduled visit to Grand Cayman on Christmas Day. Fray Tomás de la Torre, one of a group of Dominican friars aboard the vessel, kept a diary of the voyage. He recorded the incident as follows:

We were very sorry to see that we would have to spend Christmas at sea, and that we could not celebrate the birth of our Redeemer as we would have liked to, but His Majesty provided such a pleasant following wind that we sailed well, except that we were hindered in doing what we wanted, and thus sang our Christmas Eve vespers with great devotion and in the evening met together with the vicar and prayed, he giving general absolution, and we made an altar in the stern in that shed or cabin of which I have spoken, and took the baby Jesus that we carried and wrapped him in hay that was there and kept watch over him all night long, burning white candles with prayers and hymns of joy, and Our Master provided copious tears and devotion.

The first part of the night we sang many hymns, and at midnight we sang the matins and the midnight mass and afterwards the daybreak mass with all the solemnity we could without growing sleepy from the fair weather of the sea, and during our songs the sailors fell asleep, much to our great danger had not God miraculously delivered us. In the early dawn while the people were sleeping and we were quite unaware, God opened the eyes of Fray Pedro Calvo and gave him the voice to cry out "land, land."

The sailors quickly jumped up and also perceived it and with great urgency and shouts turned the ship about. Then the religious company came out to see how near we were and some declared that we were closer than others; it seemed to me that we were within two crossbow shots, which in the sea is only a short distance but nevertheless the ship was somewhat distant. God had miraculously delivered us, and gave life that day as a New Year gift. It was one of those islands called the Caimanes and was Caiman major.

It is a very small island, like that of the rivers [Deseada, where they took on water after crossing the Atlantic] where, if we were to stop and remain for sustenance, we would quickly die of thirst. Afterwards the bishop recited high mass with all solemnity, after which they gave us much to eat, although the greatest gift [life] does not supply the necessity of the sea. In the afternoon we sang our vespers and complines, and thus celebrated the holy day of the birth of our Savior.[5]

Despite the near disaster that befell this religious order at sea, the dangers of the voyage apparently only served to reinforce the faith that they were bringing to the Americas.

Dutch Castaways

Spanish mariners were not the only ones to arrive unexpectedly on the reefs of the Cayman Islands. Nearly a century later, when the Dutch began to cruise the West Indies for profit and plunder, they too were confronted with ruin on Caymanian shores. Hoping to hinder or capture the Spanish treasure fleet near Havana, the Dutch West India Company sent a squadron of ships to the Caribbean in 1629 under Admiral Pater. The fleet consisted of eleven ships, 842 sailors, 326 soldiers, 117 bronze guns, 506 iron cannons, and provisions for sixteen months. Clearly Admiral Pater meant business, since his squadron was to be reinforced along the way by thirteen additional vessels.

Several of the Dutch ships never arrived at Havana. Captain Joachim Gijsen and his ship *Dolphijn* became separated from Admiral Pater's fleet while crossing from Colombia to Cuba. Poorly sailed, the ship gradually fell downwind of Jamaica and was wrecked on Grand Cayman, allegedly because of a lack of supervision by the officers.[6] For sixteen weeks Captain Gijsen and his crew of more than 120 men and boys were marooned on the island. In that time they built a small vessel, which they named *Cayman,* from the planks of their broken ship. The castaways managed to salvage their shipwrecked artillery as well, loading four bronze and two iron cannons onto the new vessel and hiding the remainder somewhere on the island. Stocking themselves with what little provisions they had saved from the wreckage of *Dolphijn*, the intrepid Dutchmen set out to find the rest of the fleet. They eventually made it to New Netherlands (New York), where, true to the Dutch character, they sold their jury-built craft *Cayman.*

"Pyrate's Wracke"

The Cayman Islands, as we have seen, became a familiar host to highwaymen of the sea during later decades. But the same remote reefs that afforded the Brethren of the Coast refuge also took a toll. The episode of *Morning Star* demonstrates not only the foolhardiness of navigation at night in this region but also an often-understated occupational hazard of those practicing piracy:

> The beginning of August, 1722, the Pyrates made ready the Brigantine, and came out to Sea, and beating up to Windward, lay in the Track for their Correspondant in her Voyage to Jamaica, and spoke

with her; but finding nothing was done in England for their Favour, as 'twas expected, they return'd to their Consorts at the Island with the ill News, and found themselves under a Necessity, as they fan-cy'd, to continue that abominable Course of Life they had lately practis'd; in order thereto, they sail'd with the Ship and Brigantine to the Southward, and the next Night, by intolerable Neglect, they run the *Morning Star* upon the Grand Caimanes, and wreck'd her; the Brigantine seeing the Fate of her Consort, hall'd off in Time, and so weather'd the Island.[7]

Unlike the Dutch sailors nearly a century before, some of *Morning Star's* crewmen were rescued from the island by their aptly named consort *Good Fortune,* but they immediately were pursued by two warships from Ja-maica, which had been sent to apprehend them. They escaped during a lull in the wind, but had to row for their lives to avoid capture and trial for piracy. Later, another warship landed an armed party on Grand Cayman to apprehend the remaining forty-odd castaways, who were found hiding in the bush.

The Wreck of the Ten Sail

By far the greatest shipping disaster in the history of the Cayman Islands occurred one dark night in 1794 when nine British merchantmen and their naval escort crashed into the windward reefs of Grand Cayman.[8] The story of this catastrophe actually began late in 1793, when the Royal Navy man-aged to capture a French warship sailing off the island of Hispaniola.

During the French Revolutionary Wars (1792–1802), France was at war with Britain, the Netherlands, Spain, Austria, Prussia, and Sardinia. Tra-ditional rivals in the Americas, France and Britain controlled the lucrative West Indian sugar-producing industry; their most important plantation colonies, St. Domingue and Jamaica, were zealously protected by naval power. Events in Europe, particularly the French Revolution in 1789, had profound effects in the colonies. A French decree that gave mulattoes equal rights as citizens was opposed by the white planters on St. Do-mingue, and a series of slave revolts swept the island as shifting alliances created an unstable social and political environment. In 1793 the new French Republic declared war on Britain, prompting the Royal Navy to launch an expedition from Jamaica to seize St. Domingue. During this campaign, a number of French ships were captured by the British, including the frigate *Inconstante,* which was forced to surrender by HMS *Penelope* and HMS *Iphigenia.* Taken as a prize to Port Royal, Jamaica, the French warship immediately was put into Royal Navy service as a fifth-rate frigate under the new name *Convert.*[9] Probably the only conversion she received was an exchange of officers and crew, as well as new stores. Her French artillery remained on board as a valuable addition to the Admiralty's firepower.

Fifth-rate frigates were too lightly built to withstand the shock of a major battle between fleets and consequently were relegated to carrying naval intelligence, scouting for the enemy, or serving as merchant convoy escorts.[10] The latter mission was given to *Convert* under the command of newly commissioned Captain John Lawford, who received instructions in January 1794 to proceed to the west end of Jamaica, where a fleet of merchantmen was assembling for a convoy to Europe. By February 6, Lawford had taken charge of fifty-eight ships. Fifty-five of the merchantmen were bound for Europe and three schooners were bound for different ports in America.

Sailing in the vanguard of the fleet before a light wind, Lawford ordered the convoy to steer west-northwest for Cape Corrientes near the western end of Cuba. His instructions clearly stated that he was to keep all of the ships together, "and on no account or pretense whatever to leave them, but to accommodate your progress to that of the worst sailing ship among them."[11] Accordingly, Lawford directed the captain of each merchant vessel to keep astern of *Convert;* the faster ships were to shorten sail so as not to outrun the slower vessels. On the morning of the seventh, a leaking schooner gave the distress signal, causing the convoy to heave to until she was bailed out. At noon the signal to make sail was made and the convoy resumed its journey with *Convert* under foresail and topsails. After the delay that morning, Lawford was anxious to sight before nightfall the island of Grand Cayman, which normally was used as a landmark along the shipping track toward the Yucatán Channel. By midafternoon he had pulled far ahead of his consorts, one of which began firing guns to signal *Convert.* Lawford dutifully wore ship and returned to the fleet to find the same schooner again in distress, her captain afraid of being left behind.

When the fleet resumed sail, Lawford cautiously altered its course to the west; by midnight he calculated that they had safely passed to the westward of Grand Cayman to the south by some seven leagues. *Convert's* sailing master, Thomas Popplewell, then came on deck to relieve the captain as officer of the watch. He suggested to Lawford that, in the prevalence of northerly winds that night, the course should be adjusted northward, so as not to miss Cape Corrientes the next day. Before he retired, Lawford directed Popplewell to steer west-northwest, to signal the rest of the ships to do likewise, and to maintain reduced sail in order to stay with the convoy.

At three o'clock in the morning, a distress signal again was heard, this time to leeward. *Convert* made sail, running down toward the sound of the signal gun. In Captain Lawford's words,

> On my going on deck instantly after this I found that the guns had been fired by a ship ahead and that several ships of the convoy had run ahead since 12 oClock. I had not been on deck a minute before one of the men who were up loosing the topsails called out "breakers a head—close to us." As the breakers appeared in every direction and as I could not tell from the darkness of the night to what extent they might run, I immediately deemed it expedient to make the signal for the convoy to disperse and do the best for their own safety that their own judgment could suggest, and as the topsails were now sheeted home and the *Convert* certainly [would have] cleared the breakers if a Ship ahead had not unfortunately fallen onboard of us, and before it was possible to extricate ourselves we got so near to the breakers that all hope of clearing vanished and She in a few moments struck. . . . I have since learned that the Ship who fired the guns was ashore before she fired and that five or six others went ashore before Her.[12]

In the darkness, Lawford had no way of realizing that the distress signals he heard to leeward were from ships that had run up into the shallows of the eastern end of Grand Cayman. He had ordered the helm to port in order to haul his ship northward toward the sound of the gun, when Popplewell suddenly called out that another ship was looming toward them through the darkness. *Convert*'s topsails were frantically backed in an effort to slow her, but it was too late; the ships had converged on different tacks, crashing together and carrying away the frigate's jib boom. Lawford's men had just managed to get *Convert* clear and brace her yards again to the northward when the same ship crashed into her starboard bow again. Meanwhile, both ships were being carried helplessly toward the treacherous breakers that line the windward end of Grand Cayman.

Popplewell had been on the foredeck supervising the clearing of the anchors in response to the emergency and anxiously sounding the water depth below when the frigate suddenly ground to a halt in the midst of the foaming reefs. Her sails were furled immediately, and her crew attempted to get the topyards and masts down to lighten the frigate, but soon the carpenter reported that the hull had been bilged and that water had risen to the orlop deck. Lawford reluctantly concluded that it was impossible to save his ship. He ordered the boats hoisted, and the men to begin to abandon the wreck.[13]

Writing a report to the Admiralty from the beach five days afterward, Lawford ascribed the cause of his misfortune to the consorts' disobedience of his sailing instructions, suggesting that "had the ships of the convoy kept their stations and attended to signals which I am sorry to say was not generally the case with by far the greater number, this misfortune could not have happened."[14] However, the subsequent court martial of Captain Lawford and his officers and men concluded: "The Court having thoroughly examined into the several Circumstances attending the same, and having maturely and deliberately considered the whole, is of the opinion that the Misfortune was occasioned by a strong Current setting the Ships very considerably to the Northward of their Reckoning and doth therefore adjudge that the said Captain Lawford Commander of His Majesty's late Ship the *Convert,* the Officers and Company of the said Ship, be acquitted, and they are hereby acquitted accordingly."[15]

Sailing master Popplewell also had been examined by the court in an attempt to establish the cause of the navigational error and subsequent loss of the frigate. Although *Convert*'s logbook was found to contain an omission of the logged distance the day before the disaster, Popplewell blamed the currents, declaring, "I have since understood from the Different Masters of Vessels who have gone down to the Caymans from Jamaica for the purpose of carrying away the wreck of the Cargoes, that they had been considerably set to the Northward by Currents; the particulars of which are well known to the Officers of the *Convert*."[16]

The Wreck of the Ten Sail, as the episode has been called by Cayman Islanders since that unforgettable night, may have been the cause of a specific warning to mariners published a year later:

Off the east end of the Grand Cayman is a *Reef* which runs about 3/4 mile into the sea, and that end being very low land, it makes it very dangerous in the night time, when you expect to make the island. I have known several ships much out in their reckonings in running this short distance (particularly when they have met with light winds after leaving the west end of Jamaica) which is owing to the current setting to leeward or windward. I likewise recollect an instance of a ship in the year 1772, which ran ashore on this Reef, in a very fine moonlight night, when they thought they were past the island: they observed something black on the horizon, and imagined it was the reflection of the moon on the water, but it soon proved to be the island, which being low cannot be seen in the night at any great distance; and before they could rectify their mistake, they were on-shore, and the ship was totally lost.[17]

Accordingly, the first formal English sailing directions for the Cayman Islands, published in 1827, remarked, "The land [Grand Cayman] is very low and many ships have passed the island in clear moon-light nights without seeing it; hence a near approach to the eastern part, during the night, would be attended with great danger. Indeed every degree of cau-tion should be taken, as it is common for ships to be out of their reckoning, particularly with light winds and variable currents, which frequently pre-vail hereabout."[18]

Thus, at dawn on the morning of February 8, 1794, the sun rose on the horizon behind a line of jumbled hulls and twisted rigging. In addition to HMS *Convert*, nine merchantmen of the convoy—*William and Elizabeth, Moorhall, Ludlow, Britannia, Richard, Nancy, Eagle, Sally,* and *Fortune*— also had struck the reef and were wrecked.[19] A heavy sea was running and the wind blew directly onto the reef, preventing the ships still on station from approaching their wrecked consorts. Most of *Convert's* company that managed to get into the ship's boats were put aboard two or three of the merchant ships offshore; others were floated on makeshift rafts to the reef to be picked up by native Caymanian canoes that had begun to assemble around the scene of the disaster. Twenty men preferred to wait on the wrecked vessel for the weather to moderate, rather than risk getting ashore immediately. Of the total company of *Convert,* only five men lost their lives; three other casualties, including Daniel Martin, master of *Bri-tannia,* are mentioned in accounts of the wrecking, and several sick people died during the following days.[20]

A local fisherman was persuaded to brave the weather and deliver a letter from Lawford to the ships waiting offshore. Given the dangers of approaching the windward reef, they were instructed to anchor in the lee of the island at Hogsties village, where the sea was calm.[21] Only nine of the remaining ships of the convoy paid attention to Lawford's request and sailed westward to wait for survivors to be transferred there. Meanwhile, a small camp was assembled on shore, some two miles opposite the wreck-site across the lagoon. The men gathered around Lawford, who ordered them to erect huts and tents from the wreckage and to save any provisions and equipment that washed ashore. Despite rough seas, boats were sent to the bilged frigate, but unfortunately only a few casks of victuals and two puncheons of rum had survived the ordeal; the ship's stores of bread were found to be totally spoiled.

While Lawford and his men gradually collected their wits after the calamity, the islanders grew uneasy with the realization that their commu-nity suddenly contained hundreds of hungry castaways with little food and shelter. They drafted the following letter:

> Geo:Town 12th Feb[y] 1794
> Capt. John Lawford
> Sir
> We the Subscribers, Inhabitants of the the [sic] Island of Grand Camanees do Certify on Oath that from the distressed Situation of the Island in the Article of Provisions, owing to the Hurricane of the 19th Oct[r] last, Its morally impossible for the Inhabitants to support themselves, And with the Addition of the different Ship's Companys Wrecked in the East of this Island on Saturday Morning last, We the Subscribers think it Absolutely Neccessary for [our] own preserva-tion, that the diff[t] Crews belonging to the Wrecks already specified must be immediately Removed from this Island as soon as possible. We are with the utmost respect Sir
> Your most obedient Servants
> Geo[rge] Turnbull
> Geo[rge]Turnbull for W[m] Bodden
> turn over
> Joseph Dalby
> Robert Knowles Clark
> Thomas Thompson
> W[m] Gerat Prescott
> Hugh Mitchell
> James Hoy[22]

The deluge of survivors may have increased by half again the number of mouths on the island to feed. According to the first census of Grand Cay-man in 1802, the residents numbered 933 in all (see Appendix 3).[23] The closest community to the wrecksites, a village named Old Isaacs, consisted of only three families. There were, perhaps, more than 400 survivors from the wrecked ships; the muster roll of *Convert* alone listed more than 280 people on board when she left Jamaica.[24] Included in the muster were 217 officers and crew, 28 supernumeraries, 29 marines, 8 invalids, and a prisoner.[25] At least one of *Convert's* five men who perished in the disaster was buried on Grand Cayman, probably near the survivors' campsite.

In response to the islanders' petition, Lawford distributed his people on board the convoy vessels at Hog Stye Bay and dispatched them toward Cuba with letters to the governor of that island requesting aid, as they "may be under the necessity of revictualling at the Havannah."[26]

Captain Lawford chose to remain behind on the east end of Grand Cayman with his officers and thirty men to save as many of the ships' stores as possible with the help of the local boatmen. After the weather moderated, they gradually managed to salvage *Convert's* boatswain's stores, which included sails, rope, blocks, and other tackle; carpenter's stores such as tools and fasteners; and many of the gunner's stores, comprising not only ammunition and artillery implements but also swords, pistols, pikes, and axes. Four small swivel guns and eighteen of the frigate's cannon carriages also were recovered and floated to shore.[27]

But what of the cannons themselves?

In the late 1970s, coral-encrusted cannons began to appear in prominent positions outside hotels and private residences on Grand Cayman. Two cannons in particular, which ultimately were displayed in front of an aquarium at Spotts, bore curious markings on their breeches and the date 1781. Stories circulated about the guns having been recovered illegally from the lagoon at East End. Local citizens there pointed to an area known as Sand Cay, in the protected waters near the channel through the reef. Several remembered seeing a row of cannons in the sand while playing in the shallows as children. Archaeological survey by the Institute of Nautical Archaeology in 1980 confirmed the presence of at least six large artillery pieces partially buried under grass and sand. An additional cannon was found some distance away from the others, with modern ropes attached to it. This piece, which apparently had been intended for salvage but not yet recovered, bore similar inscriptions: a fleur-de-lis, a 1781 date, a serial number, a weight number, and the gunfounder's initials.

Were these cannons part of *Convert's* battery of guns? Their size, foundry date, and French markings seemed to suggest so, yet the guns were found in extremely shallow water inside the lagoon, not on the reef where historical documents indicated the frigate had wrecked.

Fig. 72. Bob Adams inspects one of several French cannons that were aboard HMS *Convert,* formerly the French frigate *Inconstante,* when she and nine merchantmen wrecked in 1794 on the eastern reef of Grand Cayman. Photo by KC Smith.

Careful scrutiny of the reef line in 1980 turned up evidence for the Wreck of the Ten Sail. An area north of the channel and Sand Cay contained concentrations of ballast stones, round shot and bar shot, ship's hardware, and hundreds of English bottle fragments, pipe stems, and ceramic sherds, all dating from the last decades of the eighteenth century. Heavier artifacts lay in pockets among the coral reef, but many of the lighter objects were strewn inside the lagoon along an underwater path toward the beach. In the 1980 aftermath of Hurricane Allen, more distinctive patterns of ships' wreckage running from the reef toward shore were discovered. Six out of more than twenty shipwreck sites studied during the survey at East End were determined to be likely candidates for the Wreck of the Ten Sail. On the beach, the hurricane had uncovered remnants of naval hardware, countless similar pottery sherds, and bottle glass in a distinct layer of mud and sand near the water's edge. This site, which the survey team hypothesized was Lawford's salvage camp, is adjacent to a submerged freshwater vent, locally called Mermaid Springs. The survey evidence suggested that the Wreck of the Ten Sail occurred near the present-day channel entrance, and that the salvage camp was directly opposite on shore.

Survey work continued at East End in the mid-1980s, conducted by the Scuba Research and Development Group of Indiana University. Designed as field activities for college students, three sessions, each lasting a few weeks, recorded several new shipwreck sites and reassessed others that had been located by the 1980 survey. Much of the fieldwork concentrated on the cannon site at Sand Cay; the positions of at least six cannons were plotted, as well as the previous positions of cannons that had been recently salvaged. Correspondence with French naval scholars established that the guns associated with the site conformed to the official French Regulations of 1779 for twelve-pounder long-pattern guns, which would have been carried by *Inconstante* when she was captured and put into British service as *Convert*.[28]

A survey of cannons salvaged from shipwreck sites in the waters off Grand Cayman was conducted by Margaret Leshikar with the help of local volunteers. By 1991, thirty cannons had been located, measured, and recorded. Nine were almost identical in dimensions and overall appearance; among these were the gun recorded by the INA team from Texas A&M in 1980—a long-pattern twelve-pounder, cast N° 45, fabricated by master founder Baynaud at the French ironworks of Forge-Neuve in 1781—and another, cast N° 25, which was recorded by Indiana University in 1986. All had been recovered from the Sand Cay site at East End.[29]

Under the auspices of the Cayman Islands National Museum, Dr. Leshikar began a five-month-long underwater search for the remains of HMS *Convert* and the nine merchantmen that wrecked in 1794. Using data from the sites previously recorded by INA and Indiana University as a foundation, the museum team returned in 1991 to Grand Cayman's windward reef to begin a systematic survey of a three-mile portion between East End Channel and Colliers Channel. More than thirty sites of shipwreck materials were examined during the course of the investigation. Two of these, which are nearly contiguous, are thought to represent the remains of HMS *Convert:* the French Cannon Site at Sand Cay and the Probable Frigate Spillage Site, which contained copper sheathing, ship's fittings, ammunition, and late eighteenth-century ceramics and glass.[30] Other eighteenth-century sites in the vicinity most likely represent vestiges of the nine wrecked merchantmen. Additional sites, some of which were previously unknown, are the remains of nineteenth- and twentieth-century shipwrecks.

Remnants of the ten ships that ran aground that night in 1794 are mere fragments of the original vessels and their cargos. After the initial salvage by Lawford's men and prominent Caymanians authorized to assist in recovery, the wrecksites undoubtedly were fished by local islanders for articles of value. A story about the Wreck of the Ten Sail is told today by elderly Caymanians. It seems that for a period of time following the convoy disaster, the island underwent a revolution in fashion apparel. Bolts of cloth obtained from the wreckage were quickly distributed by the delighted island women and transformed into dresses and other articles of clothing.[31] The only drawback to this sudden windfall was the fact that the cloth was all of the same color and design. Still other residents tell of the more recent salvage of cannons and anchors along the reef during the Second World War, when scrap iron was in great demand. And in addition to human dispersal of wreckage, countless storms have ravaged the reef line, distributing even farther afield what was left of the ships.

A historic monument park to commemorate the Wreck of the Ten Sail was unveiled by Queen Elizabeth II in February 1994—two hundred years to the month after the disaster—at a spot now called Queen's View on Gun Bluff overlooking the reefs into which the ships crashed.

A Maritime Junkyard

The Wreck of the Ten Sail was not the only disaster to occur where it did. In fact, the windward approaches to Grand Cayman comprise a veritable graveyard of ships. Captain Lawford's predicament was foreshadowed by a similar event that occurred in the same place almost thirty years previously. The early hand-drawn chart of Grand Cayman by George Gauld (see fig. 18) contains the following notation at the eastern edge of the island: "Here Capt. Hodgson with a Company of the 31st Reg.^t were Ship-

Fig. 73. In 1994, to commemorate the two-hundredth anniversary of the Wreck of the Ten Sail, this monument was erected at Queen's View on Gun Bluff overlooking the scene of the maritime disaster. Photo by KC Smith.

wreckt on a Transport from Jamaica to Pensacola in the night time in the Year 1767." The ship's name was *Cumberland;* Thomas Hodgson was not the ship's captain but a newly promoted officer in charge of recruits in the 31st Regiment of Foot, now known as the East Surreys.[32] He and all of his men, except three who drowned, were picked up by the frigate *Adventure,* as we have seen, but their ship joined what would become a growing collection of wrecks on the eastern approach to Grand Cayman. Some eighty years later, a Scottish missionary, Hope Waddell, whose ship ran aground nearby in 1845, noted "anchors, chain cables, and fragments of ships lying on the reef."[33] The 1980 archaeological survey of the island's eastern reef line confirmed his observation, revealing twenty-four distinct wrecksites in various stages of deterioration. Several were found to be lying on top of others, and many were scattered and dispersed shoreward by storm activity and the constant action of the sea.

Despite the advances of modern navigational apparatus, ships continue to wreck in the Cayman Islands, and the eastern shore of Grand Cayman still collects its share. As recently as 1962, the 7,200-ton Liberty ship *Ridgefield* struck the windward reef under full steam on a quiet night, awakening the entire village of Gun Bay with the tremendous noise of the collision.[34] Built in 1943 at the New England Ship Building Corporation in Portland, Maine, *Ridgefield* was originally commissioned as the *James A.*

Butts. During World War II she was almost struck by a Japanese torpedo in the South Pacific and later survived an air raid in the Philippines. Sold several times, she was renamed *Lone Star State, Anniston, Caldwell,* and in 1958 *Ridgefield.*[35] Sailing under the Liberian flag en route from Maracaibo to Galveston with a load of grain and beer, the 441-foot freighter crashed into the reef on the night of December 18, near the place where the Wreck of the Ten Sail had occurred almost two hundred years previously.

Two years later a 2,400-ton freighter, *Rimandi Mibaju,* smashed into the same reef, coming to rest less than a half-mile from *Ridgefield.* The 240-foot *Rimandi Mibaju* was built in Superior, Wisconsin, for the Great Lakes ore trade and was en route from Surinam with a load of bauxite when she ran ashore.[36] For almost three decades, these two wrecked vessels were prominent features on the horizon off East End; today they have collapsed beneath the relentless sea to join the remains of earlier maritime disasters. All of these submerged wrecks are reminders of the unfortunate sailors who unintentionally found themselves ashore in the Cayman Islands.

Groundings and sinkings have always been part of the Caymanian experience. One of the casualties of the notorious hurricane of 1932 was *Balboa,* a 375-foot freighter out of Jamaica that arrived in George Town

Fig. 74. This 1980 view shows the East End shipwrecks *Rimandi Mibaju,* a bauxite carrier *(foreground),* and *Ridgefield,* a former Liberty Ship. Today, only a tiny portion of the former wreck is visible above the water. Photo by KC Smith.

from Pensacola, Florida, with engine trouble. With the barometer falling, Captain Lawrence Bodden anchored his ship and landed the crew, leaving a "donkeyman," Reginald Edward, aboard on watch. Caught in shallow water off the port when the hurricane struck on November 7, the ship rode her mooring heavily as large waves passed under her. After more than twenty-four hours, *Balboa* finally capsized between 4 and 5 A.M. on November 9 and sank on her beam-ends in thirty-six feet of water.[37] During the storm, the schooners *Diamond* and *Klosking* were smashed up in South Sound, and five other schooners were washed ashore in North Sound.[38]

At dawn the next morning, Hog Stye Bay was littered with *Balboa's* cargo of lumber and kerosene oil. Reginald Edward had managed to swim ashore and was found unharmed in a small cove sitting with his cat in his arms.[39] Local residents claimed that after the sinking one could have walked from the wreck to shore on a carpet of wood without getting wet.

Some of the wood that washed ashore was used to construct waterfront buildings.[40] As a hazard to navigation, *Balboa's* hulk was reduced by explosives in 1957; today the wreck is a favorite diving attraction in thirty to thirty-five feet of water on a sandy bottom. Visitors can explore her broken hull, which is home to a variety of marine life.

Just north of *Balboa* is a large area filled with the wreckage of *Cali,* a 220-foot four-masted barkentine built in 1900 and later refitted with an engine. The steel vessel served for nearly fifty years under four different names and four different flags. She carried to the far corners of the earth a variety of cargos that included coal, nitrates, sugar, wheat, sulfur, and lumber.[41] Her last voyage began on January 9, 1949, as *Cali* left Guayaquil, Ecuador, with a cargo of rice for Santiago, Cuba. After transiting the Panama Canal, she ran into bad weather and began to leak. Course was changed for the nearest port to leeward, Grand Cayman, where the aging ship moored at George Town on January 27.[42]

Several attempts were made to dewater *Cali's* leaking hull with the assistance of pumps brought from shore, but some of her cargo had become wet and the leaks unmanageable. The ship was run ashore. For several days numerous catboats transferred what could be salvaged of the 30,000 bags of rice to shore. Some of the recovered cargo was taken to Cienfuegos, Cuba, but for months the smell of waterlogged rice hung over the harbor. Beached, salvaged, and then scrapped, *Cali* eventually was set on fire, and all her wooden furnishings and equipment were consumed.[43]

Fig. 75. The windlass of *Cali* is a prominent feature among the remains of this wrecked freighter. Photo by KC Smith.

Fig. 76. Grounded on the west end of Grand Cayman in 1944, the sailing freighter *Cali* is shown five years later in this 1949 photograph. Photo by Edwin Doran, Cayman Islands National Archive collections.

A song was written about *Cali* by Miss Aggie Bodden for the fourteen children whom she used to teach during the long midsummer holidays. One of the four verses of her song was:

On Saturday evening the first of the year,
When all the George Towners were free from care,
A boat was sighted off S. W. point,
A few hours later she almost sank in sight.
The name of the boat was the m/v Cali,
A boat that all had to keep a tally.
The Captain he was very nice
But best of all she was loaded with rice.
Rice-y, rice-y, rice-y, aye.
Rice-y, rice-y, rice-y, aye.[44]

Off Little Cayman lies a ghost ship, sitting upright on the seabed in sixty feet of water. *Soto Trader* was a 118-foot solid-refuse disposal vessel built during World War II but mothballed in Texas for thirty years before she was acquired by a Caymanian firm to be used as an island freighter.[45] On April 2, 1976, *Soto Trader* left Grand Cayman with a general cargo that included cannisters of propane gas, bulk gasoline, and several cement mixers and motor vehicles bound for Jamaica. After discharging cargo at Cayman Brac, the freighter arrived at Little Cayman on April 4 and anchored in an area called the Flats off the southwest coast. Her crew transferred a number of propane cylinders to a small barge tied alongside the ship and began to pump gasoline into fifty-five-gallon drums for transport to the island. Tragically, a spark ignited fuel fumes that had seeped into the cargo holds, and *Soto Trader* quickly was engulfed in flames and explosions. Her crew managed to get off the burning ship, but two badly burned men lost their lives. The freighter burned throughout the night and next morning slowly sank beneath the waves.[46] Today, visitors to Little Cayman can explore the ghost ship by swimming through her main cargo doors into the hold, where remains of her cargo, including the cement mixers and truck chassis, lie entombed by the sea.

On January 9, 1976, the Cayman-owned *Kirk Pride* sank off George Town harbor, despite the efforts of her captain, crew, and local waterfront volunteers. The 498-ton cargo vessel, which had been in service between Tampa and the islands for more than ten years, had undergone minor engine repairs at anchor when a strong nor'easter struck, prompting her master to attempt to move her to a safer anchorage. The ship's engine

Fig. 77. The ghost ship *Soto Trader,* which sank in 1975 after an accidental explosion, lies in fifty-five feet of water off the south coast of Little Cayman. Photo by KC Smith.

failed, and the winds blew *Kirk Pride* onto the ironshore, grounding her at the entrance to Hog Stye Bay with large holes in her starboard side. Volunteers helped dock workers pull the vessel off the rocks to an anchorage in sixty feet of water, but the pumps could not keep up with water leaking into the hold. *Kirk Pride* sank at 9:30 P.M. with the pumps still working in vain. Apparently, as the ship sank, her anchor dragged across the sandy bottom until it hooked on some coral heads. The vessel slid into deeper water to the extent of the anchor chain, which broke, sending the sunken ship over a sea wall ledge that drops off a thousand feet. Next morning, divers followed the anchor chain into deep water and over the drop-off to some 250 feet, but the ship was gone.[47]

Almost ten years later during a routine dive, a submarine from Research Submersibles Ltd. of Grand Cayman came across *Kirk Pride* sitting in 750 feet of water leaning against her stack. She had become lodged between a small pinnacle of coral at the stern and a sixty-foot-high boulder at the bow. The submarine pilot immediately confirmed the identity of the sunken ship from the name on her stern and observed that, had she landed some fifty feet to the north, she would have fallen over the wall to six thousand feet.[48] Today, visitors can take a tour of *Kirk Pride* aboard

Atlantis Submarines' two-passenger submersible. The 170-foot-long wreck still sits upright where it landed, and the cargo compartments still contain sacks of cement and a Volkswagen Thing.[49] In the clear depths of Grand Cayman's wall, *Kirk Pride* rests frozen in time.

A more obvious example of the islands' shipwreck population is the steel freighter *Gamma* that dominates the shoreline between George Town and Seven Mile Beach. She ran aground on an offshore reef during a nor'wester in 1980 and was left to rust in the sun. A later storm forced the hulk onto the beach, where she rests today as a monument to the power of the sea.[50]

The disproportionate number of shipwrecks in the Cayman Islands cannot be disputed. Archaeological research in the three islands during 1979 and 1980 located and recorded more than seventy wrecksites dating from the seventeenth century to modern times.[51] These sites, and others subsequently discovered during later investigations, form the core of the National Museum's Shipwreck Inventory. A list of historically documented shipwrecks in the islands includes at least as many as were found during these surveys. Still earlier sites of wrecked vessels may lie undetec-

Fig. 78. At a depth of 700 feet, the Caymanian freighter *Kirk Pride* is precariously lodged on the vertical coral wall that runs along the west side of Grand Cayman. Photo by Dennis Denton.

ted under the seabed or may never have been recorded in written documents. The numerous sites that have been examined and recorded thus far offer a cross section of maritime traffic over the centuries in the western Caribbean as well as several examples of vessels that relate directly to the history of shipbuilding in the Cayman Islands, as described in the previous chapter. Each of the wrecksites, whether deposited accidentally on offshore reefs or abandoned as a relic of island nautical pursuits, contributed directly to the formulation of Cayman's heritage.

Comparison of wrecks encountered during the underwater surveys revealed that most of the wrecked vessels contained little or no cargo. Although many were badly disturbed by exposure to the elements, components of the ships such as hardware and ballast still were readily identifiable. Their cargos, on the other hand, could only be discerned by minimal traces, if at all. The obvious explanation for the absence of cargo materials on these sites is that extensive salvage was conducted on the vessels subsequent to their wrecking. This conclusion is supported by the historical record. In fact, wrecked ships and especially their contents appear to have represented a resource second only to sea turtles in the development of Caymanian culture.

Salvors

Marine salvage operations always have been a part of the maritime tradition. The Cayman Islands are no exception; indeed, wrecking, salving, or scuttling ships comprised an important part of seafaring life in the islands even before they were settled permanently. The Dutch captain Joachim Gijsen, for example, depended on the salvage of his wrecked ship *Dolphijn* to end his enforced stay on Grand Cayman.

Two years later, in 1632, the ship *Amersfoort* of the fleet of Martin Thijsz en route to Havana was instructed to stop and to salvage the *Dolphijn*'s remaining guns.[52] *Amersfoort* returned to the fleet off Havana with two of the guns; it is not known whether these were all that remained on the island.

Nearly forty years later Captain John Morris, one of Henry Morgan's most valued privateers and the same captain who captured the ship of Portuguese corsair Manuel Rivero Pardal, wrecked his own frigate *Dolphin* in the Cayman Islands while returning in 1671 from the infamous raid on Panama. Shortly before, the privateer frigate *Lilly* had been abandoned nearby, her captain leaving her for a wreck. *Dolphin*, a frigate of sixty tons, carried ten guns and sixty men on the raid to Panama. *Lilly* was a smaller frigate of fifty tons, but carried fifty men and ten guns.[53] Morris salvaged what he could from his own ship, fitted out *Lilly*, and headed for the southern cays of Cuba "where he took a peragua laden with tobacco, kept the men prisoners, tormented the master, and kept the tobacco."[54]

It also should be remembered that Edward Low made use of the Cayman Islands to strip and scuttle his ship on the western coast of Grand Cayman in order to join forces with another freebooter, George Lowther, captain of the pirate ship *Delivery*.[55]

Looters

Wreck plundering for profit in the Cayman Islands first received conspicuous attention with the exploits of an opportunist named Neal Walker. Accused by the governor and Council of Jamaica in 1730 of illegally looting some 16,000 pieces-of-eight and a quantity of gold from the recently wrecked Spanish galleon *Genovesa* on the nearby Pedro Bank, Walker retreated to his hideout on the east end of Grand Cayman.[56] A proclamation was issued for his arrest, but before he could be captured and tried for piracy, Walker appeared at the scene of another Spanish wreck, the brigantine *San Miguel,* which had run aground on the reefs of Little Cayman.[57]

Instead of silver and gold, the vessel was laden with large quantities of spirits, part of which Walker managed to plunder before escaping once again. *San Miguel* had been en route from Cádiz to Veracruz in convoy with the New Spain *flota* when she came to grief. Her cargo registry, preserved in the Archives of the Indies in Spain, indicates that aside from fresh fruit for the fleet she was loaded with 1,091 barrels of *aguardiente* (brandy) and 158 barrels of wine, as well as some minor cargo.[58]

Neal Walker was not the only one to take advantage of the wrecked Spanish brigantine on the remote reef. Claiming his intentions to recover *San Miguel*'s cargo, Colin Campbell embarked in a sloop belonging to William Dove from Jamaica to Little Cayman. After fishing barrels of wine and brandy from the wreckage "in order to deposit the same in the hands of the Government for the benefit of His Catholik Majesty," the sloop itself was wrecked on the reefs. Dove and the others began to salvage their own vessel, only to have the twice-wrecked merchandise seized by suspicious authorities.

By this time, however, the word had gotten out that the wreckage of a

Spanish galleon was there for the taking. Two other vessels from Jamaica, belonging to Thomas Ware and James Jorden, were apprehended shortly afterwards with cargos looted from *San Miguel*, and the ships were seized on orders of the governor.[59] The plundered remains of the unfortunate brigantine are still visible today on the treacherous reefs of Little Cayman. Ballast stones, cannons, anchors, and fragments of earthenware storage jars are camouflaged by a mantle of time and coral.

Wreckers

The establishment of the first permanent communities in the Cayman Islands during the early 1700s included the roots of the Caymanian seafaring traditions transported from nearby Jamaica. However, the remoteness of the three islands kept them outside the close rule of law. The difference between salvage and piracy was to remain relatively unresolved in the Cayman Islands, but the occupation of wrecking, as it came to be known, was firmly entrenched. The first description of the island inhabitants of Grand Cayman, published by Edward Long in 1774, includes a discussion of their growing culture, dependent on the sea but independent of outside authority:

> Although the island is an appendage of Jamaica . . . the people upon it have never been an object of the legislature of that colony: they have a chief, or governor, of their own choosing, and regulations of their own framing; they have some justices of the peace among them, appointed by commission from the governor of Jamaica; and live very happily, without scarcely any form of civil government. . . . The Bermuda sloops have a pretty regular intercourse with them; their crews are attentive to two points, turtling and plundering of wrecks. The people of Cayman have now and then benefited likewise by such unhappy accidents. . . . Yet, to do them justice, they have generally shewn equal activity and humanity upon these occasions, in saving the lives of mariners and passengers, and preserving the cargoes, making free with a moderate share only of booty, by way of salvage.[60]

On at least one occasion, Caymanians saved the lives of passengers who were actually listed as cargo. In 1781 the African slave ship *Nelly*, en route to Jamaica, was wrecked on the Caymans and "a great many [of the slaves] were sold to pay salvage and other expenses."[61]

More than a decade later, the Wreck of the Ten Sail caused a general consternation among the inhabitants of Grand Cayman. No doubt the local populace did its share to assist in the saving of lives and property, as Captain Lawford's reports suggest, yet the disaster created unusual pressures on the islanders, who could not feed and house the survivors. In cases of lesser magnitude, the unintentional grounding of ships along Cayman's shores provided an added source of material goods that could be obtained relatively easily and cheaply. These sudden benefits often included the remains of the ships themselves. A visitor to Grand Cayman observed in 1845 that wreckage of all sorts was put to good use by the inhabitants of the east end, and that "fragments of ships seemed to form part of most of the common people's houses."[62]

The Wreck of the Ten Sail may have crystallized the tradition of wrecking among Caymanian seamen. In the late eighteenth century, the shift in turtling from Cayman to Cuba on a larger scale brought this auxiliary occupation to the forefront. The presence of Caymanian turtlers along the cays and shoals of southern Cuba did not go unnoticed by local officials. In 1798 the governor general of Cuba received a report from a Captain Don Juan Tirri, who painted an unfavorable picture of Grand Cayman and her intrepid turtlers:

> The islet is inhabited by a handful of lawless men who bear the name, and accidently carry on the trade of fisher-folk, but who are in reality nothing more than sea robbers. The island constitutes their lair and it is the place where they hide their ill-gotten gains. . . . they very often witness, or soon hear of the frequent shipwrecks of the mariners driven onto . . . reefs. Instead of giving them assistance and help that humanity demands, they hasten thither only to rob them and take to their caves even more fragments of broken vessels. They make no exception even for English boats sailing from Jamaica, many of which fall into their clutches.[63]

Captain Tirri recommended in his report that the Spanish government "wipe out this pirate's nest."

That the wreckers robbed English vessels from Jamaica is doubtful, since the Cayman Islands at that time were a dependency of Jamaica. A petition, signed around 1803 by thirteen inhabitants of Grand Cayman, asked the governor of Jamaica to consider allowing them to become exempt from the "Transient Tax on Wreck Goods, imported by them into the

Island of Jamaica."[64] The petitioners claimed that their vessels, which they described as "Turtlers entire (except when carrying the produce of this Island or Wreck Goods)" had been obliged to pay the same fees as foreign ships, and pointed out that this was unfair since the Caymans were dependencies of Jamaica.

The Reverend Hope Waddell, wrecked in *Weymouth* while en route from Jamaica to England with his family in 1845, provided a firsthand account of the activities of Caymanian wreckers the morning after the schooner ran aground on the east end of Grand Cayman:

> A fleet of canoes was making for us, and soon surrounded our helpless craft; when a host of wild, reckless-looking, coloured men sprang up the sides, like pirates or boarders greedy for prey. The head man, advancing to the captain, with one word of pity and two of business, agreed to take everything ashore, on the usual terms of half for their trouble.
>
> Then began the work of despoiling the vessel. The fellows were up in the rigging, and over the spars, and everywhere in a moment. Down came the sails and ropes, bundled into the canoes, and off ashore with amazing rapidity. Up came everything from the hold. The cabin doors, fittings, and furnishings, were by fair or foul means torn off and sent away. The people seemed to vie which would do the most, the canoes which would go and return most quickly, striving to strip the wreck during the calm of the morning, before the sea breeze rising should impede their operations. Some of them were swearing shockingly till rebuked; when they looked surprised, begged pardon, and then shouted to their companions to mind themselves, as there was a "parson" on board.[65]

Waddell took the opportunity to become acquainted with the islanders during the following days. He and his family stayed in the chief wrecker's house, which was the only two-story dwelling on the coast. Sailing by boat to the western end of the island to await a ship to England, Waddell found that George Town had a church and schoolhouse, but neither minister nor teacher. He kindly offered his services during his stay. "With avidity they received all the books and tracts we had to distribute; and implored us to make known their destitute condition, and procure them a missionary."[66] The Caymanian situation during this period is reflected further in the words of an island woman who told the minister: "Sweet potatoes will grow in some parts, and we all go a fishing, especially for turtle, to supply the English ships. But, to tell the truth sir, our main dependence is on wrecks, and we all thank God when a ship comes ashore."[67]

A legend exists on Cayman Brac, which if true could cast a shadow over this aspect of Cayman's maritime heritage. On the southeastern point of the bluff, which is one of the highest spots on the cliff overlooking the windward approach to the island, there is a section of land known as Fireburn. Today this overlook has a lighthouse, and it would have been an ideal location for a watchtower or signal fire; perhaps lookouts were posted to warn approaching Spanish fleets at night during the sixteenth and seventeenth centuries. However, in oral tradition passed down through the generations, a sinister tale of wrecking emerges. Rather than warning approaching ships at night, watchmen are said to have walked the edge of the cliff with a torch to lure mariners into thinking that the slowly moving light was another ship under way and thus cause them to sail into the cliffs.[68] A similar legend, involving a lantern and a donkey, is repeated on Grand Cayman.

Whether or not the Fireburn legend is true, ships did wreck on the windward cliffs of Cayman Brac. Early Brackers remember the fate of *Curaçao,* a merchant vessel that smashed into the bluff during a storm in 1915. A gruesome sight awaited those who climbed the bluff overlooking the wreck the morning after the storm. Severed limbs and other remains of the ship's captain and his wife had been thrown, still clad, onto the 140-foot-high cliff by the impact of the collision.[69] Five-gallon tins of kerosene, comprising part of *Curaçao's* cargo, also were found along the top of the bluff. Several days later, the people of Grand Cayman, some eighty miles to the lee, discovered scores of the same tins floating ashore at East End.[70] For months following the wrecking of *Curaçao,* lamps in the houses of families on both islands burned brightly.

A similar legend on Grand Cayman may explain the origin of the place name for Rum Point on the eastern edge of North Sound. Sometime in the eighteenth century, a ship was wrecked on the reefs guarding the sound several days before Christmas. Her cargo consisted of West Indian rum from the sugar plantations to windward. Today the villagers of East End, on the opposite side of the island, repeat the tale of a strange procession that came into their community the day following the wreck. It seems that, as the cargo of the ship was brought ashore, barrels of rum were loaded onto a cart that was headed down the trail to East End. Along the way, portions of the rum were given out to friends and relatives. By the time the cart reached its destination at the end of the trail, its owners were incoherent and the rest of the island in various stages of intoxication.[71] Those who relate this legend attest to an unprecedented Christmas celebration that year.

Wrecks that came ashore were rated "good" if they produced a large amount of salvable cargo. One such was the wreck of *Dene,* a merchant vessel that ran aground on East End in 1846. Heavily laden with a valuable cargo of dry goods, the ship was a godsend to the islanders, who had suffered a major hurricane that year. History records that one elderly resident, remembering conditions in the islands after the storm, remarked that "everyone's spirits were low until the news of the wreck of *Dene* came and revived us all for we got plenty to wear and eat."[72]

Another good wreck was that of *Prince Frederick,* which occurred on the south shore of Cayman Brac in 1895. Salvage of the full-rigged, composite-built merchantman began almost immediately after she ran aground. A popular Brac anecdote relates the consternation of one man who leapt aboard the vessel with ax in hand to chop the masts down. At the first blow, his ax was turned aside, and the surprised salvor found that the masts were made of iron.[73] As salvage proceeded, a night watchman was posted on the deck of the stricken vessel, but due to his carelessness while cooking a meal one evening, the wreck caught fire and was destroyed.

Today the remains of *Prince Frederick* lie along a shallow shelf on the seabed among submarine coral ridges. Although her wooden hull and decks have been consumed by fire and the pounding of the sea, her iron masts, anchors, hardware, and a neatly arranged assortment of reinforcing frames and knees testify to the vessel's large size and solid construction (fig. 79). The accidental fire did not prevent some of the wreck's contents from being put to use by islanders; ballast stones from *Prince Frederick* comprise the front of a large building in George Town on the largest island.

Similar examples of salvaged wreck materials put to new uses can be found throughout the Cayman Islands. At East End, the floors of several houses are covered with French tiles pulled from a wreck in the sea nearby. The house of a prominent merchant family on Cayman Brac is adorned with a mahogany staircase saved from the wreck of a German ship. A hut on Little Cayman is built from the keel timbers of an old sailing ship, salvaged from a nearby lagoon. A stranded modern freighter, *Oro Verde,*

Fig. 79. The remains of *Prince Frederick,* including this iron mast, lie on the reef off the southern coast of Cayman Brac where she wrecked in 1895. Photo by KC Smith.

was stripped, towed into deep water, and scuttled to create an underwater attraction for diving tourists. Her main derrick and boom were removed and sent to the Brac to serve as a crane on the government dock.

Sometimes, salvaged materials were sold or sent off-island rather than used locally. Such was the case with anchors and cannons from wrecks along Cayman's reefs that were collected for scrap during the Second World War. Among local fishermen, "scrapping" always has been a familiar tradition. When catches were slow, iron "fished" from wrecks represented additional income. In the 1970s and 1980s, the historical value of anchors and cannons encouraged their sale to tourist hotels. Fortunately, through the efforts of the Caymanian Heritage Trust, the National Museum was established to house relics of the maritime heritage of a unique Caribbean seafaring people.

The Caymanian people no longer rely on wrecking to supply their needs. Dramatic changes brought by air transportation, offshore finance, banking, and tourism have shifted the cultural focus from the sea to other occupations. However, the tradition of wrecking still is ingrained to a certain extent in the language and folk legends of the islanders. And, in each of the islands, the shorelines still are explored after storms to discover what the sea has cast up—a practice that was common for as long as anyone can remember.

Conclusion

The first European voyages to the New World provided explorers with a startling awareness of the abundant natural resources of the Caribbean region. Some of these resources were familiar but rare, such as alluvial gold and pearls from the sea, each serving as a catalyst for further exploration and ultimate exploitation. Others were unfamiliar, such as tobacco, maize, potatoes, or cassava, but these soon became part of the European pattern of life. Many marine resources, especially the docile manatee and the timid sea turtle, although previously unknown, quickly were realized as supplemental food sources in areas where they congregated. One such area stood apart from all others and inspired the awe of those who witnessed its profusion of marine turtles—the Cayman Islands.

For what must have been millennia, the deserted shores of these three distant isles hosted an annual arrival of swimming fleets of reptiles that went about their biological business undisturbed. This natural phenomenon did not go unnoticed by mariners who began to frequent the Caribbean Sea. As they lumbered ashore on the Caymans at night to perform their nesting ritual, the unassuming turtles soon were greeted by sea-callused hands and quickly transformed into shipboard provisions for hungry sailors. This process, like the exploitation of so many of the world's resources, was to be repeated again and again until the seemingly inexhaustible numbers of reptiles were reduced to the border of extinction.

The relationship between the sea turtle and humans most likely began in the West Indies centuries before Europeans arrived. Coastal hunting and gathering communities undoubtedly made use of the sea turtle along with other marine food resources. Indeed, the migration of aboriginal people from the mainland to the Caribbean islands may well have followed that of the sea turtle in some areas. It is clear that later European migration into the West Indies was facilitated by the availability of fresh turtle meat. The association between human and beast took on a new dimension as limited and local utilization gave way to wholesale hunting and trade in turtles during the colonial period by the French and English.

The Cayman Islands became the natural focal point for turtle fishing, which was a primary factor in the eventual settlement of the three small land forms on a permanent basis. The abundance of sea turtles had distinguished the islands initially; later, it not only insured the survival of the first settlers in a region of limited agricultural possibilities, but it also directed their course in history as a distinctively nautical people.

The insular geography of the remote islands, coupled with the relatively sparse terrestrial resources, predetermined a necessarily seaward perspective for the embryonic Caymanian culture. Not only were marine resources relied upon heavily to support the first generations of islanders, but they also contributed to the formulation of traditional pursuits such as turtling and wrecking, for which the Caymanians became widely renowned. Specialized fishing methods and vessels evolved to suit a people whose lifestyle became characterized by a tranquil pattern of isolated and independent insular existence, interrupted only by an occasional hurricane.

These islands, then, possess a maritime heritage unique to the West Indies. Historical materials gathered from archival sources have produced the testimony of events and persons that shaped their past. Archaeological investigations have recorded scores of wrecked and abandoned vessels that offer a tangible legacy to be protected and appreciated in future generations. Ethnographic data from oral histories, legends, and living memories have been collected to preserve the colloquial quality of Caymanian life.

The twilight of seafaring traditions as they have existed in the Cayman Islands is past. A rapid progression from insular isolation to instant integration with the world at large has taken place. Ancient maritime skills have fallen aside as the advantages and assurances of modern life come to bear on Caymanian lifeways. Yet, while islanders no longer go to sea as a

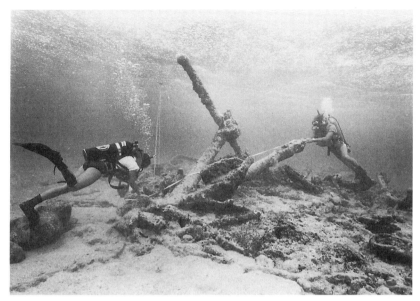

Fig. 80. The wreck of *Evening Star* on the south coast of Little Cayman is typical of many wrecked or abandoned vessels that have been documented in the Cayman Islands. Photo by KC Smith.

matter of course, their homeland still depends on maritime traffic for the importation of almost all essential raw and finished products, as well as a massive tourist trade made possible by air and cruise ship travel. Hundreds of thousands of visitors annually come to the Cayman Islands for its tropical climate and crystalline waters, which have earned a reputation as one of the world's foremost year-round diving destinations. For the Cayman Islands, the sea still represents a major resource and a munificent benefactor.

To preserve their unique seafaring past, local islanders established a small museum at Stake Bay on Cayman Brac in 1983. They worked to gather artifacts and old photographs documenting the professions by which Brackers earned their livelihoods in the past. In 1979 a law was passed to establish a Cayman Islands National Museum on Grand Cayman, based in part on the lifelong collections of Ira Thompson, which were acquired by the government. The first museum officer, Anita Ebanks, was appointed in 1984. The following year, the Memory Bank Project was created under the museum board to begin to record oral histories from elderly islanders. In 1987 the National Trust was formed as a nonprofit statutory body responsible for the preservation of Cayman's historical, natural, and maritime heritage.

Since its opening in the Old Court House in George Town in 1990, the National Museum has developed permanent exhibits on cultural and natural history and art, and an audio-visual presentation portraying island heritage. On display is a Cayman Brac catboat, built by Elford Dixon in 1964 for Nordell Jackson of East End. Constructed of plopnut, a local hardwood, with planks of imported white pine, the thirteen-foot-six-inch craft is preserved as an example of the islands' boat-building traditions. Used by Jackson and his stepfather, Carlton Pearson, to catch turtles off East End, the boat was nicknamed *Independent* because the two no longer had to rely on others for use of such a vessel.

The museum has been active in recording oral histories from elderly islanders for the Cayman Islands Memory Bank, administered by the National Archive, which opened in 1993. Since that time, memory bank records, and especially the archive collections, have grown considerably. Between 1990 and 1993, the museum and Texas A&M University helped to sponsor additional research on the 1794 Wreck of the Ten Sail, which included archival work, folklore studies, and archaeological investigations.[1] This research was directed by Dr. Margaret Leshikar, who became the museum's first full-time archaeologist in 1993. Her work resulted in a major museum exhibit that opened in February 1994, commemorating the two-hundredth anniversary of the Wreck of the Ten Sail. The exhibit,

Fig. 81. The Cayman Islands National Museum, which opened in 1990, is housed in the Old Court House, one of the islands' historic buildings. Photo by KC Smith.

Fig. 82. The Cayman Brac catboat *Independent* is preserved along with other maritime relics at the Cayman Islands National Museum in George Town. Photo by KC Smith.

which was visited by Her Majesty Queen Elizabeth II and Prince Philip, demonstrated the role of nautical archaeology and maritime history in the preservation of a national heritage.[2] At the same time, the museum worked with other organizations to bring the Wreck of the Ten Sail to the public in a Philatelic Bureau stamp issue, a Currency Board commemorative coin, a National Archive publication, a Visual Arts Society art competition, public lectures, and radio and television appearances.[3] Other public-oriented shipwreck programs have included a 1996 partnership between the museum and Parrots Landing/Calico Jack's to prepare an informational brochure for tourists and a maritime history lesson for Caymanian students on the wreck of *Cali*.[4] Recent archival, archaeological, and oral history research in conjunction with Ball State University has focused on the 1930 wreck of the schooner *Geneva Kathleen* on the northeast coast of Grand Cayman.[5]

Meanwhile, in 1992 and 1995, surveys for prehistoric sites on all three islands, including test excavations in caves on Cayman Brac, were conducted by archaeologists from the Institute of Archaeology, University College London in cooperation with the National Museum. A similar survey of Grand Cayman by the Florida Museum of Natural History was undertaken in 1993. As with a previous survey by Fewkes and a brief test on

Cayman Brac by the Institute of Nautical Archaeology, both groups found no evidence of prehistoric culture, suggesting that the Cayman Islands were not occupied by indigenous people.[6]

Like the conservation of natural resources, the preservation of Cayman's underwater and maritime cultural heritage has become an important issue in the islands. Faced with applications from prospectors who wished to salvage historic shipwrecks, the Ministry of Culture in the early 1990s formed a marine archaeology committee to advise on appropriate management measures for these significant resources. The committee reviewed the Abandoned Wreck Law of 1966, which assigns Crown ownership to abandoned wrecks of fifty years of age or older, but which does not recognize their historical and cultural value. It determined that the law should be replaced by newer legislation. By 1994 a list of points to be addressed by a new law was compiled, and in 1996 the Executive Council officially authorized work to begin on drafts of replacement legislation.[7]

The Cayman Islands National Museum has taken a leading role in the preservation of Caribbean cultural resources. When the Museums Association of the Caribbean met in the Cayman Islands in 1995, the museum conducted a workshop for participants on protecting underwater archaeological sites. Museum staff also have been active in a network involving other groups, such as the International Association for Caribbean Archaeology, the Society for Historical Archaeology, the Caribbean Conservation Association, the International Council on Monuments and Sites, the International Congress of Maritime Museums, and the United Nations Educational, Scientific, and Cultural Organization.[8]

Little Cayman now has a museum, thanks to the efforts of Linton and Polly Tibbetts, who have assembled the histories, folktales, and artifacts from this small island to share with a growing number of visitors. The museum features exhibits on the island's natural history, along with displays of local shipbuilding tools and cooking utensils.

The inventory of archaeological sites in the Cayman Islands has continued to grow. Additional shipwrecks have been recorded on all three islands, and most notably, terrestrial sites that are integral to interpretation of the unique heritage of the Cayman Islands are increasingly encountered as development is balanced with concern for natural and cultural resources.

THE DEPOSITION OF SAMUEL HUTCHINSON

This transcription of Hutchinson's eyewitness account of the 1669 Spanish corsair raid on Little Cayman is taken from the original (PRO, CO 1/25) reproduced in fig. 43:

Jamaica.

An Account given upon Oath of the Spaniard's attempt upon the English Fishermen at the Caymanns of the burning of the Governour's house and Carrying away of his Goods and of their takeing one Ship one Katch and three Great Sloops and their Cutting and Destroying all the Fisher Boates and Cannoes ye now upon ye Island.

Samuel Hutchinson Commander of the Ship Hopewell rideing at anchor in the harbour called Hudson's hole in ye little Caymanns on the 14th day of April last past Saw five Saile beeing all great Shippps Except one Tartan they appeared about fower of ye clocke in the afternoone from the South part of ye Island and came to an anchor w^{th}in Muskett Shott w^{th}out ye Rocks of ye Said Hudson's hole with English Colours flying, they fireing Six or Seaven gunns, Shott at ye Said Hutchinson's Ship upon wch ye Said Hutchinson hoisted his Colours and fired one gunn to Leeward, whereupon ye Spaniards loared ye English and hoisted the Burgonia flagg continued fireing and manned ye Tartan and Sevorall boats in order to ye boarding of Said Hutchinson's Ship, but now three tymes boates of ye Said Hutchinson lost onely one man, though he had Several great Shott placed in the hull of his Shipp, his maine yard being shot downe and mast Splintered, the Governour of ye Caymanns beeing then aboard, evening drawing on, ye boates went aboard their owne Shipps and about two of ye clocke in the morning, ye Spaniards made false fires towards the north pt of the Island, and in the meane while landed about two hundred men upon the Easternmost pt of the Island, The Said Hutchinson keepeing his Ship so long as any man Stood by him, at last went on Shoar wth the Governour, to Save their persons from beeing prisoners ye Spaniards boarding ye Shipp, ye Said Huchinson retired into the woods, and approaching the Seaside came nigh Some of ye Spanish boates, demanding of them their Admirall's name, and their reasons why they should come to destroy merchantmen and fishermen, but would make not any answer thereto. After ye they had taken ye Said Huchinson's Shipp and thrown his Salt overboarde to get her cleared of the Rockes, wch ye Said Hutchinson had runn her upon, in two days tyme they rigged her and Carryed her away wth ye Said Katch and three Sloops ye 17th day of ye Same Instant, wth about Seaventeen to Eighteen Prisoners.

Sworne unto me a true relation by Samuel Hutchinson Comander of ye Ship Hopewell on the Sixteenth day of June 1669. before me

    Robert Byndlas

[CO 125]

Appendix 2

LIEUTENANT ALFRED CARPENTER'S OBSERVATIONS

In 1880, the Royal Navy survey schooner HMS *Sparrowhawk* was detailed to conduct a hydrographic survey of the Lesser Cayman Islands and the Pedro Banks to the south of Jamaica, for the purpose of drafting an Admiralty chart for each area. Lieutenant Alfred Carpenter, the officer in charge of the expedition, and his men spent several weeks on and around Cayman Brac and Little Cayman making celestial observations, turning angles, sounding water depths, and recording geophysical features of the islands. By the time their work was completed, Lieutenant Carpenter had to requisition new boots for his men because those that had been issued to them had rapidly worn out on the ironshore of the two islands. The results of the survey produced the first navigational charts of all three islands— charts on which all modern navigation still is based. This initial survey bequeathed the name Sparrowhawk Hill to a slight elevation on Little Cayman, but has generally been forgotten or overlooked in the popular annals of the history of these islands.

Research conducted by the author at the British Ministry of Defense Hydrography Office in Taunton, Somerset, unearthed the records and handwritten reports of Carpenter's survey. Among them, the following account is of interest to the study of Caymanian heritage.

Further Information—Lesser Caymans (MDHO, OD 505)

The inhabitants of these two islands are all tall, large boned Scotchmen, slow of speech, & careful with their money-
The chief families are the Scott's, Foster's, Ryan's & Hunter's, & they are all at daggers drawn.
They multiply very fast & are careless of their children's future-
The women are very reticent-
The population is about 300 of which 100 are children-
They are friendly to strangers & anxious to trade-
Their livelihood depends on the capture of turtle, Loggerheads being the most common, then hawksbill & the green turtle-
The tortoise shell of the hawksbill & the soup meat & eggs of all are cured & carried to Jamaica Markets by schooners-

The bush has been cleared in places & yams, bananas & sugar cane grown-
Only the first of these really flourishes & they are finer even than the Jamaica Yam.

The men work in companies turning turtle & fishing at Little Cayman, but residing on Cayman Brac where the plantations are-
The turtle nets are buoyed with imitation carved wood turtles and require to be carefully avoided when approaching an anchorage-

The islanders did a good deal of wrecking at one time on the Cuban coast but have been made to desist during the disturbed state of that island.
It does not appear that they were in any way dishonest about that occupation-
There is some trade done with America in Cocoa-nuts-

From May till November the mosquitoes are very bad, and flies at all times of the year swarm about the islands finding ready food in the dead and dying flesh of the loggerhead turtles which are little eaten-
The Lion Lizard, a scaly species that carries its tail curled over its back, a few grasshoppers, & the soldier crab are the only numerous animals about-

The bush consists of Aloes, Cactuses, Sea Grape, Mangrove, a soft-beech, a little Mahogany and Candle Wood tree, all the trees being loaded with orchids-

Alligators or Caymans are on record only, & probably found their way here on driftwood of which the Southern coasts & Eastern points are covered.

The Chisel beach which is thrown up at various parts of these islands is a very remarkable collection of coral boulders & nodules combined with drift wood, seeds, conch shells & marine vegetation.

[signed] Alfred Carpenter Lieutenant in Charge

Appendix 3

THE FIRST CENSUS OF CAYMAN

Early in the year 1802, George Nugent, the governor of Jamaica, began to tour the parishes of the island on which he had taken up his post the previous year. He also made inquiries about the Cayman Islands, which at that time were a dependency of Jamaica. Nugent requested Edward Corbet of his staff to gather some unofficial information about the islands and their inhabitants. Corbet replied in a letter to the governor, dated May 25, that he had located a Jamaican merchant named Joseph Barnes who traded regularly with Caymanian vessels. Barnes estimated that on the island of Grand Cayman there were about forty-five white families, twenty free colored families, and about two hundred slaves, whose major product was cotton. The most respectable inhabitant, according to Barnes, was a gentleman named "Bowden" who claimed to hold a magistrate's commission. From what Corbet could gather, the people of Grand Cayman were "rather of a turbulent disposition," since Barnes related an occasion when it had become necessary to send soldiers from Jamaica to help keep the peace.[1] Corbet offered to make further inquiries, and the governor decided to send him immediately to the Caymans aboard a naval vessel in order to investigate the islands firsthand. Within a matter of only a few weeks, Nugent received Corbet's report, which represents the first official description and census of the Caymanian people.[2]

Corbet had sailed directly to Grand Cayman, which was the only in-habited island of the three. The first sign of settlement was the village of Bodden Town, located some four and a half leagues along its southern shore. Although this was the residence of William Bodden, for whom Corbet had a letter from Governor Nugent, the village could not be approached by sea beause of dangerous offshore reefs. Corbet's ship ran down instead to the western end of the island, where a safe anchorage was found at the southern part of Sandy Bay adjacent to a similar village of similar size, formerly called Hogstyes but recently renamed George Town. Here Corbet found a small fort, "not very well constructed," defended by three cannons of small caliber. Another fort, this one with four guns, was encountered on the road eastward into Bodden Town.

When he arrived in Bodden Town, Corbet discovered that William Bodden, considered by islanders to be their chief magistrate, was absent in the Bay of Honduras, but he was well received by his younger brother, Samuel Bodden. In response to Corbet's request on behalf of Nugent to receive their recommendations as to how best the governor could serve them, the islanders curiously deferred the question until the future return of William Bodden. While several other men held commissions as magistrates, given to them by Lord Balcarres in 1798, none came forward to act on behalf of the senior Bodden. Corbet noted that all of the magistrates resided in Bodden Town, while George Town had none. Measures adopted by the magistrates for the public good had originally been submitted by the population at large, and those who opposed the majority were pressured to leave. In fact, Corbet found that one such "ill disposed individual" had recently been shipped off to America "by the United Voice and compulsion of the Inhabitants."

More serious was the matter of a prisoner charged with murdering the husband of his sister. The man, confined for more than ten months without trial, had objected to the victim's treatment of his sister, whereupon he was challenged to fight. In returning the first blow, he had caused his brother-in-law's death. Governor Nugent had offered to send a commission for the man's trial, but the difficulty lay in finding an impartial jury, since almost all of the islanders were connected by marriage. Corbet recommended sending the man to Montego Bay, where Caymanians often resorted for marriage ceremonies, since there was no clergyman on Grand Cayman.

One of Corbet's goals on Grand Cayman was not so easily met—that of ascertaining when and by whom the island originally was settled. Most of the people he talked to had no definite idea who their ancestors were or when they came to settle the island. Some proposed the original settler to have been a soldier in Oliver Cromwell's army named Bodden. Others claimed that the first settlers had been pirates. Of much more immediate and strategic value, however, was an estimation that the island could muster only about eighty persons capable of bearing arms for their own defense. In reality, Corbet had been sent to the Cayman Islands in response to the growing presence of French forces in the West Indies. Although the islands were supposed to be under the protection of Jamaica, they had been considered too remote for Nugent's predecessors to concern themselves with. And although islanders had erected two forts to protect their major settlements, the fort at George Town had been attacked and totally destroyed by Spaniards from Cuba during the American Revolutionary War, when Spain, France, and Holland were allied against the British. Officers of the militia seem to have been chosen by popular reputation, since none had been formally commissioned for service. To Corbet, this seemed contrary to the welfare and defense of the inhabitants, especially when he learned that two officers of the militia at George Town had recently resigned because locals had disagreed with their orders.

During his stay on Grand Cayman, Corbet rode and walked across the island in different directions nearly forty miles, making an account of its geography, soil, and availability of fresh water. He found settlers growing sea-island cotton, sugar cane (from which was produced syrup), corn, yams, and plantains. He noted that sea turtles were caught in the Caymans, but most were taken off the southern cays of Cuba and brought back to trade with passing ships en route to Europe or America. In his final analysis, Corbet concluded that the Cayman Islands, despite their small size and limited soil, were a useful dependency of Jamaica. Not only were they convenient way stations for British naval vessels in need of fresh water and small provisions but, Corbet wrote (perhaps remembering the Wreck of the Ten Sail), the islands were strategically located on the track of vessels approaching the Leeward Passage and their inhabitants had provided relief to shipwrecked mariners, saving lives that otherwise would have been lost.

Corbet's visit to the islands ultimately initiated a correspondence between Governor Nugent and William Bodden, the chief magistrate of Grand Cayman. Bodden later wrote to Nugent on July 24, 1805, requesting his advice should there be another invasion of the island by the Spaniards, "as there has lately been two privateers at Geo. Town, which attacked the fort there, and was expected to land at West Bay to march against the place, but declined it."[3]

In the National Library of Jamaica in Kingston, there is a small cedar box marked Nugent Papers. Among these documents (MS.72), from the administration of Sir George Nugent, governor of Jamaica from 1801 to 1806, is Edward Corbet's report and the earliest census of the Cayman Islands (520N):

Table A3.1. First Census of the Cayman Islands, 1802

List of the Inhabitants of the Island of Grand Cayman distinguishing their place of residence, number in each Family and the slaves they possess &c.

WHITE FAMILIES	FREE PEOPLE OF COLOUR	NUMBER IN EACH FAMILY	NUMBER OF SLAVES
At the East End			
John Thomas		3	
	Charles McLean	3	1
	Charles Poncheau	4	1
At North Side			
Stephen Bodden		10	3
	Jn Tatum Sen.	4	1
	Jn Tatum Jun.	8	1
At Bodden Town			
Samuel Morton		6	9
James Bodden Esqr.		12	51
Joseph & Wm Conior		2	-
Benj McCoy Junr.		3	6
Benj McCoy Senr.		6	-
Charles Lemon		4	1
James Conior		3	1
W^m McCoy		6	3
Wm Bodden Esqr		4	51
Joseph Bodden Esqr		7	37
James Tatum		4	-
Mary Leach		8	3
James Wood		2	6
Susanna Tatum		5	2

WHITE FAMILIES	FREE PEOPLE OF COLOUR	NUMBER IN EACH FAMILY	NUMBER OF SLAVES
Wm Bodden		5	1
James Silver		1	4
John Watler		4	1
John Bodden		3	2
Waide Watler Senr.		1	31
James Watler		5	8
Susanna Watler		4	7
John Connior		6	5
Mary Ann Tatum		2	1
James Conior		1	2
	Anna Conior	7	-
	John Bodden	2	-
	Dorothy Spleen	2	-
	George Bodden	6	1
	Sarah Rosamond & Agnes Bodden	3	-
	John Tatum	4	10
	James Tatum Sr.	2	5
	Wm Tatum	1	-
At Franks Sound			
Thomas Sutherland		5	1
	Diana McLean	5	-
	Absalom Bodden	2	-
At George Town			
formerly called the Hogstyes			
John Drayton		6	23
Sarah Nixon		3	4
Abraham Bodden		6	5
Sterling Rivers		5	5
Rachal Rivers		8	17
Wm Jennett		3	-
George Bodden		7	4
Benj. Bodden		6	-
Wm L. Prescott		5	2
Eliz. Conior		1	5
Mary Savery		6	5
John Bodden		8	8

WHITE FAMILIES	FREE PEOPLE OF COLOUR	NUMBER IN EACH FAMILY	NUMBER OF SLAVES
John Edw. Rivers		4	3
Cornelia Scott		5	1
Mary Wilson		4	-
John S. Jackson		6	-
	Chloe Parsons	1	2
	James Parsons	1	5
	Wm Parsons	3	6
	Lind Rivers	1	1
	George Barrow	1	3
At West Bay			
John Bodden		6	2
Thos. Hide		8	6
Jane Walker		1	9
Wm Rivers		5	2
Isabella Hoye		1	2
Edwd. Hale		1	1
Mary Jennett		2	3
At Boatswains Bay			
	Henry Ebanks	6	8
	Augustus Ebanks	7	5
	Barnet Ebanks	6	-
Free Negroes			
Mary Mitchell		2	-
Thos. Bishop		1	-
Amazon		1	-
Free Negroes of *George Town*			
Wm Frusty		1	
Catharine Mitchell		1	
At S. W. Sound			
Wm Collins		9	7
Margaret Bush		4	5
James Bush		2	-
Wm Huggins		5	-
Christopher Chas. Bush		4	8

WHITE FAMILIES	FREE PEOPLE OF COLOUR	NUMBER IN EACH FAMILY	NUMBER OF SLAVES
Wm Toulmiry [?]		3	1
W^m & J^n Hind		2	-
At Prospect			
Waide Watler Junr.		7	17
Thomas Thompson		13	56
At Spotts			
Wm Eden		4	9
James Coe		6	6
Wm Bodden		10	21
At Little Pedro			
Wm Watler		3	6
Thos. Knowles Eden		1	3

A General Account of the Number of Inhabitants in the Island of Grand Caymanes distinguishing their Colour place of Residence &c.

PLACE OF RESIDENCE	WHITES			PEOPLE OF COLOUR		
	NO. OF FAMILIES	NO. IN ALL	SLAVES	NO. OF FAMILIES	NO. IN ALL	SLAVES
East End	1	3	2	7	1	
Frank Sound	1	5	1	2	7	
Bodden Town	24	104	233	8	21	16
Little Pedro	2	4	9			
Spotts	3	20	36			
Prospect	2	20	73			
South W. Sound	7	29	21			
George Town formerly called the Hog Styes	17	90	95	5	7	17
				(2 free negroes)		
West Bay	8	24	25			
Boatswain Bay				3	19	13
				(4 free negroes)		
North Side	1	10	3	2	12	2
Total	66	309	496	22	73	49
				(6 free negroes)		

A List of Persons acting in the Island of the Grand Cayman as Officers of Militia having been chosen by the Inhabitants of the respective Quarters

At Bodden Town

Wm Bodden Senr. Esq.	Captain
James Bodden Esq.	Lieutenant
Joseph Bodden Esq.	Ensign

At George Town

Jⁿ Edw. Rivers	Captain
Jⁿ S. Jackson	Lieutenant

It was understood that those two Gentlemen were about to resign their Situations in consequence of meeting with some opposition to their orders

South West Sound

Wm Collins	Captain

Prospect, Spotts & Little Pedro

James Coe	Captain

A List of the Magistrates now acting in the Island of the Grand Cayman appointed under a Commission from the Right Honb^{le} The Earl of Balcarres Lie^t. Governor of Jamaica dated 13 Jany 1798-

Wm Bodden Senr.	Chief Magistrate
James Bodden	
Joseph Bodden Junr.	

Two other Gentlemen were appointed magistrates by this Commission, but who are since dead.

Notes

PREFACE

1. Ware, *George Gauld,* 148.
2. "Sailing Directions," MDHO, OD 505.
3. Davies and Brunt, "Scientific Studies," 2.
4. Fewkes, "Prehistoric Island Culture Area," 49–281.
5. Lowe, "Birds of the Cayman Islands"; Bangs, "Collection of Birds"; Savage English, "Birds of Grand Cayman"; Davis, "Cicadas"; Fisher, "New Species of Cerambycidae"; Hale Carpenter and Lewis, "Collection of Lepidoptera"; Blackwelder, "Staphylinid Beetles"; Grant, "Herpetology"; Lewis, "Marine Turtle"; Carr, *Windward Road;* Pilsbry, "Land Mollusca"; Pilsbry, "Land Mollusks of Cayman Brac"; Salisbury, "Mollusca"; Abbott, *Marine Mollusks.*
6. Mately, "Geology"; Doran, "Land Forms."
7. Billmyer, "Cayman Islands"; Doran, "Physical and Cultural Geography."
8. Davies, "Mosquitoes," 357.
9. Wickstead, *Natural Resources Study.*
10. Stoddart and Giglioli, "Geography and Ecology."
11. Davies and Brunt, "Scientific Studies," table 1.1, 10.
12. Davies, "Bibliography."
13. Brunt and Davies, *Natural History and Biogeography.*
14. Hirst, *Notes;* Williams, *History;* Bingner, *Brief History;* Elder and Elder, *Thesis on Cayman.*
15. Hannerz, *Caymanian Politics;* Goldberg, "East End."

CHAPTER 1. THE CAYMAN ISLANDS PROJECT

1. Roger C. Smith, "Cayman Islands Survey, 1980."
2. Roger C. Smith, "Cayman Islands."
3. Roger C. Smith, "Cayman Islands Survey."
4. KC Smith, "The Treasure They Seek Is Cayman's History."
5. Graves, "History Beneath the Waves."
6. Roger C. Smith, "Archaeology of the Cayman Islands," 22.
7. KC Smith, "Shipwrecks and Documents."

CHAPTER 2. FOUNDED UPON THE SEAS

1. Brunt et al., "Pleistocene Rocks."
2. Mately, "Geology," 385; Folk, Roberts, and Moore, "Black Phytokarst from Hell."
3. Stoddart and Giglioli, "Geography and Ecology."
4. Rigby and Roberts, "Geology, Reefs, and Marine Communities."
5. Grant, "Herpetology," 5.
6. Hirst, *Notes*, 30.
7. Captain William Jackson, "Brief Journall," 24.
8. Morgan and Patton, "Occurrence of Crocodylus."
9. Barnett, "Cayman on the Map," 50.
10. Captain William Jackson, "Brief Journall"; "Sir Thomas Lynch to Joseph Williamson," January 27, 1672, *Calendar of State Papers,* vol. 7, 322.
11. Sloane, *Voyage,* vol. 1, 342; Long, *History of Jamaica,* vol. 1, 309.
12. Keeler, *Drake's West Indian Voyage,* 113.
13. Scott, *The Pirate,* 188.
14. Whistler, "Henry Whistler's Diary," 338–46.
15. "Col. Edward D'Oyley to Commissioners of the Admiralty," April 13, 1661, *Calendar of State Papers,* vol. 5, 23.
16. Dampier, *Dampier's Voyages,* vol. 2, 133–34.
17. Ware, *George Gauld,* 148.
18. "Gage to War Office," PRO, CO 5/233.
19. "Log of HMS *Adventure,*" PRO, ADM 51/52.
20. Hirst, *Notes,* 24.
21. Huntress, *Shipwrecks and Disasters,* 53–54.
22. Hirst, *Notes,* 109.
23. "Log of HMS *Jamaica,*" PRO, ADM 51/4225.
24. "Court Martial of Captain Francis Knighton," PRO, ADM 1/5271.
25. Burton, "Climate and Tides," 58, 60.
26. Hirst, *Notes,* 177.
27. Ibid., 278.
28. Ibid., 280.
29. McLaughlin, *The '32 Storm,* 177.
30. Williams, *History,* 73–74.
31. McLaughlin, *The '32 Storm,* 15–48, 149–78.

32. Captain Ashlan Foster, personal communication, 1980.
33. Captain Callen Ritch, personal communication, 1980.
34. Ibid.; McLaughlin, *The '32 Storm,* 71–78, 169.
35. Kohlman, *Wotcha Say,* 20.
36. Ibid., 21.
37. "Presbyterian Church and Grand Cayman 1846–1946," quoted in Doran, "Physical and Cultural Geography," 243.

CHAPTER 3. SHOAL OF SEA TURTLES

1. Morison, *Journals . . . of Christopher Columbus,* 353.
2. Anghiera, *Historie,* 21.
3. Gudger, "Sucking Fish," 289–311, 446–67, 515, 525.
4. Parsons, *Green Turtle and Man,* 85.
5. Considine and Winberry, "Green Sea Turtle," 52.
6. Parsons, *Green Turtle and Man,* 6; Lewis, "Marine Turtle," 56–65.
7. Considine and Winberry, "Green Sea Turtle," 52.
8. Ibid.
9. Carr, *So Excellent A Fishe,* 160–207, 269.
10. Long, *History of Jamaica,* vol. 1, 311.
11. Dampier, *Dampier's Voyages,* vol. 1, 113.
12. Long, *History of Jamaica,* vol. 1, 62.
13. Fernández de Oviedo y Valdes, *Historia General y Natural,* 231.
14. Purchas, *Hakluytus Posthumus,* vol. 19, 191–92.
15. Hughes, "Notes."
16. Willis, "Archeology of 16th-Century Nueva Cadiz."
17. Laet, *West-Indische Compagnie,* vol. 1, 40–41.
18. Gage, *New Survey,* 26.
19. Purchas, *Hakluytus Posthumus,* vol. 19, 24–25.
20. Dampier, *Dampier's Voyages,* vol. 2, 399.
21. Bigges, *Drake's West Indian Voyage,* map facing p. 28.
22. Andrews, *English Privateering Voyages,* 214.
23. Oldmixon, *British Empire in America,* vol. 2, 406–7.
24. Laet, *West-Indische Compagnie,* vol. 1, 42.
25. Ibid., vol. 2, 125–26.
26. Ibid., 27.
27. Ibid., 169–70.
28. Ibid.
29. Haring, *Buccaneers in the West Indies,* 83.
30. Esquemeling, *Buccaneers of America,* 61–62; Rochefort, *Histoire Naturelle et morale,* 224.
31. "Declaraciones hechas por los franceses," AGI, Indiferente General 2542.
32. Captain William Jackson, "Brief Journall," 24.
33. Battick, "Rooth's Sea Journal," 20.
34. *Calendar of State Papers, 1574–1733,* vol. 9, 595.

35. Osbourne and Taylor, "D'Oyley's Journal," 71.
36. Ibid., 80.
37. Ibid., 83–87.
38. *Calendar of State Papers*, vol. 9, 119; addenda, 290.
39. "Instructions for Thomas Windsor," PRO, CO 308/1.
40. *Calendar of State Papers*, vol. 11, 721.
41. Gardiner, *History of Jamaica*, 510.
42. Parsons, *Green Turtle and Man*, 11.
43. Oldmixon, *British Empire in America*, vol. 2, 407–8.
44. Dampier, *Dampier's Voyages*, vol. 1, 399.
45. Ibid.
46. Parsons, *Green Turtle and Man*, 23.
47. Squier, *Waikna*, 54.
48. "Sharpe . . . to Duke of Newcastle," PRO, CO 137/48.
49. Long, *History of Jamaica*, vol. 1, 312.
50. Doran, "Physical and Cultural Geography," 346.
51. Aguilar and Saunders, *Postal History*, 11.
52. Doran, "Physical and Cultural Geography," 344.
53. Duncan, "Capturing Giant Turtles," 183; Langley, "Capturing Green Turtles," 62.
54. Matthiessen, *Far Tortuga*, 206–7.
55. Ibid., 300.
56. Vaquero, *Life and Adventure*, 19.
57. Hirst, *Notes*, 274.
58. Carr, *Windward Road*, 232–35.
59. Hirst, *Notes*, 274.
60. Goldberg, "East End," 108–10.
61. Hirst, *Notes*, 251.
62. Lee Jervis, personal communication, May 1980.
63. Hirst, *Notes*, 276.
64. England, "Grand Cayman," 17.
65. Henry Watson, personal communication, May 1980.
66. McLaughlin, *The '32 Storm*, 50–51.
67. Hirst, *Notes*, 270.
68. Hannerz, *Caymanian Politics*, 41.
69. Rebel, *Turtle Fishery*, 122–23.
70. Doran, "Physical and Cultural Geography," 359.
71. Williams, *History*, 88; Considine and Winberry, "Green Sea Turtle," 53.
72. S. O. "Bertie" Ebanks, *Cayman Emerges*, 16–17.
73. Fosdick and Fosdick, *Last Chance Lost?* 79–107.
74. Sefton, "Now They're Farming Turtles," 34.
75. Fosdick and Fosdick, *Last Chance Lost?* 109–24.
76. Considine and Winberry, "Green Sea Turtle," 53.

77. Walker, "Cayman Turtle Farm," 49.
78. Fosdick and Fosdick, *Last Chance Lost?* Appendix 1.
79. Walker, "Cayman Turtle Farm," 51–52.
80. Fosdick and Fosdick, *Last Chance Lost?*, 281–97.
81. Wood and Wood, "Sea Turtles," 234.

CHAPTER 4. CROCODILES AND PIRATES

1. Barrie, *Peter and Wendy*, 6–7.
2. Bigges, *Drake's West Indian Voyage*, map facing p. 28.
3. Rochefort, *Histoire naturelle et morale*, 224.
4. Captain William Jackson, "Brief Journall," 24.
5. Dampier, *Dampier's Voyages*, vol. 2, 133–34.
6. Chapman Grant, "Herpetology," 14.
7. Morgan and Patton, "Occurrence of Crocodylus."
8. Ibid.; Morgan, Franz, and Crombie, "Cuban Crocodile," 153.
9. Morgan, "Late Quaternary Fossil Vertebrates," 474–78.
10. Ibid., 476.
11. Gosse, *History of Piracy.*
12. Thornton, "Modyfords and Morgan," 53–56.
13. "Deposition of Cornelius Carstens," PRO, CO 1/25.
14. "Thomas Modyford to Lord Arlington," March 18, 1670, *Calendar of State Papers*, vol. 7, 58, 59.
15. "Deposition of Samuel Hutchinson," PRO, CO 1/25.
16. "Rivero Pardal's Reprisal Commission," PRO, CO 1/25.
17. "Deposition of Cornelius Johnson," PRO, CO 1/25.
18. "Deposition of Joan Boys," PRO, CO 1/25; "Deposition of Julian de Cobino," PRO, CO 1/25.
19. "Don Pedro de Ulloa a Su Magestad," AGI, Indiferente General 2542.
20. "Rivero Pardal's Letters," PRO, CO 1/25.
21. Avery, "Pots as Packaging."
22. "Richard Browne to Lord Arlington," PRO, CO 1/25.
23. "Governor Modyford to Lord Arlington," PRO, CO 1/25.
24. Williams, *History*, 10.
25. Hirst, *Notes*, 20.
26. Defoe, *Pyrates*, 100.
27. Ibid., 191.
28. Ibid., 271.
29. Ibid., 293.
30. Ibid., 306.
31. S. O. "Bertie" Ebanks, *Cayman Emerges*, 22.
32. Vernice Ebanks, Cayman Islands Memory Bank, 1989.
33. B. B. Grant, personal communication, May 1980.

CHAPTER 5. CATBOATS AND SCHOONERS

1. Laet, *West-Indische Compagnie*, vol. 1: 42.
2. William A. Baker, "Notes on a Shallop."
3. William A. Baker, *Sloops and Shallops*, 33.
4. Taylor, *Western Design*, 137.
5. *Calendar of State Papers*, vol. 5, 240.
6. Robinson, "Admiralty and Naval Affairs," 35.
7. Baker, *Sloops and Shallops*, 41–42.
8. Goldenberg, *Shipbuilding in Colonial America*, 39.
9. "Deposition of Samuel Hutchinson," PRO, CO 1/25.
10. "Shipps under . . . Admirall Morgan," PRO, CO 308/1.
11. "Shipps, etc., that Trade for Logwood," PRO, CO 308/1.
12. "Deposition of John Dorell, of the sloop *Blessing*," and "Deposition of Boucher Clausen, of the sloope *Hereford*," November 15, 1684, *Calendar of State Papers*, vol. 11, 724, 725.
13. "Deposition of John Greene, master of the sloop *Blessing*," "Captain Stanley, R.N., to Lieutenant-Governor Hender Molesworth," and "Deposition of Anthony Griffin, master of the sloop *Prosperous*," November 15, 1684, *Calendar of State Papers*, 1574–1733.
14. Dampier, *Dampier's Voyages*, vol. 1, 134–35.
15. Doran, "Physical and Cultural Geography," 149–50.
16. William A. Baker, *Sloops and Shallops*, 111–13.
17. Chapman, *Architectura Navalis Mercatoria*, plate 57.
18. Chapelle, *American Sailing Craft*, 171–72.
19. Sloane, *Voyage*, vol. 1, xvii.
20. Anderson, *Seventeenth Century Rigging*, 45.
21. Harrington, "Dating Stem Fragments," 63–65.
22. Davey, *Clay Tobacco Pipe*, vol. 2, 85, plate 7.
23. Green, *Vergulde Draeck*, 159, fig. 35B.
24. Morison, *Journals . . . of Christopher Columbus*, 66.
25. McKusick, "Aboriginal Canoes."
26. "Captain John Lawford to Philip Stephens, Secretary of the Admiralty," February 13, 1794, PRO, ADM 1/2059.
27. Waddell, *Twenty Nine Years*, 214.
28. Davidson, *Bay Islands*, 74–79.
29. Squier, *Waikna*, 58.
30. Young, *Mosquito Shore*, 76.
31. Captain Ashlan Foster, personal communication, May 1980.
32. Lee Jervis (son of Daniel), personal communication, May 1980.
33. McLaughlin, *The '32 Storm*, 101.
34. Burton, *Wild Trees*, index.
35. Doran, "Physical and Cultural Geography," 314.
36. Burton, *Wild Trees*, 111.

37. Ibid., 32.
38. Roger C. Smith, "Caymanian Catboat."
39. Ansel, *Whaleboat.*
40. Leshikar, *1794 Wreck of the Ten Sail,* 370.
41. Williams, *History,* 35.
42. Hirst, *Notes,* 267.
43. Captain Ashlan Foster, personal communication, May 1980.
44. Hirst, *Notes,* 267.
45. Captain Keith Tibbetts, personal communication, May 1980.
46. Ibid.
47. Burton, *Wild Trees,* 119.
48. Captain Keith Tibbetts, personal communication, May 1980.
49. Kohlman, *Under Tin Roofs,* 97; McLaughlin, *Cayman Yesterdays,* 49–51.
50. Captain Keith Tibbetts, personal communication, May 1980.
51. Williams, *History,* 77; Sayward, "Under Sail," 25.
52. Joy Baker, "*Goldfield:* The Pride of Old Cayman," 11.
53. Lee A. Ebanks, Cayman Islands Memory Bank, June 1978.
54. Kohlman, *Under Tin Roofs,* 54.
55. Webster, *Beyond the Iron Shore,* 144–47; Will Jackson, *Up from the Deep,* 48.
56. H. C. Dixon, *Cayman Brac, Land of My Birth,* 42–44.
57. Ibid., 51–52.
58. Jackson, *Up from the Deep,* 58–63.
59. Radley Gourzong, Cayman Islands Memory Bank, September 1992.
60. Lee A. Ebanks, *Lest It Be Lost,* 58.
61. Eddie Lou Dixon, Cayman Islands Memory Bank, 1978.
62. Ibid.
63. Radley Gourzong, Cayman Islands Memory Bank, September 1992.
64. Matthiessen, "To the Miskito Bank," 161.
65. Jackson, *Up from the Deep,* 63.
66. Ibid., 143.
67. Ibid., 63.
68. Kohlman, *Under Tin Roofs,* 100.
69. Jackson, *Up from the Deep,* 54; Ebanks, *Lest It Be Lost,* 56.
70. Williams, *History,* 74.
71. Jackson, *Up from the Deep,* 54.
72. Baker, "*Goldfield:* The Pride of Old Cayman," 11.
73. Ibid., 14; Jackson, *Up from the Deep,* 52–53.
74. Baker, "*Goldfield:* The Pride of Old Cayman," 11.
75. Williams, *History,* 69–70.
76. Ibid., 79; Will Jackson, *Smoke-Pot Days,* 26.
77. Jackson, *Smoke-Pot Days,* 30.
78. Jackson, *Up from the Deep,* 70.
79. Williams, *History,* 70.
80. Jackson, *Up from the Deep,* 70–71.

CHAPTER 6. A GRAVEYARD OF SHIPS

1. *Description of the Windward Passage,* 14.

2. Orbe, "Ship Course from Sanlúcar."

3. Ware, *George Gauld,* 148.

4. "Remarks of HMS *Parthian,*" MDHO, Miscellaneous Papers, vol. 47.

5. Torre, *Desde Salamanca,* 114.

6. Laet, *West-Indische Compagnie,* vol. 7, 173.

7. Johnson, *History of the Pyrates,* 294.

8. Leshikar, *1794 Wreck of the Ten Sail;* Leshikar-Denton, *Wreck of the Ten Sails* and "Ten Sail, Wreck of the."

9. College, *Ships of the Royal Navy,* vol. 1, 135.

10. Falconer, *Falconer's Marine Dictionary,* 237–38.

11. "Commodore Ford to Captain Lawford," January 5, 1794, PRO, ADM 1/5331.

12. "Captain John Lawford to Philip Stephens, Secretary of the Admiralty," February 13, 1794, PRO, ADM 1/2059.

13. "Testimony of First Lieutenant B. Bogue," PRO, ADM 1/5331.

14. See note 12 above.

15. "Court Martial of Captain John Lawford," PRO, ADM 1/5531.

16. "Testimony of Master Thomas Popplewell," PRO, ADM 1/5531.

17. Roberts, *Observations on the Gulf Passage,* 2.

18. *West India Directory,* 46.

19. Leshikar-Denton, *Wreck of the Ten Sails,* xiv; Leshikar, *1794 Wreck of the Ten Sail,* 218–31.

20. "*The Royal Gazette*: A Passenger's Account of the Disaster," in Leshikar-Denton, *Wreck of the Ten Sails,* 25–28; Leshikar, *1794 Wreck of the Ten Sail,* 206–7

21. "Captain Lawford to the Merchant Ships Off East End," PRO, ADM 1/2059.

22. "Inhabitants of the Island of Grand Camanees to Captain Lawford," PRO, ADM 1/2059.

23. "Report . . . by Edward Corbet," NLJ, MS.72, 520N.

24. "Muster Roll of HMS *Convert,*" PRO, ADM 36/11476.

25. Leshikar, *1794 Wreck of the Ten Sail,* 182, 184.

26. "Captain Lawford to His Excellancy the Governor of Havannah," PRO, ADM 1/2059.

27. Leshikar, *1794 Wreck of the Ten Sail,* 209–12.

28. Ibid., 291.

29. Ibid., 292.

30. Ibid., 31–331.

31. Hebe Foster, personal communication, 1980.

32. "Muster Roll of the 31st Regiment of Foot," PRO, WO 12/4648.

33. Waddell, *Twenty Nine Years,* 214.

34. Marshall Watler, personal communication, 1980.

35. Berg and Berg, *Tropical Shipwrecks,* 82.
36. Hudson, *Adventurer's Guide,* 140, 278–79.
37. McLaughlin, *The '32 Storm,* 132–35, 171.
38. Ibid., 171.
39. Ernest Panton, Cayman Islands Memory Bank, 1978.
40. McLaughlin, *The '32 Storm,* 105.
41. "The 'Cali' Story," parts 1 and 2.
42. Ibid., part 2.
43. Ibid., part 3.
44. "The 'Cali' Song."
45. "The Soto Trader," 67.
46. "Soto Trader explosion"; "Soto's Trader wreckage."
47. "*Kirk Pride* Sinks."
48. "Sunken Ship Found."
49. Berg and Berg, *Tropical Shipwrecks,* 75–78.
50. Ibid., 74.
51. Roger C. Smith, "Archaeology of the Cayman Islands."
52. Laet, *West-Indische Compagnie,* vol. 9, 119.
53. "Shipps under . . . Admirall Morgan," PRO, CO 308/1.
54. "Sir Thomas Lynch to John Williamson," January 27, 1672, *Calendar of State Papers,* vol. 7, 322.
55. Williams, *History,* 14.
56. *Calendar of State Papers, 1574–1733,* December 24, 1730.
57. "Governor Hunter to the Council of Trade and Plantations," December 24, 1730, *Calendar of State Papers,* vol. 37, 413.
58. "Rexistro del Bergantín San Miguel," AGI, Contratación 1326.
59. "Affidavit of Martin Admunson," PRO, CO 137/54.
60. Long, *History of Jamaica,* vol. 1, 312–13.
61. Williams, *History,* 21.
62. Waddell, *Twenty Nine Years,* 214.
63. Hughes, "Notes," 152.
64. "Humble Petition," NLJ, MS.72, 639N; *Edward Corbet's Report and Census,* 31–33.
65. Waddell, *Twenty Nine Years,* 214.
66. Ibid., 215.
67. Ibid., 216.
68. Captain Keith Tibbetts, personal communication, 1980.
69. Nolan Foster, personal communication, May 1980.
70. Marshall Watler, personal communication, 1980.
71. Ibid.
72. S. O. "Bertie" Ebanks, *Cayman Emerges,* 7.
73. Nolan Foster, personal communication, May 1980.

CONCLUSION

1. Leshikar, 1794 *Wreck of the Ten Sail;* Leshikar-Denton, "Cayman Islands," 92, and *Wreck of the Ten Sails.*
2. Leshikar-Denton, "Underwater Cultural Resource Management: A New Concept," 35.
3. Leshikar-Denton, "Cayman Islands," 92, and *Wreck of the Ten Sails.*
4. Leshikar-Denton, "Underwater Cultural Resource Management: A New Concept," 36.
5. Ibid.
6. Ibid.; Drewett, "Cayman Islands"; Stokes and Keegan, "Settlement Survey"; Drewett, "Archaeological Survey."
7. Leshikar-Denton, "Underwater Cultural Resource Management: A New Concept," 35.
8. Leshikar-Denton, "Underwater Cultural Resource Management in Mexico and the Caribbean," 60.

APPENDIX 3. THE FIRST CENSUS OF CAYMAN

1. "Edward Corbet to Governor Nugent," NLJ, MS.72, 637N; *Edward Corbet's Report and Census,* 27–28.
2. "Report . . . by Edward Corbet," NLJ, MS.72, 520N; *Edward Corbet's Report and Census,* 3–8.
3. "William Bodden to Governor Nugent," NLJ, MS.72 (unnumbered).

Bibliography

MANUSCRIPT SOURCES

Jamaica: National Library of Jamaica, Institute of Jamaica, Kingston (NLJ)

Nugent Papers (MS.72), 520N "Report on the Cayman Islands by Edward Corbet,"
June 21, 1802; 637N "Edward Corbet to Governor Nugent," May 25, 1802; 639N
"The Humble Petition of the Inhabitants of the Island of Grand Caymanas,"
1803; (unnumbered) "William Bodden to Governor Nugent," July 24, 1805.

Great Britain: Ministry of Defence, Hydrography Office, Taunton (MDHO)

OD 505, "Sailing Directions for the Lesser Cayman Islands," Lieutenant Alfred
Carpenter, 1880.
S 126, "Letter of Proceedings, HMS *Sparrowhawk*," July 7, 1880.
S 105, "Reporting Proceedings, HMS *Sparrowhawk*," July 4, 1881.
Miscellaneous Papers, vol. 42, "Remarks of HMS *Sybille*," 1818; "Remarks of HMS
Tamar," 1819–20; "Remarks of HMS *Hyperion*," 1882–83.
Miscellaneous Papers, vol. 47, "Remarks of HMS *Parthian*," 1820.

Great Britain: Public Record Office, Kew (PRO)

ADM 1/2059, "Captain John Lawford's Letters," 1794–95.
ADM 1/5271, "Court Martial of Captain Francis Knighton of His Majesty's Sloop
Jamaica," March 10, 1716.

ADM 1/5331, "Court Martial of Captain John Lawford, the Officers and Company of the *Convert*," April 1, 1794.

ADM 36/11476, "Muster Roll of HMS *Convert*," 1793–94.

ADM 51/52, "Log of HMS *Adventure*," January 13–31, 1768.

ADM 51/4225, "Log of HMS *Jamaica*," September 23–October 15, 1715.

CO 1/25, "Deposition of Cornelius Carstens, Purser of ye Shipp Mary and Jane," March 21, 1669; "Deposition of Mr. Lane," April 30, 1670; "Deposition of Edward Attenbury," June 16, 1670; "Manuel Rivero Pardal's Reprisal Commission," June 16, 1670; "Manuel Rivero Pardal's Letters"; "Deposition of Cornelius Johnson," June 5, 1670; "Deposition of Samuel Hutchinson," June 16, 1670; "Deposition of Julian de Cobino," June 20, 1670; "Deposition of Joan Boys," June 22, 1670; "Richard Browne to Lord Arlington," December 12, 1670; "Governor Modyford to Lord Arlington," March 15, 1670.

CO 5/233, "Major General Thomas Gage to War Office," January 30, 1768.

CO 37/10, "Lieutenant Governor Hope to Council of Trade and Plantations," February 21, 1723.

CO 137/48, "Memorial of John Sharpe on behalf of the inhabitants of Jamaica and merchants trading there, to Duke of Newcastle," November 13, 1738.

CO 137/54, "Governor Hunter to Duke of Newcastle," January 18, 1730; Affidavit of Martin Admunson," January 18, 1730.

CO 308/1, "Instructions for Thomas Windsor, Lord Windsor, Governor of our Island of Jamaica," April 1662; "Copy of a Commission of Warre . . . , Being a Translation of the Originall in Spanish," February 5, 1670; "Copy of an Order of Sir Thomas Modyford and Councill declaring Warre against the Spaniards in the West Indies," June 29, 1670; "Captaine Manuell Riveros Challenge"; "A List of the Shipps under the Command of Admirall Morgan"; "A List of what Shipps and Vessells have arrived in Port Royal Harbour . . . 1st of January 1668 untill the 1st of January 1670"; "A List of Shipps etc., that Trade for Logwood at Campechy and belong to this Harbour of Port Royal in Jamaica," March 4, 1670.

Interregnum, Entry Book, vol. 105, "Warrent for Robt. Thompson and Francis Willoughby . . . ," August 5, 1656.

WO 12/4648, "Muster Roll of the 31st Regiment of Foot," 1765–68.

Spain: Archivo General de Indias, Seville (AGI)

Contratación 1326, "Rexistro del Bergantín San Miguel," 1730.

Indiferente General 1611, "Relación de las pérdidas que los ingleses han padecidos a manos de Españoles en Indias Occidentales," Cartagena, June 25, 1671.

Indiferente General 2541, "El Virrey de Nueva España al Rey," México, June 14, 1669.

Indiferente General 2542, "Testimonio de las declaraciones hechas por los franceses que se aprehendieron en la embarcación . . . ," Cartagena, April 24, 1670.

Indiferente General 2542, "El Gobierno Don Pedro de Ulloa a Su Magestad," Cartagena, April 24, 1670.

PRINTED SOURCES

Abbott, Robert Tucker. *The Marine Mollusks of Grand Cayman Island, British West Indies*. Philadelphia: Academy of Natural Sciences of Philadelphia, 1958.

Aguilar, E. F., and P. T. Saunders, *The Cayman Islands: Their Postal History, Postage Stamps and Post Marks*. George Town, 1962.

Alcedo, Antonio de. *Diccionario Geográfico de las Indias Occidentales o América*. 5 vols. 1786–89. Reprint, Madrid: Real Academia Española, 1967.

Anderson, R. C. *Seventeenth Century Rigging*. Hemel Hempstead: Model and Allied Publications, 1955.

Andrews, Kenneth R., ed. *English Privateering Voyages to the West Indies, 1588–1595*. Hakluyt Society Publications, 2d series, no. 111. Cambridge, 1959.

Anghiera, Pietro Martire. *The Historie of the West Indies, containing the Acts & Adventures of the Spaniards. . . .* Translated by M. Lok, Ghent. London, 1622.

Ansel, Willits D. *The Whaleboat: A Study of Design, Construction and Use from 1850 to 1970*. Mystic, Conn.: Mystic Seaport Museum, 1978.

Askew, R. F. "The Butterfly (Lepidoptera, Rhopalocera) Fauna of the Cayman Islands." *Atoll Research Bulletin* 30 (1980): 1–7.

Avery, George. "Pots As Packaging: The Spanish Olive Jar and Andalusian Transatlantic Commercial Activity, 16th–18th Centuries." Ph.D. dissertation, University of Florida, 1997.

Baker, Joy. "*Goldfield*: The Pride of Old Cayman." *Nor'wester*, April 1983: 8–17.

Baker, William A. "Notes on a Shallop." *American Neptune* 17 (1957): 105–13.

———. *Sloops and Shallops*. Barre, Mass.: Barre Publishing Company, 1966.

Bangs, Outram. "A Collection of Birds from the Cayman Islands." *Bulletin of the Museum of Comparative Zoology* 60, no. 7 (1916): 303–20.

Barnett, Curtis. "Cayman on the Map." *Nor'wester* (March 1978): 48–52.

Barrie, Sir James Matthew, *Peter and Wendy*. London, 1906. Reprint, New York: Charles Scribner's Sons, 1940.

Battick, John F. "Richard Rooth's Sea Journal of the Western Design, 1654–1655." *Jamaica Journal* 5:4 (December 1971): 3–22.

Berg, Daniel, and Denise Berg. *Tropical Shipwrecks: A Vacationing Diver's Guide to the Bahamas and Caribbean*. East Rockaway, N.Y.: Aqua Explorers, 1989.

Bigges, Walter. *Sir Frances Drake's West Indian Voyage*. London, 1589. Facsimile edition, Amsterdam: Da Capo Press, 1969.

Billmyer, James H. S. "The Cayman Islands." *Geographical Review* 35 (January 1946): 29–43.

Bingner, Alice Grant. *A Brief History of the Cayman Islands: A Unique Community "Founded Upon the Seas."* N.p.: privately printed, 1982.

Blackwelder, Richard E. "The Staphylinid Beetles of the Cayman Islands." *Proceedings of the United States National Museum* 97, no. 3213 (1947): 117–23.

Brunt, M. A., and J. E. Davies, eds. *The Cayman Islands: Natural History and Biogeography*. Dordrecht: Kluwer Academic Publishers, 1994.

Brunt, M. A., M. E. C. Giglioli, J. D. Mathes, D. J. W. Piper, and H. G. Richard.

"The Pleistocene Rocks of the Cayman Islands." *Geological Magazine* 110 (1973): 209–22.

Burton, F. J. "Climate and Tides of the Cayman Islands." In *The Cayman Islands: Natural History and Biogeography,* edited by M. A. Brunt and J. E. Davies, 51–60. Dordrecht: Kluwer Academic Publishers, 1994.

———. *Wild Trees in the Cayman Islands.* George Town: National Trust of the Cayman Islands, 1997.

"The 'Cali' Song." *Caymanian Weekly* (George Town), December 7, 1966, 4.

"The 'Cali' Story." Parts 1–3. *Caymanian Weekly* (George Town), November 2, 1966, 9; November 9, 1966, 9; November 16, 1966, 6.

Carr, Archie. *The Windward Road: Adventures of a Naturalist on Remote Caribbean Shores.* Gainesville: University Presses of Florida, 1956. Reprint, 1979.

———. *So Excellent A Fishe: The Classic Study of the Lives of Sea Turtles.* New York: Charles Scribner's Sons, 1967. Reprint, 1984.

Chapelle, Howard I. *American Sailing Craft.* New York: Bonanza Books, 1936.

Chapman, Frederick Henrick. *Architectura Navalis Mercatoria.* Stockholm, 1798. Reprint, London: Adlard Coles, 1975.

College, John. *Ships of the Royal Navy: An Historical Index.* 2 vols. New York: A. M. Kelley, 1969.

Considine, James L., and John J. Winberry. "The Green Sea Turtle of the Cayman Islands." *Oceanus* 21, no. 3 (1978): 50–55.

Daily Gleaner (Kingston, Jamaica), February 6, 1968, 8.

Dampier, Capt. William. *Dampier's Voyages 1679–1701.* 2 vols. Edited by John Masefield. London: E. Grant Richards, 1906.

Davey, Peter. *The Archaeology of the Clay Tobacco Pipe.* Vol. 2. British Archaeological Reports, International Series, no. 60. Oxford, 1969.

Davidson, William V. *Historical Geography of the Bay Islands, Honduras: Anglo-Hispanic Conflict in the Western Caribbean.* Birmingham, Ala.: Southern University Press, 1974.

Davies, J. E. "Bibliography of the Cayman Islands." In *The Cayman Islands: Natural History and Biogeography,* edited by M. A. Brunt and J. E. Davies, 543–56. Dordrecht: Kluwer Academic Publishers, 1994.

———. "Mosquitoes of the Cayman Islands." In *The Cayman Islands: Natural History and Biogeography,* edited by M. A. Brunt and J. E. Davies, 357–76. Dordrecht: Kluwer Academic Publishers, 1994.

Davies, J. E., and M. A. Brunt. "Scientific Studies in the Cayman Islands." In *The Cayman Islands: Natural History and Biogeography,* edited by M. Λ. Brunt and J. E. Davies, 1–12. Dordrecht: Kluwer Academic Publishers, 1994.

Davis, William T. "Cicadas Collected in the Cayman Islands by the Oxford University Biological Expedition of 1938." *Journal of the New York Entomological Society* 47, no. 3 (September 1939): 207–13.

Defoe, Daniel. *A General History of the Robberies and Murders of the Most Notorious Pyrates.* London, 1724. Facsimile edition, New York: Garland Publishing, 1972.

A Description of the Windward Passage. London, 1720.

Dixon, Reverend H. C. *Cayman Brac, Land of My Birth*. New York: Shining Light Survey, n.d.

Doran, Edwin B. "A Physical and Cultural Geography of the Cayman Islands." Ph.D. dissertation, University of California, Berkeley, 1953.

———. "Land Forms of Grand Cayman Island, British West Indies." *Texas Journal of Science* 6, no. 4 (December 1954): 360–77.

Drewett, P. L. "The Cayman Islands: Their Potential in Prehistoric Research." University College London Institute of Archaeology Report, London, 1992.

———. "An Archaeological Survey of Cayman Brac and Little Cayman, Together with a Test Excavation in Great Cave, Cayman Brac, 1995." University College London Institute of Archaeology Report, London, 1996.

Duncan, David D. "Capturing Giant Turtles in the Caribbean." *National Geographic* 84 (August 1943): 177–90.

———. *Yankee Nomad: A Photographic Odyssey*. New York: Holt, Rinehart and Winston, 1966.

Ebanks, Lee A. *Lest It Be Lost: Eighty Years in the Life of a Caymanian*. George Town: privately published, 1985.

Ebanks, S. O. "Bertie." *Cayman Emerges: A Human History of Long Ago Cayman*. George Town: Northwester Company, 1983.

Edward Corbet's Report and Census of 1802 on the Cayman Islands. Our Islands' Past, vol. 1. George Town: Cayman Islands National Archive and Cayman Free Press, 1992.

Elder, Thomas C., and Ann R. Elder. *A Thesis on Cayman*. Hamilton, Ind.: privately published, 1975.

England, George A. "Grand Cayman." *Saturday Evening Post* 201, no. 3 (July 21, 1928).

Esquemeling, John. *The Buccaneers of America*. 1681. Reprint, New York: Dover Publications, 1967.

Falconer, William. *Falconer's Marine Dictionary*. 1780. Reprint, New York: A. M. Kelley, 1970.

Fernández de Oviedo y Valdes, Gonzalo. *Historia General y Natural de las Indias Occidentales*. Translated by Richard Eden. In *The First Three English Books on America*, edited by Edward Arber. 1885. Reprint, New York: Kraus Reprint Company, 1971.

Fewkes, J. Walter. "Prehistoric Island Culture Area." *Annual Report of the Bureau of American Ethnology* 34 for 1912–13 (1922): 49–281.

Fisher, W. S. "Results of the Oxford University Cayman Islands Biological Expedition, 1938: Descriptions of Nine New Species of Cerambycidae (Col)." *The Entomologist's Monthly Magazine* 77, no. 924 (May 1941): 108–15.

Folk, Robert L., Harry H. Roberts, and Clyde H. Moore. "Black Phytokarst from Hell, Cayman Islands, British West Indies." *Geological Society of America Bulletin* 84: 2151–2360.

Fosdick, Peggy, and Sam Fosdick. *Last Chance Lost? Can and Should Farming Save the Green Sea Turtle? The Story of Mariculture Ltd.—Cayman Turtle Farm.* York, Penn.: Irvin S. Naylor, 1994.

Gage, Thomas. *A New Survey of the West Indies, 1648.* New York: Robert M. McBride, 1929.

———. *Thomas Gage's Travels in the New World.* Edited by J. Eric Thompson. Norman: University of Oklahoma Press, 1958.

Gardiner, W. J. *A History of Jamaica.* 1873. Reprint, London: Frank Cass, 1971.

Goldberg, Richard S. "East End: A Caribbean Community Under Stress." Ph.D. dissertation, University of Texas, 1976.

Goldenberg, Joseph A. *Shipbuilding in Colonial America.* Charlottesville: University of Virginia Press, 1976.

Gosse, Philip. *The History of Piracy.* 1932. Reprint, New York: Burt Franklin, 1968.

Grant, Chapman, ed. "The Herpetology of the Cayman Islands, with an Appendix on the Cayman Islands and Marine Turtle." *Bulletin of the Institute of Jamaica,* Science Series No. 2, 1940.

Graves, Jim. "History Beneath the Waves," *Caribbean and West Indies Chronicle* 95, no. 1554 (March 1980): 24–25, 28.

Great Britain. Public Record Office. *Calendar of State Papers, Colonial Series, America, and the West Indies.* 46 vols. London: Her Majesty's Stationery Office, 1860–1994.

Green, Jeremy N. *The Loss of the Vereenigde Oostindische Compagnie Jacht Vergulde Draeck, Western Australia 1656.* British Archaeological Reports, Supplementary Series, no. 36. Oxford, 1977.

Gudger, E. W. "The Use of the Sucking Fish for Catching Fish and Turtle: Studies in Echeneis or Remora." *American Naturalist* 53 (1919): 289–311, 446–67, 515–25.

Hale Carpenter, G. D., and C. Bernard Lewis. "A Collection of Lepidoptera (Rhopalocera) from the Cayman Islands." *Annals of the Carnegie Museum,* vol. 29, article 13 (1943): 371–96.

Hannerz, Ulf. *Caymanian Politics: Structure and Style in a Changing Island Society.* Stockholm Studies in Social Anthropology, 1. Stockholm: Universitetet Socialanthropologiska Institutionen, 1974.

Haring, C. H. *Buccaneers in the West Indies in the Seventeenth Century.* 1910. Reprint, Hamden, Conn.: Archon Books, 1966.

Harrington, J. C. "Dating Stem Fragments of Seventeenth and Eighteenth Century Clay Tobacco Pipes." In *Historical Archaeology: A Guide to Substantive and Theoretical Contributions,* edited by R. L. Schuyler. Farmingdale, N.Y.: Baywood, 1978.

Hirst, George S. S. *Notes on the History of the Cayman Islands.* Kingston, Jamaica: P. A. Benjamin Manufacturing Company, 1910.

Hudson, George I. *An Adventurer's Guide to the Unspoiled Cayman Islands: The Islands Time Forgot.* Miami: Cayman Islands Information Center, 1973.

Hughes, H. B. L. "Notes on the Cayman Islands." *Jamaican Historical Review* 1, no. 2 (December 1942): 154–58.

Huntress, Keith, ed. *Narratives of Shipwrecks and Disasters, 1586–1860*. Ames: Iowa State University Press, 1974.

Jackson, Captain William. "A Brief Journall or a Succinct and True Relation of the Most Remarkable Passages Observed in that Voyage Undertaken by Captain William Jackson to the Westerne Indies or the Continent of America. Anno Domini 1642." *Camden Miscellany* (London) 13, Camden Third Series 34 (1924).

Jackson, Will. *Up from the Deep: The Beginnings of the Cayman Islands*. St. Petersburg, Florida: privately published, 1996.

———. *Smoke-Pot Days*. George Town: Cayman National Cultural Foundation, 1997.

Johnson, Captain Charles. *A General History of the Pyrates*. 1724. Reprint, Columbia: University of South Carolina Press, 1972.

Keeler, Mary. *Sir Francis Drake's West Indian Voyage, 1585–86*. London: Hakluyt Society, 1981.

"*Kirk Pride* Sinks," *Caymanian Compass* (George Town), January 15, 1976, A3.

Kohlman, Aarona Booker. *Wotcha Say: An Introduction of Colloquial Caymanian*. George Town: Cayman ArtVentures, 1978.

———. *Under Tin Roofs: Cayman in the 1920s*. George Town: Cayman Islands National Museum, 1993.

Laet, Joannes de. *Iaerlyck Verhael van de Verrichtinghen der Geoctroyeerde West-Indische Compagnie*. 13 vols. The Hague: Martinus Nijhoff, 1931–37.

Langley, William Wright, Jr. "Capturing Green Turtles Off Nicaragua." Master's thesis, School of Public Communication, Boston University, 1964.

Leshikar, Margaret E. *The 1794 Wreck of the Ten Sail, Cayman Islands, British West Indies: A Historical Study and Archaeological Survey*. Ph.D. dissertation, Texas A&M University. Ann Arbor, Mich.: University Microfilms, 1993.

Leshikar-Denton, Margaret E., ed. *The Wreck of the Ten Sails*. Our Islands' Past, vol. 2. George Town: Cayman Islands National Archive and Cayman Free Press, 1994.

———. "Underwater Cultural Resource Management in Mexico and the Caribbean." *Underwater Archaeology*, 1996: 57–60.

———. "Underwater Cultural Resource Management: A New Concept in the Cayman Islands." *Underwater Archaeology*, 1997: 33–37.

———. "Caribbean." In *Encyclopaedia of Underwater and Maritime Archaeology*, edited by James P. Delgado, 86–89. London: British Museum Press, 1997.

———. "Cayman Islands." In *Encyclopaedia of Underwater and Maritime Archaeology*, edited by James P. Delgado, 91–92. London: British Museum Press, 1997.

———. "Ten Sail, Wreck of the." In *Encyclopaedia of Underwater and Maritime Archaeology*, edited by James P. Delgado, 416. London: British Museum Press, 1997.

Lewis, C. Bernard. "The Cayman Islands and Marine Turtle." In "The Herpetology of the Cayman Islands," edited by Chapman Grant, 56–65. *Bulletin of the Institute of Jamaica*, Science Series, no. 2, 1940.

"Little Cayman Sleuths Unveiling Our History," *Cayman Times* (George Town), July 20, 1979, 10–11.

Long, Edward. *The History of Jamaica.* 3 vols. 1774. Reprint, London: Frank Cass, 1970.

Lowe, Percy R. "On the Birds of the Cayman Islands, West Indies." *Ibis,* 9th series, vol. 5 (1911): 137–61.

McKusick, Marshall B. "Aboriginal Canoes in the West Indies." *Yale University Publications in Anthropology,* no. 63 (1970).

McLaughlin, Heather R. *Cayman Yesterdays: An Album of Childhood Memories.* George Town: Cayman Islands National Archive, 1991.

———, ed. *The '32 Storm: Eyewitness Accounts and Official Reports of the Worst Natural Disaster in the History of the Cayman Islands.* George Town: Cayman Islands National Archive, 1994.

Maloney, John. "The Islands Time Forgot." *Saturday Evening Post* 222, no. 41 (April 8, 1950).

Mately, C. A. "The Geology of the Cayman Islands (British West Indies), and Their Relation to the Bartlett Trough." *Quarterly Journal of the Geological Society of London* 82 (1926): 352–87.

Matthiessen, Peter. "A Reporter at Large: To the Miskito Bank." *New Yorker* 43 (October 28, 1967).

———. *Far Tortuga.* New York: Random House, 1975.

Millás, José C. *Hurricanes of the Caribbean and Adjacent Regions.* Miami: Academy of Arts and Sciences of the Americas, 1968.

Morgan, Gary S. "Late Quaternary Fossil Vertebrates from the Cayman Islands." In *The Cayman Islands: Natural History and Biogeography,* edited by M. A. Brunt and J. E. Davies, 465–508. Dordrecht: Kluwer Academic Publishers, 1994.

Morgan, Gary S., Richard Franz, and Ronald I. Crombie. "The Cuban Crocodile, *Crocodylus rhombifer,* from Late Quaternary Fossil Deposits on Grand Cayman." *Caribbean Journal of Science* 29, no. 3–4 (1993): 153–64.

Morgan, Gary S., and Thomas H. Patton. "On the Occurrence of Crocodylus (Reptilia, Crocodilidae) in the Cayman Islands, British West Indies." *Journal of Herpetology* 13, no. 3 (1979): 289–92.

Morison, Samuel Eliot. *Journals and Other Documents in the Life and Voyages of Christopher Columbus.* New York: Heritage Press, 1963.

National Oceanic and Atmospheric Administration (NOAA). *Tropical Cyclones of the North Atlantic Ocean, 1871–1992.* Historical Climatology Series, 6, no. 2. Asheville, N.C.: NOAA, National Weather Service, 1993.

Oldmixon, John. *The British Empire in America.* 2 vols. London, 1741.

Orbe, Juan Antonio de. "Ship Course from Sanlúcar, Spain, to San Juan de Ulúa and Back to Spain" (AGI Contratación 4890, November 22, 1712). In McDonald, David, and J. Barto Arnold, *Documentary Sources for the Wrecks of the New Spain Fleet of 1554,* 309–10. Austin: Texas Antiquities Committee, 1979.

Osbourne, Francis J., and S. A. G. Taylor. "Edward D'Oyley's Journal, Part One." *Jamaican Historical Review* 10 (1973): 33–112.

Parsons, James J. *The Green Turtle and Man.* Gainesville: University of Florida Press, 1962.

Pilsbry, Henry A. "Land Mollusca of the Cayman Islands Collected by the Oxford University Biological Expedition, 1938." *Nautilus* 56, no. 1 (July 1942): 1–9.

———. "Land Mollusks of Cayman Brac." *Nautilus* 63, no. 2 (October 1949): 37–48.

Purchas, Samuel, ed. *Hakluytus Posthumus or Purchas His Pilgrims.* 20 vols. Glasgow, 1905–19.

Rebel, Thomas B. *Sea Turtles and the Turtle Fishery of the West Indies, Florida and the Gulf of Mexico.* Coral Gables: University of Miami Press, 1974.

Rigby, J. Keith, and Harry H. Roberts. "Geology, Reefs, and Marine Communities of Grand Cayman Islands, British West Indies." Brigham Young University Special Publication no. 4. Provo, Utah: Brigham Young University Department of Geology, 1976.

Roberts, Charles. *Observations on the Gulf Passage, or the Passage from Jamaica Through the Gulf of Florida by the Grand Cayman and Cape St. Antonio; and on the Bahama Islands.* London: W. Faden, 1795.

Robinson, Gregory. "Admiralty and Naval Affairs, May 1660 to March 1674." *Mariner's Mirror* 36 (1950): 11–40.

Rochefort, Charles de. *Histoire naturelle et morale des îles Antilles de l'Amérique.* Lyon: Christofle Fourney, 1667.

Salisbury, A. E. "Mollusca of the University of Oxford Expedition to the Cayman Islands in 1938." *Proceedings of the Malacological Society of London* 30 (May 1953): 39–54.

Sauer, Jonathan D. "Cayman Islands Seashore Vegetation." University of California Publications in Geography, no. 25 (November 1982). Berkeley and Los Angeles: University of California Press.

Savage English, T. M. "Notes on Some of the Birds of Grand Cayman, West Indies." *Ibis,* 10th series, vol. 4 (1916): 17–35.

Sayward, Gilbert. "Under Sail to Grand Cayman, Part Two: The Regatta." *Motor Boating,* June 1939: 23–25, 110.

Scott, Sir Walter. *The Pirate.* Waverly Novels, vol. 25. Edinburgh, 1902.

Sefton, Nancy. "Now They're Farming Turtles." *Oceans* 7, no. 5 (1974): 34–35.

———. "Seafarers of the Caymans." *Sea Frontiers* 35, no. 2 (March–April 1989): 106–13.

Sloane, Sir Hans. *A Voyage to the Islands of Madeira, Barbados . . . and Jamaica with a Natural History. . . .* 2 vols. London: British Museum (private printing), 1707.

Smith, KC. "The Treasure They Seek Is Cayman's History," *Nor'wester* 8, no. 10 (September 1979), 14–17.

———. "Shipwrecks and Documents Tell Cayman's History," *Nor'wester* 9, no. 4 (March 1980), 39–44.

Smith, Roger C. "Cayman Islands." *INA Newsletter* 6, no. 3 (fall 1979): 10–11.

———. "Cayman Islands Survey." *International Journal of Nautical Archaeology* 9, no. 1 (1980): 85–86.

————. "Cayman Islands Survey, 1980." *INA Newsletter* 8, no. 1 (spring 1981): 1–2, 4–7.

————. "Archaeology of the Cayman Islands." *Archaeology* 36, no. 3 (September–October 1983): 16–24.

————. "The Maritime Geography of the Cayman Islands." *Caribbean Geography* 1, no. 4 (November 1984): 247–54.

————. "The Caymanian Catboat: A West Indian Maritime Legacy." *World Archaeology* 16, no. 3 (1985): 329–36.

"The Soto Trader," *Northwester* 4, no. 5 (May 1975): 67–69.

"Soto Trader explosion that killed two under police investigation," *Caymanian Compass* (George Town), April 6, 1976, A1–2.

"Soto Trader wreckage seen on the ocean bed," *Caymanian Compass* (George Town), April 15, 1976, A1.

Squier, Ephraim George. *Waikna or, Adventures on the Mosquito Shore.* 1895. Reprint, Gainesville: University of Florida Press, 1965.

Stoddart, D. R., and M. E. C. Giglioli, eds. "Geography and Ecology of Little Cayman." *Atoll Research Bulletin* 241 (1980): 1–181.

Stokes, A. V., and W. F. Keegan. "A Settlement Survey for Prehistoric Archaeological Sites on Grand Cayman." Florida Museum of Natural History, Department of Anthropology Miscellaneous Project Report no. 52. Gainesville, 1993.

"Sunken Ship Found." *Caymanian Compass* (George Town), November 26, 1985, A1.

Tannehill, Ivan R. *Hurricanes, Their Nature and History, Particularly Those of the West Indies and the Southern Coasts of the United States.* Princeton: Princeton University Press, 1944.

Taylor, S. A. G. *The Western Design: An Account of Cromwell's Expedition to the Caribbean.* Kingston: Institute of Jamaica, 1965.

Thompson, Ernest F. "The Fisheries of the Cayman Islands." *Development and Welfare of the West Indies* (Bridgetown), no. 23 (1946).

Thornton, H. P. "The Modyfords and Morgan." *Jamaican Historical Review* 2, no. 2 (October 1952): 36–60.

Torre, Tomás de la. *Desde Salamanca, España, hasta Ciudad Real, Chiapas: Diario del viaje 1544–1545.* Edited by Franz Blom. Mexico City: Editorial Central, 1945.

Vaquero [pseud]. *Life and Adventure in the West Indies.* London: John Bale, Sons and Danielsson, 1914.

Waddell, Reverend Hope M. *Twenty Nine Years in the West Indies and Central Africa: A Review of Missionary Work and Adventures 1829–1858.* 1863. Reprint, London: Frank Cass, 1970.

Walker, Tom A. "The Cayman Turtle Farm." *Aquaculture Magazine* 18, no. 2 (March–April 1992): 47–55.

Ware, John D. *George Gauld, Surveyor and Cartographer of the Gulf Coast.* Gainesville: University Presses of Florida, 1982.

Webster, Bonnie-Lee E. *Beyond the Iron Shore.* George Town: privately printed, 1991.

West India Directory. London: J. W. Norie, 1827.

Whistler, Henry. "Henry Whistler's Diary for the Year 1655," *Journal of the Institute of Jamaica* 1 (1893): 338–46.

Wickstead, J. H., ed. *Cayman Islands Natural Resources Study.* 6 vols. London: Ministry of Overseas Development, 1976.

Williams, Neville. *A History of the Cayman Islands.* 1970. Reprint, George Town: Government of the Cayman Islands, 1992.

Willis, Raymond F. "The Archeology of 16th Century Nueva Cádiz." Master's thesis, University of Florida, 1976.

Wood, F. E., and J. R. Wood. "Sea Turtles of the Cayman Islands." In *The Cayman Islands: Natural History and Biogeography,* edited by M. A. Brunt and J. E. Davies, 229–36. Dordrecht: Kluwer Academic Publishers, 1994.

Young, Thomas. *Narrative of a Residence on the Mosquito Shore: With an Account of Truxillo, and the Adjacent Islands of Bonacca and Roatan; and a Vocabulary of the Mosquitian Language.* London, 1847. Reprint, New York: Kraus Reprint Company, 1971.

ORAL SOURCES

Dixon, Eddie Lou. Resident of Cayman Brac. Interviewed by Doren Miller, Radio Cayman broadcast, Cayman Islands Memory Bank, 1978.

Ebanks, Lee A. Resident of West Bay, Grand Cayman. Interviewed by Grace Wright, Cayman Islands Memory Bank, June 17, 1978.

Ebanks, Vernice. Resident of Newlands, Grand Cayman. Interviewed by Ethel Jackson, Cayman Islands Memory Bank, August 28, 1989.

Foster, Captain Ashlan. Resident of Stake Bay, Cayman Brac. Personal communication, May 1980.

Foster, Hebe. Resident of the Rock, Cayman Brac. Personal communication, May 1980.

Foster, Nolan. Resident of the Point, Cayman Brac. Personal communication, May 1980.

Gourzong, Radley. Resident of Grand Cayman. Interviewed by Heather McLaughlin, Cayman Islands Memory Bank, September 29, 1992.

Grant, B. B. Resident of Cayman Brac. Personal communication, May 1980.

Jervis, Lee. Resident of Bamboo Bay, Cayman Brac. Personal communication, May 1980.

Panton, Ernest. Resident of Grand Cayman. Interviewed by Doren Miller, Radio Cayman broadcast, Cayman Islands Memory Bank, 1978.

Ritch, Captain Callen. Resident of Cayman Brac. Personal communication, May 1980.

Tibbetts, Captain Keith. Resident of the Watering Place, Cayman Brac. Personal communication, June 1980.

Watler, Marshall. Resident of Gun Bay, Grand Cayman. Personal communication, July 1980.

Watson, Henry. Resident of the Watering Place, Cayman Brac. Personal communication, May 1980.

Index

Italicized page numbers refer to illustrations.

Abandoned Wreck Law, 17, 182
Adams, Bob, 11, *159*
Adams, Charles, 4
Africa, 57, 105. *See also* Royal African
   Company
agouti, 83
Algemeen Rijksarchief, 10
alligators, 26, 61, 86, 87, 187
aloe, 186
American Revolutionary War, 191
Amsterdam, 10
Anchor's Point (Grand Cayman), 48
Anchorage Bay (Little Cayman), 29, 47
anchorages, 22, 28, 29, 30, 31, 34, 35, 37,
   42, 46, 48, 166, 167, 186, 190
anchors, 6, 8, 9, 14, *15*, 30, 114, 118, 131,
   136, 137, 141, 162, 171, 175, 176, *179*.
   See also tackle, marine
Anstis, Thomas, 105, 106
Antilles, Greater, 88, 148; Lesser, 148
Arch, H. E., 153
Arch, James, 140
Archer, Lt., 35
archaeological sites, xvii, 7, 16, 17, 39,
   48, 49, 95–100, 140–43, 158–61. *See*

also shipwrecks; Wreck of the Ten
   Sail
architecture, marine. *See* marine architecture
Archivo General de Indias, 10, 11, 170
Arlington, Lord, 91
artifacts, 4, 8, 17, 35, 36, 39, 143, 159,
   179, 182; ammunition, 8, 96, 100, 159,
   161; animal bones, 39, 49, 57, 95, 100,
   117, 118, 120, 141, 142; ballast stones,
   14, 39, 41, 49, 95, 98, 116, 117, 118, 140,
   159, 168, 171, 175; barrel hoops, 98,
   118; bottle glass, 30, 39, 141, 142, 159,
   159, 161; buttons, 30; ceramics, 8, 29,
   39, 95, 118, 120, 141, 142, 175; ceramics,
   English, 16, 142, 159, 160, 161; ceramics, French, 16; ceramics, Spanish olive jars, 4, 16, 17, 98, 100, *101*, 118, 171;
   matchlock musket, 98, *99*, 100; ships'
   fittings, 8, 14, 39, 40, 95, 140, 141, 142,
   159, 161, 168, 175; slow match, 96, *97*, ;
   stingray spine, *41*; thimble, 96, *97*; tobacco pipes, 8, *16*, 30, 95, 96, 118, 120,
   159. *See also* anchors; cannons;
   tackle, marine

Ascension Island, 81
Atlantic Ocean, 148
Atlantis Submersibles, Ltd., 168
Australia, 54, 120
Austria, 152

Bahamas, 27, 29, 57
Balcarres, Lord, 190, 196
Ball State University, 181
bananas, 140, 146, 186
Banks, Capt. James, 88
Barbados, 46, 87, 90
Barcelona, 111
Barnes, Joseph, 187
Barranquilla, 144
Barrie, James M., 84
Bartlett Deep, 19
Bass, Dr. George F., 3, 4
Bath Town, 105
Battle of Bloody Bay, 30
bauxite, 163
Bay Islands, 121, 144, 190
beaches, 3, 18, 20, 26, 29, 33, 47, 48, 57,
    86, 111, 131, 133, 138, 155, 160, 168, 187;
    turtle nesting, 22, 31, 33, 53, 55, 57, 59,
    60, 65, 80, 81, 82, 113, 121,
Beetle, Charles, 128
Bermuda, 57, 65, 106
Bernard, Capt., 91
Bight, The (Cayman Brac), 29
birds, xvi, 2, 20, 35, 60, 79, 83, 136; eggs,
    79
Blackbeard. See Teach, Edward
Blathwayt, William, 63
Bloody Bay (Little Cayman), 29, 30
Blossom Village (Little Cayman), 36, 46
Bluefields (Jamaica), 47
Bluefields (Nicaragua), 136
boats, 4, 5, 13, 49, 57, 78, 106, 109, 110–
    16, 120, 122–28, 136, 138, 166, 173. See
    also canoes; catboats; piraguas;
    schooners; shallops; sloops
Boatswains Bay (Grand Cayman), 110,
    194, 195
Bodden, Aggie, 166
Bodden, Capt. Haman, 136
Bodden, Capt. Lawrence, 164
Bodden, Capt. Rayal, 139

Bodden, Capt. Steadman, 137, 138
Bodden, Capt. Warren, 140
Bodden, Frankie and Jody, 6
Bodden, Samuel, 190
Bodden, William, 190, 191, 192
Bodden Town (Grand Cayman), 36, 37,
    190, 192, 193, 195, 196
Boeckman, Kathryn, 7, 9
Bogue, The, 48
Bonnet, Maj. Stede, 103
Bouse Bluff (Grand Cayman), 48
Bradley, George, 105
brandy, 170
Brasiliano, Rock, 90
Brayne, Lt. Gen. William, 62
breadfruit, 13
Brethren of the Coast, 103, 151. See also
    buccaneers; pirates
Bristol, 103
British Broadcasting Corporation, 1
British Central Land Company, 121
British Merchant Service, 146
British Ministry of Overseas Develop-
    ment, xvi
Brown, Surgeon, 101
buccaneers, 8, 90; origins of, 89. See also
    pirates
Byndlas, Robert, 184

Cabo Cruz, 148
Cabot, Sebastian, 26
cactus, 186
Cádiz, 170
caimans, 26, 60, 86, 87, 187
Calvo, Fray Pedro, 150
Campbell, Colin, 170
Campeche, 91, 149; Bay of, 121
Canal Point (Grand Cayman), 146
cannon carriage, 118, 158
cannons, 4, 6, 8, 34, 37, 38, 151, 158, 159,
    169, 170, 171, 176, 190. See also weap-
    ons, cannons
canoes, 93, 109, 115, 121; Caymanian,
    122, 156; dugout, 74, 115, 120. See also
    dories; piraguas; pitpans
Cardinall, Sir Allen, 131
careening, 39–42, 42, 64, 110
Careening Place (Grand Cayman), 38,

39, 40, 41, 140, 142, *143*

Caribbean Conservation Association, 182

Caribbean Sea, 1, 18, 29, 76, 83, 90, 147, 148, 177

Carolina, 106. *See also* North Carolina; South Carolina

Carpenter, Lt. Alfred, 185, 187. *See also* Appendix 2

Carr, Dr. Archie, 75

Carstens, Cornelius, 91

Cartagena, 61, 86, 94, 148

cassava, 20, 77

Cat Head Bay (Cayman Brac), 48

catboats, 122–28, *70, 71, 74, 125, 126, 127, 131, 133, 135,* 138, 164, 180; *Ajax, 126, 127,* 128; construction of, 123, 124; *Defiance, 125; Independent, 180, 181; Terror,* 122, 123. *See also* boats; equipment, marine; equipment, fishing; marine architecture; tackle, marine

caves, 9, 12, 20, 37, 47, 88, 89, 111, 172, 181

Cayman Brac, description of, 20, 59, 60; economy of, 79; map of, *21;* maritime geography of, 29; origin of name, 28; population of, 20, 186; settlement of, 77; shipbuilding on, 77, *129, 130;* shipwrecks of, 174, 175, *176,* 182. *See also* shipbuilding; shipwrecks

Cayman Energy, Ltd., 6

Cayman Islands: aboriginal populations of, xv, 12, 181, 182; agriculture in, 20, 22, 30, 31, 35, 67, 173, 174, 178, 186, 191; census of, 9, 157 (*see also* Appendix 3); coat of arms of, *52;* description of, 18, 19, 59, 60, 87, 171, 185–87; discovery of, 25, 52; early government of, 67, 171; economy of, 67, 77, 79–81; fortification of, 63, 190, 191; geography of, xvi, 28, 29, 178, 191; geology of, xvi, 19, 20; government of, 3, 4, 9, 16, 17, 36, 82, 176, 179, 182; governor of, 16, 63, 67, 171, 183, 184; history publications about, xvii; location of, 18, *19;* maps of, Cantino, Alberto, 25; maps of, Münster, 25; maps of, Porcacchi, Tomaso, 26; maps of, Ribiero, Diogo, 26; maps of, Wolfenbüttel, 26; naming of, 25–28; place names of, 47–49; population of, 22, 37, 186 (*see also* Appendix 3); sailing directions for finding, 148; seasonal settlement by English, 63; seasonal settlement by French, 60, 61; settlement from Jamaica, 66, 171; weather patterns of, 29, 35, 43. *See also* forts; shipwrecks

Cayman Islands Currency Board, 181

Cayman Islands Executive Council, 16, 182. *See also* Cayman Islands, government

Cayman Islands Memory Bank, 179, 180

Cayman Islands Ministry of Culture, 182

Cayman Islands National Archive, 180, 181

Cayman Islands National Museum, 17, 168, 176, 179, *180, 181,* 182

Cayman Islands Philatelic Bureau, 181

Cayman Islands Project, 1–17, *7, 11*

Cayman Islands Visual Arts Society, 181

Cayman National Trust, 34, 179, 180

Cayman Trench, 19

Cayman Turtle Farm, Ltd., 82

Caymanian Heritage Trust, 4, 9, 17, 176

cedar. *See* wood

cement, 2, 13, 48, 81, 166, 168

Central America, 64, 121, 140

Channel Bay (Cayman Brac), 35, 36

Charles Bay (Little Cayman), 88

Cienfuegos (Cuba), 164

clippers, Baltimore, 116

coal, 164

coconuts, 13, 22, 30, 36, 144, 186

Colliers Channel (Grand Cayman), 161

Colombia, 91, 151

Colonial Development Corporation, 81

Columbus, Christopher, 11, 25, 52, 53, 120

Columbus, Ferdinand, 52

commerce, maritime, 22, 28, 29, 34, 35, 36, 48, 64, 66, 67, 74, 76, 77, 79, 80, 82, 90, 115, 120, 128, 140, 144, 146, 163, 166, 178, 179, 186, 189, 191

Connolly, Capt. McNeil, 138

Convention on International Trade in Endangered Species, 82

Corbet, Edward, 189–91. *See also* Appendix 3
corn, 67, 177, 191
Corrientes, Cape, 153, 154
corsairs, French, 63; Spanish, 63. *See also* buccaneers; pirates; privateers
Costa Rica, 81
cotton, 69, 189, 191
Council of Jamaica, 64, 102, 170
cows, 86, 89. *See also* livestock
Crawl Bay (Cayman Brac), 48
Crawl Bay (Grand Cayman), 48
Crawl Bay (Little Cayman), 48
crocodiles 11, 26, 33, 61, 83, 84, 85, 87, 88
Cromwell, Oliver, 61, 62, 90, 191
Crow, Bill, 7
crustaceans, 22, 54, 186
Cuba, 1, 3, 26, 111; Caymanian turtlers at, 67, 76, 172, 191; crocodiles at, 26, 88, 89; English turtlers at, 63, 114, 115; en route to, 59, 151, 158, 164; governor general of, 91, 158, 172; hostilities with Caymanians, 67, 68, 191; hurricanes in, 10, 43; islands of, 29, 53, 55, 148, 170, 172, 191; mountains of, 19; navigation near, 148, 149, 153; pirates at, 106; privateers at, 101; turtles at, 54, 56, 57, 68, 128, 191; wrecking at, 186. *See also* crocodiles; wrecking
Cubagua, 57

D'Oyley, Col. Edward, 62
Dampier, William, 31, 33, 55, 58, 64, 87, 115
Darroch, Alison, 7
Denton, Dennis, 11
Deseada, 150
Dixon, Eddie Lou, 137, 138
Dixon, Elford, 180
dories, 121, 122, 127. See also canoes, dugout
Dove, William, 170
Drake, Sir Francis, 27, 58, 86
Drayton, John, 128
Driftwood Village (Grand Cayman), 111
Duck Pond (Grand Cayman), 38, 39, 41
Duck Pond Wreck, 142, *143*. *See also* Grand Cayman, shipwrecks

duppies, 16
Dutch West India Company, 10, 151
DuTertre, Jean Baptiste, 60

East End (Grand Cayman), 13, 37, 88, 137, 138, 139, 158, *163*, 173, 174, 175, 192, 195
East End Channel (Grand Cayman), 161
East End Sound (Grand Cayman), 2, 4, 5
East Sound (Little Cayman), 36
Ebanks, Anita, 179
Ebanks, Capt. Allie, 75, 76
Ebanks, Gideon, 111
Edward, Reginald, 164
Egypt, 61, 87
Engemann, Ed, 144
England, 77, 91, 95, 102, 103, 106, 113, 114, 152; Charles II, 113; en route to, 173; king of, 102, 106; queen of, 45, 161, 181; seal of, 63
English Channel, 10
equipment, fishing, floats, 69; harpoon, 57, 64, 122, 126; kelleck, 69; lead weight, 142; line, 69, 126; muntle, 126; nets, 65, 67, 70, 124, 137, 186; nets, "drop," 122; nets, "long," 69; nets, "swing," 69; nets, "trap," 78; traps, 13, 121; turtle decoys, 69, 186; water glass, 5, 74, 78, 126. *See also* rope; tackle, marine
equipment, marine: oars, 48, 69, 78, 109, 113, 114, 115, 122, 124, 126, 127, 128, 138; paddles, 124, 126; windlass, 14, 141, *165*. *See also* tackle, marine
Esquemeling, John, 60
Europe, navigation to, 148, 153
Evans, John, 109

Farrington, Capt. Charles, 144
Farrington, Rayburn, 144
Fewkes, Jesse Walter, xv, 181
fireburn (Cayman Brac), 174
fishes, 3, 5, 13, 39, 48, 53, 54, 56, 57, 74, 118, 124, 136, 137, 147. *See also* equipment, fishing; remora fish; sharks
fishermen, 4, 6, 13, 22, 29, 34, 36, 39, 47,

51, 56, 57, 66, 68–81, 95, 117, 135, 137, 156, 172, 176, 183, 184, 186. *See also* turtle, fishing; turtle, hunters
Fitzherbert, Capt. Thomas, 33
Flats, The (Little Cayman), 166
Florida, 88; Keys, 29; Straits, 148
Florida Museum of Natural History, 181
forts: Bodden Town, 36, 37, 190, 191; Fort George, 34, 190, 191; Gun Bluff, 37; Little Cayman, 30; Tortuga, 89
Foster, Ashland, 47
Foster, Lambert and Alice, 139
France, 60, 103, 152, 191
Frank Sound (Grand Cayman), 193, 195
French Revolutionary Wars, 152
frigates, 91, 95, 101, 102, 113, 153, 154, 155, 157, 158, 162, 169, 170. *See also* ships
Fryer, John, 64

Gage, Maj. Gen. Thomas, 31
Gage, Thomas, 57, 58
galleys, 64, 115
Galveston (Texas), 163
Gambia River, 107
Gauld, George, xv, 32, 37, 44, 45, 148, 149, 161
George Town (Grand Cayman), 33, 34, 35, 37, 48, 75, 111, 129, 138, 139, 144, 163, 164, 166, 168, 173, 175, 180, 190, 191, 192, 193, 194, 195, 196
George Town Barcadere, 111
Gibson, Pat, 11
Giglioli, Marco, xvi, xvii
Gijsen, Capt. Joachim, 151, 169
Gloucester (Maine), 131
Goat Island (Jamaica), 63
Goat Rock (Grand Cayman), 81
Goldfield Foundation, 144
Gracias, Cape, 136
Grand Cayman: description of, 22, 149, 150, 156; discovery of, 25; map of, 24, 32, 39, 45; population of, 37, 67, 157 (*see also* Appendix 3); settlement of, 66, 67, 190, 191; shipbuilding in, 129, 130, 139, 140, 143; shipwrecks of, 3, 10, 14, 15, 16, 31, 101, 106, 121, 140–43, 151, 152–70, 160, 161, 163, 165, 168, 173, 175, 182; warning to mariners

about, 155, 156. *See also* shipbuilding; shipwrecks
Great Lakes, 163.
green turtles. *See* turtles, green
Grizzel, "Uncle Joe," 6, 7, 8
guano, 22, 30, 79
Guinea, 106
Gulf Oil Company, 146
Gulf Stream, 148
Gun Bay (Grand Cayman), 162
Gun Bluff (Grand Cayman), 13, 37, 161, 162

Hague, The, 10
Haiti, 3, 67; hurricanes in, 10
Hands, Israel, 104
hardwood. *See* wood
Harvard University, Peabody Museum, xv
Havana, 18, 57, 58, 93, 148, 158, 169
hawksbill turtles. *See* turtles, hawksbill
Hendricksz, Adm. Boudewijn, 59
Hispaniola, 52, 61, 89, 90, 106, 148; navigation near, 152
Hodgson, Capt., 161
Hog Stye Bay (Grand Cayman), 158, 164, 167
Hogsties (Grand Cayman), 33, 37, 156, 190, 195
Holland, 10, 152, 191
Honduras, 87, 106, 146; Gulf of, 55, 104, 106, 107, 121
Hook, Capt., 84
Hornigold, Benjamin, 103
House of Commons, 106
House of Trade, 11
Hoyt, Denise, 11, 15
Hoyt, Steve, 11
Hundley, Paul, 7
hurricanes, 10, 18, 42–47, 137; Allen, 1–3, 160; David, 9; Frederick, 9; Gilbert, 43; of 1751, 44, 45; of 1838, 45, 46; of 1846, 175; of 1876, 20, 46, 138; of 1903, 46; of 1932, 46, 47, 123, 163, 164, 175. *See also* Table 2.1
Hutchinson, Samuel, 91, 183; deposition of 91, 92, 93, 183, 184. *See also* Little Cayman, attack on the turtling station

Hydrography Office, 10, 185
Hyndes, Joseph, 110

iguanas, 26, 83, 85, 87
Imperial Oil of Canada, 146
Indian Ocean, 54
Indiana University, 160
Indians, Carib, 122; Miskito, 64, 65, 66, 74, 122, 136
Institute of Jamaica (National Library), 9, 88, 192
Institute of Nautical Archaeology, xvii, 3, 5, 158, 160
International Association for Caribbean Archaeology, 182
International Congress of Maritime Museums, 182
International Council on Monuments and Sites, 182
ironshore, 7, 19, 37, 79, 130, 167, 185. See also geology; limestone
Island Record Office (Jamaica), 9
Isle of Wight, 113
Ita, Adm. Pieter, 57, 59

Jackson, Capt. Nelson, 47
Jackson, Capt. William, 26, 61, 87
Jackson, Nordell, 180
Jackson's Point (Little Cayman), 29
Jacobs, A. D., 136
Jamaica, 18, 25, 26, 31, 36, 47, 61, 64, 91, 102, 106, 109, 113, 115, 120, 136, 171, 189; English invasion of, 27, 61, 62, 90, 113; en route to, 106, 151, 166, 171; government of, 8, 9, 63, 64, 67, 93, 100; governor of, 9, 26, 27, 36, 63, 90, 102, 103, 106, 139, 170, 171, 172, 189, 190, 191, 192, 196; hurricanes in, 1, 3; islands dependent on, 63, 67, 171, 172, 173, 189, 191; land grants for Cayman Islands, 66; merchant crews recruited in, 146; navigation from, 25, 35, 59, 87, 106, 148, 149, 151, 152, 153, 155, 157, 158, 162, 163, 172, 173; navigation to, 47, 151; soldiers from, 189; Spanish raids on, 91, 93, 100, 102; sugar colony, 152; trade with, 67, 73, 79, 123, 129, 135, 139, 166, 172, 186,

187; vessels from, 114, 115, 128, 152, 170, 171, 172
James River (Virginia), 105
James, Capt., 62
Jardinella de la Reina, 53
Jervis, Daniel, 122, 123
Jervis, Lee, 127, 128
Johnson, Bradlee, 144
Jordan, James, 171

Keimanos Museum, 4
Key West, 48, 73
King, Capt. William, 58
Kingston (Jamaica), 73, 75, 90, 192
Kirkconnell brothers, 146
Kirkconnell, Louisa, 12
Knighton, Capt. Francis, 37

Labat, Pierre, 56
Laet, Johann de, 59
Lavasseur, Mons., 60, 89
Lawford, Capt. John, 153–61. See also Wreck of the Ten Sail
leatherback turtles. See turtles, leatherback
Legrand, Pierre, 90
Leshikar, Dr. Margaret, 11, 12, 160, 180
Library of Congress, U.S., 10
lighthouse, 4, 174
limestone, xvi, 19, 20, 28, 29, 117. See also geology; ironshore
line. See equipment, fishing; rope; thatch palm
Little Cayman: attack on the turtling station, 8, 11, 36, 91–94, 98, 114, 120, 121, 183, 184; description of, 20, 22, 60; geography of, 29, 30; map of, 23; museum of, 182; population of, 22, 186; shipwrecks of, 7, 8, 95, 119, 166, 167, 170, 171, 175, 179, 182. See also shipwrecks
Little North Sound (Grand Cayman), 111
Little Pedro (Grand Cayman), 195, 196
livestock, 34, 67. See also cows; pigs; poultry
Lloyd, Capt., 149
Lockyer, E., 67

loggerhead turtles. *See* turtles, logger-
head
logwood. *See* wood
Lolonois, François, 90
London, 10, 63, 67, 106, 181
Long Bay (Grand Cayman), 31, 33
Long, Edward, 26, 55, 171
looters, 170, 171
Los Alteres (Cuba), 148
Low, Edward, 106, 107, 108, 109, 170
Lowther, George, 107, 108, 170
lumber. *See* wood
Luna Erreguerena, Pilar, 11
Lynch, Sir Thomas, 26, 102, 103

Madrid, Treaty of, 102
mahogany. *See* wood
manatees, 64, 115
mangroves, xvi, 3, 20, 22, 38, 41, 72, 88,
111, 124, 138, 143, 186. *See also* wood
Maracaibo, Venezuela, 8, 91, 163
Mariculture, Ltd., 81
Marine Archaeology Council, 182
marine architecture: copper sheathing,
141, 142, 161; fasteners, nails, 123, 130,
140, 141; fasteners, screws, 123; fasteners, treenails, 123, 130, 141; floors, 123,
130; frames, 5, 116, 117, 118, 122, 123,
129, 130, 140, 141, 142, 143, 175; keel,
122, 123, 124, 128, 129, 130, 140, 141,
142; keelson; planking, 122, 123, 124,
129, 130, 142; planking, ceiling, 141,
142; planking, garboard; rudder, 124;
stem, 123, 129, 130, 140; sternpost, 123,
129, 130, 140; stringer, 123; thwarts,
122, 123, 124. *See also* catboats, construction of; schooners, construction
of; shipbuilding
marooning, 4, 60, 136, 151, 169
Martin, Capt. Daniel, 156
Martyr, Peter, 53
masts. *See* tackle, marine
Maynard, Lt., 105
McLaughlin, Woody, 4, 5
McTaggart, Dr. Roy, 137
Menes, Ricardo, 11
merchant marine, 80, 146. *See also* commerce, maritime

Mermaid Springs (Grand Cayman), 160
Merren, H. O., 146
Mexico, 88, 144, 148; Gulf of, 35, 147,
148, 149
Miami, 4, 82
militia, 37, 68, 191, 196
Miskito Cays, 74, 75, 77, 79, 102, 111, 137,
138; Caymanian turtlers at, 68–77, 69,
74, 79
Miskito Coast, 64, 65, 68, 121, 143
Misteriosa Deep, 19
Mobile, 129
Moddyford, Sir Thomas, 36, 90, 91,
102
Molesworth, Col. Hender, 63
mollusks, xvi, 5, 7, 13, 48, 54, 187
Montego Bay, 128, 136, 190
Moore, James, 110
Moorings, The (Grand Cayman), 48
Morgan, Sir Henry, 8, 91, 93, 95, 101, 114,
116, 169
Morris, Capt. John, 101, 169, 170
Mosquito Research and Control Unit,
xvi
mosquitoes, xvi, 3, 186
Muddy Foots (Little Cayman), 36
Museums Association of the Caribbean,
182

Nantucket, 109
National Bulk Carriers, 146
Nederlands Scheepvaartmuseum, 10
nets. *See* equipment, fishing
New England, 106, 127, 128, 130
New England Shipbuilding Corporation,
162
New York, 114, 146, 151
Newcastle, Duke of, 66
Newfoundland, 65, 109
Newlands (Grand Cayman), 45
Newport (Rhode Island), 109
Nicaragua, 129, 140; dispute over tur-
tling rights, 79–81
Nine Years (King William's) War, 103
nitrates, 164
nor'easter, 166
nor'wester, 35, 168
North Carolina, 104, 105

North Side (Grand Cayman), 192, 195
North Sound (Grand Cayman), 22, 37, 48, 49, 81, 140, *141*, 142, *143*, 144, 146, 164, 174
North Sound Deep Wreck, 140–42, *141*. *See also* Grand Cayman, shipwrecks
Nova Scotia, 129, 130, 131
Nueva Cádiz (Venezuela), 57
Nugent, Sir George, 189, 190, 191, 192

oars. *See* equipment, marine
Old Isaacs (Grand Cayman), 37, 157
oral history, 12, 47, 111, 161, 174, 175, 178, 179, 180, 181
orchids, 187
Oriente Deep, 19
Oviedo y Valdes, Gonzalo Fernández, 56
Owen Island (Little Cayman), 20
Oxford University, xvi

Pan, Peter, 84
Panama, 139, 146; English raid on, 91, 100, 101, 114, 170
Paris, 61
Parrots Landing/Calico Jack's, 181
Parry, Adm., 31
Parsons, Capt. Reginald, 144
Parsons, Edmund, 77
Pater, Adm., 151
PBY flying boat, 3
Pearson, Carlton, 180
Pedro (Grand Cayman), 45
Pedro Banks, 47, 170, 185
Penn, Adm. William, 113
Pensacola, 31; en route from, 163; en route to, 162
Philip, Prince, 181
Philippines, 163
Pidgeon Island (Jamaica), 63
pigs, 34, 67, 89. *See also* livestock
pine. *See* wood
piraguas, 115. *See also* canoes, dugout
pirates, 4, 20, 27, 30, 37, 84, 85, 90, 103–11, *105*, *107*, *108*, 151, 152, 170, 172, 173, 191; Pirates Week, 34. *See also* buccaneers
pitpans, 121, 122. *See also* canoes, dugout
Pixon, Jean, 61

plantains, 20, 72, 191
Pliny, 87
Point of Sand (Little Cayman), 20, 36
Popplewell, Thomas, 153, 154, 155. *See also* Wreck of the Ten Sail
Port Morant, 93
Port Royal, 31, 35, 38, 48, 102, 109, 139, 153
Port Royal: buccaneers at, 90, 91, 103; turtle trade at, 48, 63, 64, 65, 73, 76, 77, 79, 114, 115
Porter, William, 110
Portland (Maine), 162
Portobelo, 8, 91
potatoes, 20, 177, 191
poultry, 67. *See also* livestock
privateers: English, 36, 58, 64, 86, 87, 89, 90, 91, 101, 102, 103, 114, 169; Spanish, 8, 192. *See also* buccaneers; Dampier, William; Drake, Sir Francis; Jackson, William; King, William; Rivero Pardal, Manuel
Prospect (Grand Cayman), 36, 37, 45, 46, 195
Providencia, 91, 139
provisions, 20, 28, 30, 31, 42, 46, 58, 60, 61, 62, 63, 64, 72, 112, 113, 118, 136, 137, 144, 151, 157, 177, 191
Prussia, 152
Public Record Office, 10
Puerto de Cuba, 148
Puerto Príncipe, 91
Pull-and-Be-Damned Point (Grand Cayman), 48

Quita Sueño Bank, 77

Rankine, Alejandro, 144
Red Bay (Grand Cayman), 45
reefs, 4, 19, 26, 28, 49, 52, 68, 69, 74, 85, 103, 112, 121, 131, 147, 151, 169, 172, 176; of Cayman Brac, 29, 35, 46; of Grand Cayman, 2, 3, 4, 5, 7, 13, 14, 22, 31, 36, 37, 38, 121, 148, 149, 152, 155, 156, 158, 159, 160, 161, 162, 163, 168, 174, 190; of Little Cayman, 20, 22, 36, 60, 91, 93, 117, 148, 170, 171
regattas, 131, 132, *133*

remora fish, 53, 54. *See also* fishes
reptiles, xvi, 26, 85, 86, 186. *See also* alligators; caimans; crocodiles; iguanas
Research Submersibles, Ltd., 167
rice, 164, 166
ridley turtles. *See* turtles, ridley
Rivero Pardal, Manuel, 8, 91, 93–95, 94, 114, 120, 169
Rivers, Evans, 111
Roberts, Bartholomew, 105, 106
Rochefort, Charles de, 60, 86
rope: hemp, 84, 96, 118; thatch, 69, 71, 72, 112, 118, 122, 124, 132–35, *134*, *136*, 146. *See also* tackle, marine; thatch palm
Royal African Company, 107
Royal Navy, xv, 10, 30, 31, 62, 139, 146, 149, 152, 153, 185
Royal Navy, Trinidad Royal Navy Volunteer Reserve, 146
Royal Society, xvi
rum, 36, 67, 157, 174, 175,
Rum Point (Grand Cayman), 83, 174
Ruyters, Adm. Dirk, 59
Ryan, Capt. Bernard, 47

sailing routes, Caribbean, 147, 148
sails. *See* tackle, marine
St. Domingue, 152
St. Kitts, 87
salt, 58, 78, 79, 93, 115, 137, 184, 137. *See also* turtle meat, salted
Salt Creek (Grand Cayman), 81
Salt Island (Jamaica), 63
Salt Rocks (Little Cayman), 20
salvage, 118, 121, 151, 158, 160, 161, 164, 169, 170, 171, 175, 176, 182
San Andrés, 139, 144
Sand Cay (Grand Cayman), 158, 160
Sandy Bay (Grand Cayman), 190
Santo Domingo, 86
Sardinia, 152
Saunders, Robert, 110
Savannah (Grand Cayman), 45
schooners, 41, 68, 78, 123, 128–32, 153; *Acme*, 47; *Adams*, 69, 71, 72, 73, 75, 76, 131, 132; *Alsons*, 132, 139; *Arbutus*, 132; *Arbutus II*, 140; *Armistice*, 132, ; *Blake*,

132; *Bloomfield*, 136; *Carmena*, 47; construction of, 129–31, *129*, *130*; *Diamond*, 164; *Dreadnought*, 132; *E. A. Henning*, 132; *Fernwood*, 47; *Franklin*, 132; *Georgiana*, 136; *Gleaner*, 132; *Goldfield*, 131, 132, 143–46, *145*, ; *Hustler*, 139; *Klosking*, 164; *Laguna*, 132; *Majestic*, 131, 137, 138; *Melpomene*, 47; *Merico*, 139; *Polly and Betsy*, 128; *Rainbow*, 75; *Rembro*, 132, 133, 137, 138; *Sparrowhawk*, HMS, 10, 185; turtling, crew makeup of, 68; *Two Friends*, 128; *Village Belle*, 132; *Wembley*, 132; *Wilson*, 75, 76, 131, 132, 138, 140; *Woodlark*, 132; *Ziroma*, 132
Schouten, Cdr. Pieter, 113
Scott Bay (Cayman Brac), 29
Scott, G. R., 136
Scott, Sir Walter, 27
Seattle, 144
Seranilla Bank, 77, 136, 148
Serrana Bank, 77, 79, 136, 148
Seven Mile Beach (Grand Cayman), 33, 81, 168
Seville, 10, 11
shallops, 113, 114
sharks: danger to turtles, 68, 69, 70; fishing for, 74, 137. *See also* fishes
shipbuilding, 19, 28, 29, 34, 77, 123, 124, 128–31, *129*, *130*; Bermuda, 115; Jamaica, 113. *See also* catboats; construction of; schooners, construction of
ships: *Adventure*, HMS, 31, 33, 162; *Amersfoort*, 169; *Anniston*, 163; *Antares*, 146; *Arms of Holland*, 61; *Bodner*, 146; *Bulk Oceanic*, 146; *Bulk Oil*, 146; *Bulk Star*, 146; *Bulk Trader*, 146; *Caldwell*, 163; *Capitana*, 25; *Cayman Mariner*, 6; *Cayman*, 151; *Cimboco*, 139, *139*; *Commander*, 146; *Curaçao*, 174; *Defiance*, 146; *Delivery*, 107, 108, 170; *Dove*, 61; *Drake*, HMS, 38; *Falmouth*, 61; *Gambia Castle*, 107, 108; *Good Fortune*, 105, 152; *Greyhound*, HMS, 109; *Hopewell*, 91, 92, 93, 94, 183, 184; *Inconstante*, 153, 160. *See also* Wreck of the Ten Sail; *Iphigenia*, HMS, 153; *James A. Butts*,

ships—*continued*
162, 163; *Lady Slater*, 139; *Lilly*, 169, 170; *Lone Star State*, 163; *Mary and Jane*, 91; *Merco*, 146; *Mizpah*, 146; *Nelly*, 171; *Nunoca*, 139; *Ontario*, HMS, 149; *Orion*, HMS, 144; *Parthian*, HMS, 149; *Penelope*, HMS, 153; *Petro Emperor*, 146; *Petro King*, 146; *Petro Sea*, 146; *Phoenix*, HMS, 35; *Queen Anne's Revenge*, 103, 104, 105; *Salomon*, 58; *San Pedro y la Fama*, 91, 101, *Santiago*, 25, *Trans Lake*, 146, *Transea*, 146, *Transpan*, 146, *Transpar*, 146, *Trial*, 131, *Universe Leader*, 146

shipworms, 122, 130

shipwrecks, 2, 3, 4, 5, 6, 7, 10, 12, 13, 14, 15, 16, 17, 37, 46, 95, 105, 106, 121, 147, 149, 151–76, 160, 161, 162, 163, 168, 169, 172, 174, 175, 176, 178, 182; *Arbutus II*, 140; *Balboa*, 163, 164; *Britannia*, 156; *Cali*, 164, 165, 166, 181; *Convert*, HMS, 153–61, 159 (*see also* Wreck of the Ten Sail); *Cumberland*, 31, 162; *Curaçao*, 174; *Dene*, 175; *Dolphijn*, 10, 151, 169; *Dolphin*, 101, 169, 170; *Eagle*, 156; *Evening Star*, 179; *Fortune*, 156; *Fred Lowrie*, 136; *Gamma*, 168; *Geneva Kathleen*, 181; *Genovesa*, 170; *Jamaica*, HMS, 37, 38; *Kirk Pride*, 166, 167, 168; *Ludlow*, 156; *Maggie Gray*, 9; *Majestic*, 131, 137, 138; *Moorhall*, 156; *Morning Star*, 106, 151, 152; *Nancy*, 156; *Oro Verde*, 175, 176; *Prince Frederick*, 175, 176; *Richard*, 156; *Ridgefield*, 6, 162, 163; *Rimandi Mibaju*, 163; *Sally*, 156; *San Miguel*, 170, 171; *Soto Trader*, 166, 167; *Vergulde Draeck*, 120; *Weymouth*, 173; *William and Elizabeth*, 156. *See also* Grand Cayman, shipwrecks of; Little Cayman, shipwrecks of; Cayman Brac, shipwrecks of; Wreck of the Ten Sail

slaves, 57, 58, 64, 93, 152, 171, 189. *See also* Appendix 3

Sloane, Sir Hans, 26, 64, 116

sloops, 78, 106, 109, 114, 116, 128, 129; Bermudan, 109, 115, 171; *Betty*, 114;

English turtling, 63, 64, 115; *Fancy*, 109; *Fred Lowrie*, 136; Jamaican, 114, 115; *Lambe*, 114; *Le Lyon*, 114; *Le Serfe*, 114; *Ranger*, 109; *Revenge*, 103, 104, 105; *Scourer*, 110; *William*, 114

Smith, KC, 7, 11

Smith, Roger, 7, 8, 11, 30, 99

Smith, Sheli, 7, 9

Society for Historical Archaeology, 182

South America, 57, 88, 140

South Carolina, 104

South China Sea, 54

South Hole Sound (Little Cayman), 6, 20, 36, 48, 91, 95, 96, 97, 98, 101, 116, 117, 183

South Sound (Grand Cayman), 36, 48, 164

South West Sound (Grand Cayman), 194, 195

Southwest Cay (Serrana Bank), 79

Spain, 11, 26, 57, 58, 90, 100, 102, 103, 152, 170, 191; king of, 11, 94; queen of, 91; navigation from, 57, 148; royal standard of, 93, 102

Spanish Town, 9

Sparrowhawk Hill (Little Cayman), 20, 185

Spotts (Grand Cayman), 37, 45, 47, 158, 195, 196

Stake Bay (Cayman Brac), 29, 179

sugar, 67, 110, 164, 174, 186, 191

sulfur, 96, 164

Superior (Wisconsin), 163

Surinam, 81, 163

survey tools: digital trisponder, 6; magnetometer, 6, 95; towboards, 13; water scooters, 13, 14

tackle, marine: masts, 124, 131, 175, 176; rigging, 93, 141, 173; rope, 69, 96, 112, 114, 118, 122, 124, 132, 134, 135; sails, 41, 114, 122, 124, 127, 129, 137, 153, 154, 155, 158, 173; yards, 109, 114, 154, 155, 184. *See also* anchors; equipment; rope

Tampa, 73, 129, 139, 144, 166

Teach, Edward (aka Blackbeard), 103–5, 105

Texas, 166

Texas A&M University, xvii, 3, 180
Texas Oil Company, 146
thatch palm, 41, 69, 71, 72, 94, 112, 122, 124, 126, 131, 132, 133, 135, 146. *See also* rope; tackle, marine
Thijsz, Adm. Martin, 169
31st Regiment of Foot (East Surreys), 162
Thompson, Ira, 4, 179
Tibbetts, Linton and Polly, 182
Tiburon, Cape, 148
Tirri, Capt. Juan, 57, 172
tobacco, 170, 177. *See also* artifacts, tobacco pipes
Topsail Inlet, 104
Torre, Fray Tomás de la, 149
Tortuga (Hispaniola), 60, 61, 89, 90
treasure, 111, 170
treasure hunters, 4, 117, 182
Turks and Caicos Islands, 29, 79
turtle, cannery, 81; crawls, 38, 48, 67, 72, 73, 74, 75, 76, 83, 86; eggs, 22, 33, 52, 55, 58, 59, 61, 64, 83; eggs, ban on taking, 67; eggs, imported for farming, 81; eggs, "red eggs," 79; eggs, "white eggs," 79; farming, 81–83; fishing, xvii, 22, 34, 35, 69, 70, 71, 72, 73, 178, 191; fishing, Cayman Brac method from boats, 78, 122; fishing, description of seasons, 68; fishing, division of catch, 73, 74, 77, 79; fishing, equipment (*see* equipment, fishing); fishing, Indian methods, 53, 54, 64, 65, 66; grass, 53, 68, 72, 81, 95, 98, 116; hunters, Dutch, 59, 60, 61; hunters, English, 58, 59, 61, 62, 65, 178; hunters, French, 60, 61, 66, 67, 86, 87, 90, 178; hunters, Indian, 64, 65, 66, 178; meat, 67, 81, 82, 178, 186; meat, dried, 58, 64, 78; meat, grilled, 64; meat, opinions of, 58, 60, 64, 79, 86; meat, salted, 58, 61, 64, 78, 79, 83; oil, 65, 82; rangers, 74, 136, 137; shell, 65, 66, 77, 78, 79, 81, 82, 83, 137, 186; soup, 81, 82, 186; stew, 83. *See also* salt
Turtle Wreck, 95, 96, 97, 100, 116–20, 117, 119
turtles, xvi, 22, 25, 26, 28, 31, 52, 55, 56, 177, 178; English consumption of, 62; 64; freshwater, 83; green, 54, 60, 67, 70, 71, 72, 73, 74, 75, 80, 83, 122, 137, 186; green, food-to-meat conversion ratio of, 82; hawksbill, 54, 60, 65, 67, 77, 78, 79, 83, 122, 137, 186; leatherback, 54, 60; loggerhead, 54, 60, 83, 186; navigational ability of, 55, 76; ridley, 54, 60, 83; "shelling" of, 65; Spanish consumption of, 57, 58

U.S. Department of Commerce, 82
United Nations Educational, Scientific and Cultural Organization, 182
United States: prohibition on turtle imports, 82; ships of, 146; trade with, 76, 77, 129, 139, 140, 144
University College London, Institute of Archaeology, 181
Utrecht, Treaty of, 103

vegetables, 67. *See also* Cayman Islands, agriculture in; provisions; yams
Venezuela, 57, 87
Veracruz, 57, 170
Volkswagen Thing, 168

Waddell, Hope, 162, 173
Walker, Neal, 170
Walton, Capt. Edwin, 136
War of Spanish Succession (Queen Anne's War), 103
Ware, Thomas, 171
Warwick, Earl of, 87
water, fresh, 2, 28, 29, 30, 33, 34, 58, 67, 86, 87, 89, 113, 160, 191; lack of, 30, 60, 138, 150
water glass. *See* equipment, fishing
Watering Place (Cayman Brac), 29, 47
Watler, Conwell, 143
Watler, Marshall, 13
Watler, Victorine, 13
weapons: axes, 158; clubs, 87; cutlasses, 111; grenades, 101; guns, 90; muskets, 86, 98, 99, 100, 106; pikes, 86, 158; pistols, 104, 108, 110, 158; stink pots, 101; swivel guns, 101, 158; swords, 110, 158. *See also* cannons

Weary Hill (Little Cayman), 20
wells, 29, 30, 30, 89. *See also* water
West Bay (Grand Cayman), 31, 48, 75,
    108, 132, 192, 194
West End (Cayman Brac), 136
Western Design, 113. *See also* Jamaica,
    English invasion of
whaleboat, 109; New England, 127, 128.
    See also boats
wheat, 164
Windsor, Gov. Thomas, 63
Windward Islands, 43, 110
Windward Passage, 147, 148
wine, 16, 64, 100, 170
wood: bitter plum, 123; buttonwood,
    123; candle wood, 187; cedar, 115, 121,
    123, 129, 192; driftwood, 187; dye-
    wood, 49; fiddlewood, 123, 129; fir,
    129; gourd, 126; hardwood, 20, 49,
    112, 121, 128, 133, 142, 143; jasmine,

123, 129; logwood, 106, 114, 115, 121;
    lumber, 146, 164; mahogany, 121, 129,
    130, 143, 187; mangrove, 124; pine,
    123, 124, 128, 129, 130, 143, 180;
    plopnut, 123, 180; pompero, 123, 129;
    sea grape, 123, 186; Spanish elm, 124;
    strawberry, 124; whitewood, 123; wild
    ginep, 124; wild sapodilla, 123, 129.
    See also shipbuilding
World Turtle Conference, 83
World War II, 144, 146, 161, 163, 166, 176
Wreck of the Ten Sail, 5, 33, 121, 152–61,
    159, 162, 172, 180
wreckers, 4, 170–76
wrecking, 22, 37, 178, 186

yams, 20, 186, 191
yards. *See* tackle, marine
Young, Thomas, 121
Yucatán Channel, 43, 147, 148, 149, 153

Roger C. Smith is state underwater archaeologist for the Division of Historical Resources, Florida Department of State. He is adjunct faculty at the University of West Florida in underwater archaeology and the author of *Vanguard of the Empire: Ships of Exploration in the Age of Columbus* (1993) and coauthor of *An Atlas of Maritime Florida* (University Press of Florida, 1997).